not to be in the EU and on what terms is an issue that dominates endless political debate so far this century. Denis MacShane knows the Europe issue as few others. He has lived and worked in different European countries, speaks languages, and has a contacts book of politicians and journalists in most EU member states. The first edition of this book argued that if we got to a referendum then Britain would vote to leave the EU. He was right and it is important to know the arguments and passions that have made the Brexit question important in contemporary political discourse.'

Mathew Taylor, Chief Executive, Royal Society of Arts

'This is an important study of the forces in Britain that have led Britain out of the EU, which is bad news for Britain and for Europe.'

Pascal Lamy, former Director, World Trade Organization

BREXIT
HOW BRITAIN LEFT EUROPE
DENIS MACSHANE

I.B. TAURIS
LONDON · NEW YORK

Fully revised edition published in 2016 by I.B.Tauris & Co. Ltd
London • New York
Reprinted twice 2016
www.ibtauris.com

First edition published in 2015 by I.B.Tauris & Co. Ltd
Second edition published in 2015

ISBN: 978 1 78453 784 5
eISBN: 978 0 85773 906 3
ePDF: 978 0 85772 542 4

A full CIP record for this book is available from the British Library

A full CIP record is available from the Library of Congress
Library of Congress Catalog Card Number: available

Typeset in AGaramond
Printed and bound by CPI Group (UK) Ltd, Croydon, CR0 4YY

MIX
Paper from
responsible sources
FSC
www.fsc.org   FSC® C013604

CONTENTS

ACKNOWLEDGEMENTS   vii

PREFACE TO NEW EDITION   x

PREFACE   xiii

1   A CENTRIFUGAL EUROPE   1

2   CHURCHILL INVENTS THE UNITED STATES OF EUROPE   28

3   THE FIRST ANTI-EUROPEAN PARTY   35

4   LABOUR SAYS *NON, MERCI* TO EUROPE   47

5   THE TORIES BECAME THE PARTY OF EUROPE,
    OR DID THEY?   57

6   JACQUES DELORS LAUNCHES BRITISH
    EUROSCEPTICISM   63

7   FROM MAGGIE TO MAJOR: THE DRIFT TO
    CONSERVATIVE EUROSCEPTICISM   79

8   TONY BLAIR: WAS HE PRO-EUROPEAN?   84

9   WILLIAM HAGUE AND DAVID CAMERON HELP
    CREATE UKIP   108

10 WHERE'S THE VISION THING? ASK FRIEDRICH HAYEK   126

11 HOW THE CITY FINANCES EUROPHOBIA   139

CONTENTS

12 THE BRITISH LIKE THEIR PARLIAMENT, BUT NO OTHER   151

13 MYTHS, MURDOCH, LIES: THE PRESS AND EUROPE   166

14 HOW THE EUROZONE HAS MARGINALIZED BRITAIN   183

15 WILL BRITAIN EVER FALL IN LOVE WITH EUROPE?   196

AFTERWORD: WHAT HAPPENS NOW?   212

EPILOGUE   227

FURTHER READING   254

INDEX   258

ACKNOWLEDGEMENTS

This book arose from a lunch early in 2013 in the place de la Bourse in Paris – where else should books be born? – with my friend Laurent Joffrin, then editor of the *Nouvel Observateur*, now of *Libération*, and other media friends. It was just after David Cameron made his promise of an in–out referendum in 2017 if re-elected.

My French friends snorted and said that the prime minister's dramatic pledge was just a bone thrown to Rupert Murdoch – whom many across the Channel credit with a degree of mind-control over British prime ministers that only they can say is true or not – as well as something to shut Ukip up. I disagreed and set out my thesis that a number of different forces had steadily grown in Britain which were now coming together and which could result in Britain leaving the EU.

As I explained my thinking both they and I realized I was telling them about the passions over Europe which had risen to prominence in Britain. Passions about which they knew little. Politicians, editors, business leaders, writers, *saloniers* and the man or woman in the street all had pronounced and often hostile views on Europe.

So although this is a book for my fellow Brits, it stems from a political and writing life which has been, in part, devoted to explaining to people on the continent how my country thinks about Europe. I left London to work on the continent soon after Margaret Thatcher's election in 1979 and did not permanently return until the summer of 1994 when elected an MP. Then my parliamentary life, other than constituency duties, was taken over by the European question. I spent eight years as a parliamentary private secretary and minister at the Foreign and Commonwealth Office and then five serving as Tony Blair's political envoy to Europe and as UK delegate on the Council of Europe. My interest in Europe, some countries whose languages I speak and where I had spent time in prison for committing a criminal offence in Poland in 1982, running money to the underground trade union, NSZZ Solidarnosc, took over much of my life.

It would be impossible to list all the fellow politicians, thinkers, writers and officials who have made me see Europe in a different way. Among journalists I would like to single out the *Guardian*'s Europe correspondents, John Palmer, Martin Walker, Nick Watt and Ian Traynor, as well as the BBC's Mark Mardell and *The Economist*'s David Rennie and John Peet.

Britain is blessed with quality think-tanks and academics on EU issues, and any conversation or a chance to listen to or read Charles Grant, Tim Garton Ash or Mark Leonard, among others, has informed this book. A number of very able Foreign and Commonwealth Office officials, John Kerr, Stephen Wall, Colin Budd, Paul Lever, Nigel Sheinwald, Kim Darroch and Peter Westmacott, have made me think harder about Europe, as have colleagues like Pascal Lamy, Jacques Lafitte and Jean-Claude Piris.

Tony Blair remains for me the prime minister who did the best for those in Britain the Labour Party exists to serve and seeing him in action on European affairs and talking to him about Europe was always fascinating. Chris Patten, Giles Radice, Tam Dalyell and John Monks encouraged me as an MP to challenge the myths and disinformation about the EU that I encountered daily on arriving in the Commons 20 years ago. I have lost count of all the debates in Parliament on Europe I took part in, and I remain grateful to all the MPs, pro- and anti-EU alike, who have made me think about our country and the rest of our region of the world.

I had the privilege of chairing or taking part in fascinating annual get-togethers between British politicians, business leaders, academics, journalists and intellectuals and opposite numbers in France, Germany, Spain and Italy. Peter Mandelson and Alan Donnelly have been consistent as Labour political animals in their pro-Europeanism and have taught me much, as have Richard Corbett MEP and his former colleagues Glyn Ford and Carole Tongue.

I would hate to count the millions of words in the form of articles, books and diary notes that I have produced on Europe, but I am grateful to all the editors who in the past have taken my thoughts on Europe. I remember in the first decade of this century going regularly to see the editor of the *New Statesman*, where I published my first article on European politics in 1974. He was indifferent to any articles on Europe and indifferent to winning circulation for the paper, and one of the major reasons why Britain may quit the EU is not so much the hostility of anti-EU editors as the indifference of editors who think they are pro-European but will not give space to fight Europhobe arguments and distortions.

I am grateful to Jo Godfrey at I.B.Tauris, whose sharp editorial eye led to reshaping and rewriting early drafts. Christopher Feeney removed many infelicities as did the sharp eyes of Laura MacShane. I would like to dedicate this book to the memory of my father and mother, one from the far east of Europe, the other rooted in its far west. The world they grew up in was devoured by the politics of populist nationalism and a dislike of neighbouring nations and people that I had never experienced until once again the politics of contempt for the other was reborn this century. It is also for my four children, Sarah, Laura, Emilie and Benjamin, in the hope they will see out their days as citizens of the EU as well as having the passports of the countries of their mother and father. If they don't, I fear the worst.

PREFACE TO NEW EDITION

In January 2015 I wrote the first edition of this book in which I set out the reasons why I believed that if it came to a referendum on Brexit – a term I had coined in an article for the *Yorkshire Post* in January 2012 – there would be a vote to leave the European Union.

At the time, no one knew who would win the May 2015 general election. There was a clear divide between David Cameron, who had announced his plan to hold an EU plebiscite if the Conservatives won a second term, and the Labour leader of the opposition, Ed Miliband. He refused to pledge an EU referendum in Labour's manifesto despite a great deal of pressure from Labour MPs and most shadow cabinet members.

David Cameron emerged from the 2015 general election with an overall majority. He may also have felt that, having seen off a pointless and irrelevant referendum on changing the voting system in 2011 and having defeated the Scottish separatist movement plebiscite in September 2014, his luck would hold in 2016 for his Europe referendum.

If so, it was a massive miscalculation. A second edition of this book was published in September 2015 to take into account David Cameron's victory and the announcement that there would be a referendum on 23 June 2016. I underlined all the reasons why I still thought Brexit was the likely outcome. The British political-media establishment had been largely Eurosceptic for some years. The business establishment, in the shape of the Confederation of British Industry (CBI) and the British Chambers of Commerce (BCC), had published report after report critical of the European Commission and few business leaders were ready to find a good word for Europe. It was fashionable on the left to blame all the woes of Greece, Spain or Portugal on the EU, without looking at the internal politics of clientelism and corruption that had left southern EU members exposed when the financial crash hit.

Not all Conservative MPs were out-and-out Leavers but they used the EU as a whipping boy to stir up votes and, so they hoped, keep Ukip at bay. But the more the Conservative Party establishment and the anti-EU press kept banging on about how rotten the EU was, the more the Ukip vote grew.

In addition, Cameron ordered ministers to change the way voters in Britain registered to vote. This resulted in a massive drop in the number of young people on the electoral register. Only 37 per cent of the total registered voters in the UK voted for Brexit. While as a percentage the votes cast were higher than in general elections, there was widescale disenfranchisement which may have tilted the vote to Brexit. A total of 1.9 million young voters were removed from the Electoral Register, more than the 1.3 million majority for Leave. In addition, relatively few of the two million plus British citizens who live in Europe and who are the most directly affected were able to vote because of bureaucratic obstacles placed in their way by UK voting rules.

The core underlying reasons for Brexit had been set out in the first edition of this book published in January 2015. Others will pore over the minutiae of the campaign and already there are endless debates interpreting the vote and the reasons why so many did not, or were not able to, vote. However the underlying currents hostile to the EU had been flowing strongly for years and had indeed been strengthened by Cameron's Eurosceptic leadership of the Conservative Party after 2005 and then his premiership after 2010. For 15 years he had been hostile to Europe. For 15 weeks of the campaign he found words of praise for the EU. The voters preferred the 15 years of Cameron's anti-Europeanism to the 15 weeks of his latter-day conversion to pro-Europeanism. What you sow you reap.

I have no idea if David Cameron ever read my book. We always had the most cordial of personal relationships when I was an MP and I did send a flyer for the book to every MP and even received a telephone call from Michael Gove during the 2015 general election campaign to talk about it.

Now he has left Number 10 perhaps David Cameron will have time to read it and realise that from the moment he switched British democracy from its representative parliamentary tradition to populist plebiscitary politics he was doomed. If Lord North is in our history as the prime minister who lost America, David Cameron now enters history as the prime minister who lost Europe. He asked the people of Britain for a vote of confidence on 23 June 2016, they gave him their answer. Now someone else must clear up the mess. May the new prime minister be lucky. But no one should hold their breath.

Denis MacShane, September 2016

PREFACE

This book is not about Europe. It is about Britain, my country. It sets out the reasons why Britain on the sixtieth anniversary of the Treaty of Rome will leave the European Union unless there is a major change of direction in British politics. This will mean the end of Britain in Europe. It may also be the first step in the end of Europe, in the sense of the union of European states that over decades have agreed to share important elements of sovereign power in order to achieve something bigger than any individual European nation could create on its own, as well as having laid to rest the demons that destroyed European civilization in the first half of the twentieth century.

Brexit seeks to argue that different tributaries – political, economic, much of the press, cultural, identity, historical – are coming together in one powerful confluence that – unless Britain awakes to the danger of where we are heading – will take Britain out of Europe. The book will explain where these tributaries originated and why they are now powerful.

The political direction of travel of the Conservative Party over the last 20 years has been firmly against the EU. Labour has been silent and not made a pro-European case with vigour and impact. The economic attraction of Europe that generated support in the years between 1950 and 1990 as mainland economies outperformed the UK has faded as the Eurozone, in particular, has become associated with slow- or no-growth economies in contrast to the better performance, especially this century, of Britain. The press mocks and scorns the EU whenever it can. There is no mass-impact media coverage and comment in favour of Europe. British identity and cultural confidence are depicted as being under threat from forces in Brussels and Strasbourg that show no respect for British frontiers, traditions or needs. British history has always been suspicious of full-scale entanglement with continental forces. The EU is presented as the latest in a long line of alien practices and beliefs that do not mesh with British, or English, requirements and identity.

All these different force-fields are now uniting and if a vote in the form of an in–out referendum actually happens – and it probably will – then both we British and our friends in other countries should not assume it will be a vote to say Yes to Europe.

Since entering the European Economic Community, as it was then called, in 1973, Britain has always been a net contributor to the European budget, a position the richer France did not arrive at until the end of the twentieth century. Germany was the major paymaster for European construction from the Treaty of Rome (1957) and remains so today. Germany did not have Britain's security obligations to defend democratic Europe during the Cold War era. For 40 years, the common cry of Eurosceptics has been that each British taxpayer is making a contribution of thousands of pounds to France's agro-industry multinationals or to corrupt businessmen and politicians building bridges to nowhere in southern Italy. (In fact, the contribution to the EU budget of everyone in the UK is 37p a day!) Even the most pro-European of British politicians has had to attack the Common Agricultural Policy in order to be listened to. The concept of getting a fair share of money back (*le juste retour*, in Eurospeak) is seen as alien to European construction by the keepers of the faith in Brussels. They are right. But if one wants a reason why the British have never fully shared the European 'dream', the fact that the 'dream' has meant that so much money has gone from the British taxpayer to richer nations is part of the answer. Now Britain is paying even more thanks to its recent economic success measured in strong GDP growth. The German taxpayer may feel relief that

Britain is paying more, but for those who want Britain to quit the EU the argument that no more money will go to Brussels resonates.

Yet the facts are that the total EU budget does not exceed 1 per cent of the total European GDP. And of that 1 per cent about four-fifths goes straight back to member states, including Britain, in the form of payments to farmers and poor regions. Britain got £700 million from the EU in the late 1990s for northern regions where the standard of living had fallen to below 75 per cent of the EU average, and between 2014 and 2020 the UK will receive €11 billion in different cohesion funds. Despite the myth that the EU makes most laws in Britain, the House of Commons Library can never find more than about 7 per cent of primary legislation that emanates from Europe. The controversial laws of recent years like raising student tuition fees or gay marriage are all made-in-Westminster laws, as is most legislation.

Other books have been and are being written about the merits and de-merits of Britain leaving the EU. That is not the purpose of this book, even though it will not take much effort by the reader to discover I do not think that Britain outside the EU will have the rosy future depicted by the 'better-off-out' enthusiasts. The purpose of this account is to answer the question so many outside Britain are beginning to ask with increasing intensity: how has the United Kingdom come to the point when for the first time in its history it may be about to repudiate a major set of treaty obligations and quit an important international institution, which, while much criticized, surely, on balance, has done much good in the modern world?

So although this is a book about British politics, the impact of Britain leaving Europe will have an impact far beyond its shores. It is not inevitable. On a spectrum which at one end has Britain staying an EU member state much as it stays a NATO member and which, at the other end, has the UK leaving the EU in the foreseeable future, I believe and will explain in this book that we are much closer to the latter position than the former.

The reason is simple: Prime Minister David Cameron has pledged an in–out referendum in 2017. He will campaign for a vote to stay in the EU only if major concessions are made. To begin with many Conservative MPs called for a quota or a cap on the number of EU citizens allowed to work in Britain. The catch-all term 'immigrant' replaced describing Europeans in Britain by their nationality. The prime minister was told firmly by EU heads of government that such a formal quota breached the core principle of free movement of people. Instead he came up with the suggestion that European citizens should not travel to Britain unless a job awaited them. Quite how this would be policed, as all EU citizens, including the British, can go anywhere in Europe without let or hindrance, was not spelled out. He also said that unlike British citizens in low-paid jobs who get a form of subsidy via the tax system to provide slightly more income, anyone from Ireland, Poland or other EU member states should have to wait four years before being eligible for such payments.

Thus workers doing the same job for the same employer would have different income according to whether they were British or other EU citizens. Mr Cameron's view that European employees should be treated differently from British employees doing the same job produced an angry reaction from Poland, whose prime minister, Donald Tusk, became president of the European Council in December 2014. Poland's deputy foreign minister, Rafal Trzaskowski, told BBC's *Newsnight* that the prime minister's proposals would 'be against all the existing laws of the EU and obviously that would be a red line for us'. The Czech Europe minister, Tomáš Prouza, was more sarcastic. He tweeted a picture of Czech pilots who fought in the Battle of Britain with the RAF noting that they hadn't 'worked in the UK for over four years'. In December 2014, the EU Commission President, Jean-Claude Juncker, told the *Guardian* that Mr Cameron was 'beating up' on European working in Britain, seeing them as 'criminal'.

Legal experts also said such discrimination would be illegal under existing EU treaty law and Mr Cameron did indeed admit that changes in the EU Treaty law would be necessary. This, in turn, means that any of the 27 other EU member states can veto such treaty change or be required to ratify it by referendum. The chances of that happening by 2017 – the year of French and German elections as well as the year of Mr Cameron's in–out referendum – are slim, if it's actually possible at all. So the question then arises as to whether Mr Cameron would campaign strongly to stay in Europe without treaty change to accommodate his demands and do so against a Eurosceptic press, hostility from Eurosceptic Conservative MPs and vocal anti-European politicians, and against a background of business disenchantment with the poorly performing Eurozone. One of his senior colleagues, the cabinet minister, Oliver Letwin, said in November 2014 that if Mr Cameron failed to gain a better deal for Britain in Europe, he 'would want to recommend leaving'. So if the present government is re-elected, the chances of Britain leaving the EU are high. Even if there is a non-Conservative government in the next few years the clamour for a referendum will grow in intensity.

We are in a transformatory moment in British politics. The long hegemony of two big parties alternating in power is over. Polls show the Scottish Nationalist Party winning more MPs than Labour in Scotland and the Greens overtaking the Liberal Democrats. Britain now has to live with four-, five-, even six-party politics. In October and November 2014, the United Kingdom Independence Party (Ukip), dismissed a few years previously by David Cameron as 'a bunch of fruitcakes and loonies and closet racists' won its first seat in the House of Commons. Ukip's main *raison d'être* is to take Britain out of Europe. The votes Ukip candidates won in the European and local elections in 2014 as well as in parliamentary by-elections point the direction of travel of British public opinion and voting intentions.

The question of Europe has merged with a growing dissatisfaction with political elites and the way Britain is governed. Bertolt Brecht famously wrote after the 1953 East Berlin uprising that since the people could not elect a new government, the government would elect a new people. Voters in Britain still have to elect MPs who become ministers and take decisions that affect all of us. However, it is clear that many voters, perhaps half of them, don't want either David Cameron or Ed Miliband and don't much like any long-standing party. The one way they can show their discontent and unhappiness is to give the Westminster elites a great big kick by voting for Ukip. If they get a referendum they can give vent to their anti-politics mood by voting against whatever the London elites tell them to do.

Following the first Ukip by-election victory, the very Eurosceptic Mayor of London, Boris Johnson, a Conservative Party leader-in-waiting, told the BBC, 'It's obviously axiomatic that if we don't get the reform that we need in 2016 or 17, then I think we should campaign to come out.'

When in January 2013 David Cameron first announced he would campaign to win the 2015 general election by pledging an in–out referendum senior Liberal Democrats dismissed the idea as a gesture to Eurosceptic political passions. As the *Financial Times* reported in July 2013, 'The Liberal Democrat leader on Monday said his party did not support the prime minister's planned referendum in 2017 following a "so-called renegotiation" of Britain's relationship with the EU.' By October 2014 the Lib Dems had done a volte-face. Nick Clegg's close political friend Danny Alexander briefed journalists at the party conference in Glasgow that the Lib Dems would drop their opposition to the 2017 in–out referendum if that was price of holding on to ministerial posts. This left Ed Miliband alone in opposing Cameron's proposed 2017 plebiscite.

To win the referendum David Cameron needs major concessions from Europe. Top of the list are some control of entry of EU citizens who seek to live and work in Britain. Another demand is a return to the position prior to 1997 when Britain was not covered by EU social policy obligations. The EU Social Chapter was agreed in 1991 as part of the Maastricht Treaty. The Social Chapter allows EU leaders by majority vote to legislate directives which were contained in the EU Social Charter, which in turn was based on Conventions agreed by the International Labour Organization and the Council of Europe. Most of its provisions, such as maternity leave, paid holidays, the right to join a trade union, were already the norm in Britain and other EU member states. But British labour relations were based on convention and contract, not on law. Under Mrs Thatcher the law was used to weaken social rights of workers, and trade union membership declined by half as a result. The idea of European law supporting workers and unions was a red rag to the Conservatives in 1992 and it still is today.

In 1992, the construction of Europe based on a common set of rules which all accepted and lived by came to an end as the British government obtained an opt-out from the Social Chapter provisions of the Maastricht Treaty. In truth, the Social Chapter was largely symbolic. EU states clung to their own traditions of labour relations. Trade unions remained traditional, cautious and conservative institutions. But for Conservatives after 1997, and for many businesses who liked to blame EU 'red tape' and social regulations, there has long been a desire to return to a prelapsarian Europe with Brussels having no right to impose social rules. So today, a common demand from business leaders if they are to support a Yes vote in a referendum is that 'Social Europe' has to go.

Unfortunately for Mr Cameron and businesses hoping for a Yes vote, the surge in Ukip votes in 2014 coincided with a succession of European leaders politely but firmly saying they could not agree to changes in the EU treaties or an end to free movement of European citizens so that Britain could impose quota limits on Europeans who live and work in Britain. In a visit to London, the French prime minister, Manuel Valls, said there would be no new EU Treaty before 2017 and that there was no question of abolishing the free movement of people that had led to Eastern European immigration into Britain in the last decade. This line was repeated by Italy's Europe minister, visiting London at the same time. The new European Commission president, Jean-Claude Juncker, said at his inauguration by the European Parliament just before taking office on 1 November 2014 that he was not prepared to compromise on the basic EU principle of freedom of movement for citizens. The German chancellor, Angela Merkel, also said that free movement of people could not be changed to satisfy Mr Cameron. She later went further. In November 2014 *Der Spiegel* reported Mrs Merkel as believing Britain might be on the point of leaving, as Europe had reached the point of no return on Mr Cameron's insistence that the UK could opt out of the principle of free movement within the EU.

Across the Channel, the incoming commissioners in charge of EU social policy told members of the European Parliament at their confirmation hearings that they had no plans to reduce or abolish the various EU policies and laws supporting worker rights and trade unions. The Commission President, Jean-Claude Juncker also told MEPs that in his period of office, 2014–19, he would ensure 'the handwriting of the European Social Model is clearly visible in everything we do'.

So while ruling political and business elites in London were insisting that the EU had to conform to their wishes, the leaders of European nations and the newly arrived chiefs of EU institutions in Brussels said core demands like abolishing the right of free movement or Social Europe could not be conceded.

There has long been a debate in British political and public life on the pros and cons of European integration and construction. Now suddenly the question was being changed. It was no longer about Europe, but about a fundamental change in the course of Britain's island history. Britain's most successful engineer and businessman, Sir James Dyson, told the BBC in November 2014 he would vote to leave the EU if there was a referendum. On the left, the influential political commentator Mehdi Hassan, once a pro-European, wrote in the *New Statesman* that 'it's pretty difficult to mount a credible defence of the single currency or, for that matter, the EU itself'. To leave the EU would be as big a decision as any in the great moments of British history – Parliament's decision to execute a king; the abolition of the corn laws and embrace of free trade; votes for all citizens; the Irish war of independence; the loss of empire; or the decision to invade Iraq alongside George W. Bush. Each led to a fundamental change in the way Britain saw or felt about itself or was seen beyond British borders.

Modern politics is said to be more transactional than transformatory. This book will argue that Europe had and is having a transformatory impact on British politics, in particular on the Conservative Party in the past 20 years. Between 1945 and 1995 the Conservative Party had a pragmatic, transactional approach to Europe. In the last two decades Britain's oldest governing party has been changed by the European question. This is not what its leaders and MPs intended when they started down the Eurosceptic piste. What began as criticism, much of it reasonable, as the EU is an imperfect body, turned into barely hidden contempt for the EU and the 'federasts', to use William Cash MP's phrase to describe supporters of the UK's membership of the EU.

What was a minority opinion, namely that Britain should leave the EU, has morphed into open discussion about the possibilities and usefulness of leaving. So the arguments in this book also reveal the transformation of the Conservative Party into a new political body. This has happened before in Tory history, and we should not be surprised at the party's historical ability to change itself and to promote a radical new vision of what Britain should be.

There are many books on Europe by fine historians, journalists and polemicists. They can be divided into three categories. Histories, descriptions and arguments. There is a large academic community devoted to European studies with careful, methodical professors publishing worthwhile studies on aspects of Britain's relationship with Europe. Some of these are written by insiders, diplomats who worked as European specialists for the government in Downing Street and still exercise influence as members of the House or Lords.

Others are technical descriptions of the evolution of EU policy and the workings of the EU institutions such as the European Council, Commission or Parliament. The third group consists of the foes and fans of European integration. They produce books galore setting out their position. They hope to convert opponents or doubters or to demonstrate the wrongness and folly of the 'pro' or 'anti' camps. British journalists and intellectuals, in particular, have a solipsistic, finger-wagging style as they pronounce or preach on Europe.

For the avoidance of any doubt, I am in the European camp. I sat though hours and hours, morning, afternoon, evening and night, in the House of Commons listening to partisan speeches and made not a few myself. Indeed my maiden speech in 1994 was on Europe when I spoke just after Edward Heath, the prime minister who took Britain into Europe. My very last speech in the Commons in 2012 was also on the EU.

But in this book I try to describe and work out why Britain has got to a stage in its history when such a momentous decision as quitting the EU – as big in its own way in geo-political and historical terms as the decision of the United States to quit Europe in 1919 and retreat across the water to an isolationism lasting two decades – is talked about openly. For some it is a worry; for others highly desirable.

Many try and draw up a balance sheet of EU membership, an exercise never applied to, say, membership of NATO, the World Trade Organization or the UN. But few are willing to ask if Britain really is a European nation. I write this in Switzerland, which is quintessentially European. It is German, French and Italian in language – and lots of others, including English. Thirty-four per cent of its population are immigrants or the children of immigrants. The Swiss people's commitment to the highest levels of Europe's culture as well as an ingrained belief in liberal democracy, rule of law and support for high social-environmental standards are taken for granted.

In Britain we are in the EU, in contrast to the Swiss, who are not. Yet Switzerland, where I was based in the 1980s, feels a completely European country in a way my own county of Britain does not. To be sure, the Swiss have changed many of their rules and laws to be in compliance with EU norms as defined in Brussels. They now have a tricky set of decisions to take following a referendum in February 2014, changing the constitution to impose limits on the number of European citizens who can live or work in the Swiss Confederation. The future of Britain's tortured relationship with the EU and the negotiations over a reformed EU and a possible in–out referendum will coincide with, and impact on, Switzerland's own renegotiation of its relationship with the EU.

As I waited in Gatwick Airport at 5.30 a.m. for my flight to Geneva, the airport bars were open as British travellers sat drinking dawn pints of beer, gently getting drunk before boarding their flights. It was a reminder of why Britain never quite feels European. Having a drink is part of life, but the ferociously fast and furious public consumption of alcohol is quintessentially British. Young British men and women on Spanish or Greek islands get outstandingly and outrageously drunk in the way their continental brothers and sisters never do. When I wrote to the Slovakian ambassador asking for his help in dealing with Slovakian Roma who were behaving badly in South Yorkshire he politely suggested I might come to Bratislava to see young Yorkshire men drunk, vomiting in the streets and having endless paid-for sex in brothels with trafficked girls sold into sex slavery from further east. *Touché*!

One continental town or city looks a bit like another. The standardized global chain stores or coffee shops are there. But they keep a specific identity separate from us. Individually owned or managed shops still exist. Cafés sprawl onto the streets. There is a rattle of trams. Taxis are ordinary saloon cars, not purpose-built black cabs. Double-decker trains exist but not double-decker buses. The smell of sausages, crêpes or galettes is subtly different from that of food fried in cheap oil that pervades every British town.

The continent has giant rivers that are industrial and transport arteries with lakes like inland seas. There is nowhere in Britain more than a short drive from big, tidal seas with cold, rolling waves. Most Europeans live in countries with big mountain ranges and have more severe weather, hotter in summer, colder in winter, than temperate Britain, where the highest peak barely reaches a thousand metres. Central heating heats an entire block of apartments, not single flats one by one.

The police across the Channel look different, with every country having a medley of police forces, all armed, unlike the usually unarmed British bobby under a pointed blue helmet. French and German towns still have bookshops supported by the *prix du livre* (France) or *Preisbindung* (Germany) – agreements that protect authors, publishers and bookshops unlike Britain, where Amazon and discount books on sale in supermarkets have all but killed bookshops.

Europe drinks coffee and cold lager beer. Britain prefers tea and enjoys warm bitter beer. All European nations have written constitutions. Not Britain. They are republics and even when the head of state is a king or queen they are citizen monarchs who retire when old. Britain's head of state lives by convention, not a constitution, is head of the official national church, whose bishops are also unelected legislators. One British king has abdicated in the last few centuries but none has retired. Other than Sweden, every EU member state has been invaded, occupied or lived under authoritarian despotism in living memory or has, like Ireland, been carved bloodily from its masters between 1916 and 1921. In short, Britain is not, in truth, European. It has been the EU's awkward neighbour and partner, but few Brits see or think of themselves as European.

So in the forthcoming debate over Britain's future in Europe it is necessary to start with the reminder that Britain is not European. We constitute Europe's major off-shore island nation and we are members of the EU, save that we do not use the common currency and we do not have identity cards but instead insist that our citizens cannot travel across a border without a passport.

The Scottish referendum highlighted how much strain there is within the British Union itself, as the battle was fought to keep the two main nations within the UK linked to each other. The Union of the United Kingdom was only saved by a last-minute bribe by the London political establishment in the form of offering a permanent enhanced payment to the Scots to buy their acquiescence, as well as a promise of more transfer of sovereign powers from the UK Parliament to Edinburgh. Even these panic-stricken, last-minute promises could not persuade Scotland's biggest city, Glasgow, to vote in favour of continuing union. And far from the Scottish referendum settling the issue, there has been a surge of support for the Scottish Nationalist Party, which is looking to hold a second referendum as it exploits the tensions in English politics as so many south of the border look to break up the other union England is part of – the European Union.

So if there is this much internal tension within the component elements of the UK, no one should be surprised if there is equal or even greater tension in the union of Britain with 27 other EU member states.

Unlike the Scottish–English marriage, which was consummated in 1707 and until recently has not been much questioned, the four-decade-long cohabitation, living as it were in separate rooms, between the UK and Europe has been permanently scratchy and under challenge and faces stress tests that could easily lead to divorce.

Brexit argues that it is time to take very seriously indeed the possibility of such a divorce. It is organized in three sections. The first looks at the current forces and actors that might lead to a Brexit – Britain exiting the EU. The second delves into the political history of Britain's relations with the EU. In part, the later moments of that history are based on my own experience as an MP and minister engaged mainly in European political affairs in addition to constituency duties. I kept a daily diary over this period on which I draw. This is not to assert that my evidence is worth more than that of others, but at least it was a contemporaneous record of what I took part in as an MP and minister specializing in Europe during the governments of Tony Blair and Gordon Brown between 1997 and 2010. The third part looks at the different tributaries – media, economic, business, intellectual, social-cultural – that are coming together into a confluence that can take us out of Europe.

Everyone on the pro-union side involved in the two-year-long Scottish referendum campaign was convinced that there was no real challenge to worry about. Time and again political pundits, elite London journalists and London-based political grandees told us it would be an easy win in favour of staying in the Union. We now know better. Brussels cannot come up with the generous political-financial bribe offered by David Cameron that closed the deal for the British Union. So if a referendum takes place on the EU we should not assume the answer will be Yes to Europe.

1

A CENTRIFUGAL EUROPE

The most popular play in recent years in London has been *One Man, Two Guvnors*. It is a modern version of the mid-eighteenth-century playwright Carlo Goldoni's play *Arlequin, serviteur de deux maîtres*. In the updated English version, the main actor invites two members of the public sitting in the front stalls on to the stage to help him in a scene. He asks them their names and what they do for a living. Then like a music-hall comedian he gets laughs, but not in an unkind way, as he makes gentle fun of them.

One evening in March 2013 the actor called up his victims. After the name, he asked one man where he worked. The reply was a muffled, hard-to-hear 'Commission'. The actor asked the man to repeat more clearly where he worked and again the reply was a whispered 'Commission'.

'Not the European Commission?', asked the actor, speaking in an incredulous tone of voice, as if no decent Englishman could possibly work for the European Commission. The poor man on stage sadly nodded his head.

'THE EUROPEAN COMMISSION!', bellowed the actor as the audience in the Theatre Royal, Haymarket started to boo and hiss at the very mention of Europe. The audience consisted of ordinary people keen to see a play which had transferred from the Royal National Theatre to the bigger theatre in the Haymarket and which was still pulling in crowds. There was middle England, not rich, not poor, not left, not right, not young, not old. If the mere mention of Europe produced such a hostile reaction, how would they vote in the in–out referendum announced by David Cameron in January 2013?

To be sure, endless conversations, a few minutes listening to any radio phone-in on Europe or a glance at papers like the *Sun* or *Daily Mail* would provide evidence of deep public hostility to Europe, now fused with the even more toxic issue of immigration. Yet when a whole theatre would as one boo and jeer the mention of the European Commission, something profound was taking place.

That is why Mr Cameron's decision in January 2013 to promise an in–out referendum was the most important of his premiership. It demolished the centuries-old tradition that Parliament should decide Britain's international engagements and treaties. Certainly a referendum in 1975 had confirmed the decision of Parliament to sign the Treaty of Rome and thus enter into a mesh of international treaty obligations embodied in the European Community and now European Union. But never before in British history had a prime minister proposed a plebiscite to repudiate an international treaty.

The 1975 referendum turned out to be a damp squib. All major forces – political chiefs, business leaders, the press, the TUC – were aligned in favour of a Yes vote. A 2017 referendum will be a very different affair. Parties will be divided. It is hard to imagine the press suddenly becoming evangelists for Europe. Businesses are very nervous of displaying any European enthusiasms. In 1975, foreign workers from Europe were not an issue. Britain has not really ingested referendums into its political life. They have their own dynamic. Voters can say No on the basis that a better nego-tiation will produce better results. They can say No to punish an unpopular government. They can say No because they do not like the idea of foreigners living and working in Britain. They can say No because they don't like paying increasing sums of money to Brussels. They can say No to rulings from the European Court of Human Rights, which has nothing to do with the EU. They can say No because they fear their national culture and iden-tity is not what it was. A referendum is about emotion, anger, disappointment – it is not a rational profit-and-loss judgement. The nineteenth-century historian Lord Acton described referendums as 'the triumph of democratic force over democratic freedom'. A referendum 'overrules [...] the representative principle' as 'it carries important measures away from the [...] legislature to submit them to the votes of the entire people, separating decision from deliberation'.

This passion for plebiscite in place of parliament is now embedded in the unwritten British constitution and nearly led to the end of the UK in the Scottish referendum. Tony Blair sprinkled around referendum promises. The euro, the Mayor of London, Scottish and Welsh devolution, the Northern Ireland peace settlement, regional government for the north-east of England and the EU constitutional treaty were all subjects of Blair's plebiscite pledges. Both the Conservatives and the Liberal Democrats promised an EU referendum in their 2010 election manifestos. They wriggled out of those promises, but referendums were held on changing the voting system and local ones on having directly elected mayors. Advocates of referendums argued that they would renew democracy and encourage citizens to participate in politics. There is no evidence that the plethora of plebiscites under Tony Blair and David Cameron has had any such effect. Every poll shows the public more disenchanted than ever with political elites, no matter how many referendums they offer.

The question of how Britain was linked to continental Europe as an EU member has always been contested political terrain. There has never been a moment since 1945 when there was broad national agreement on Britain's relationship with Europe. There have always been powerful political voices arguing against Europe. Since January 2013 Mr Cameron's in–out referendum has moved that debate to a different level. Parliament would be bypassed. In 1975, the referendum result was predictable, and everyone recognized the process as a fig-leaf to allow Labour, then in power, to keep Britain in Europe. Thirty-eight years later, Mr Cameron's in–out referendum is a very different political project full of risk and with the definite possibility it might end in Britain exiting the EU.

By the time of the prime minister's announcement in January 2013, I was using the term 'Brexit' – Britain exiting the EU. This was derived from the then fashionable concept of 'Grexit' – Greece exiting the euro, which newspapers like the *Financial Times* popularized, as the Greeks were told that a return to their former currency, the drachma, was the solution to their ills. Ignoring this advice, the Greeks are still using the euro.

Friends pooh-poohed my worries and warnings that Brexit could easily happen. 'Don't worry,' I was repeatedly told. The British people will never vote to quit the EU. This complacency pervades all of the non-Eurosceptic elites in politics, posh journalism, diplomatic circles, the long-established business federations, university European studies department and the important think-tanks that opine on Europe.

In the first months of 2014, several books by thoughtful, intelligent analysts such as Hugo Dixon, David Charter, Lord (Anthony) Giddens, Philip Legrain, Anton la Guardia and John Peet, Lord (Roger) Liddle and Roger Bootle all came out with different perspectives on the UK and Europe. Only Roger Bootle, the right-wing economics commentator, was prepared to countenance and make the case for Brexit. For the rest of the London elite commentariat, it was not going to happen.

The one group ignored in these high-level discussions on Britain and Europe were the voters. In the space of 18 months, between the prime minister's announcement of an in–out referendum and the surge of Ukip votes in the European Parliamentary elections followed by the arrival of the first Ukip Member of Parliament, the stakes were raised and Brexit became more likely. If in 2013 any mention of the European Commission was booed in a West End theatre audience, a year later voters were going to the polls with a devastating message to the political-business-media elite in London.

In European and local elections in May 2014 voters endorsed Brexit. They gave the biggest share of votes to Ukip, founded two decades ago with only one object – to obtain a referendum which would take Britain out of the EU. For the first time in a century neither the Conservatives nor Labour topped a nationwide election.

The broadcasters and press turned the 2014 election and the triumph of Ukip into as big a media event as a general election. The Eurosceptic 'Business for Britain' organization was quick off the mark with a statement insisting the response to the Ukip surge was to adopt the Ukip policy of a referendum. The EU-critical business community took advantage of the absence of any clear leadership from the more mainstream Confederation of British Industry or British Chambers of Commerce. Their declaration was duly given prominence by the press and broadcasters. 'A referendum is not only needed to address the gaping hole in the democratic legitimacy of our membership of the EU, but is also a vital component in efforts to reform the EU and its sprawling institutions. Without a referendum, it is difficult to take seriously claims of a desire to reform the EU, or to trust the people.'

One of the more forthright Eurosceptic Conservative MPs, Douglas Carswell, wrote: 'We need a pact with Ukip. If David Cameron is serious about an in–out vote in 2017 as he says he is and if Nigel Farage is as serious about Brexit as he claims, the two of them need to do a deal.' No deal has emerged – so far – but Carswell followed his own logic by defecting to Ukip. This forced a parliamentary by-election which turned into a stunning triumph for Ukip voters clamouring for Brexit. In a by-election held the same day in a hitherto ultra-safe Labour seat in north-west England, Ukip came within 600 votes of winning the seat. All over England citizens were voting in favour of Brexit, it appeared.

The landscape and alignments of British politics were changing fast. Pouring petrol on the Brexit flames, the outgoing European Commission announced that Britain would have to pay an extra €2.1 billion contribution to EU coffers. The reason given was that Britain's economy and tax revenues had done so much better than the rest of Europe, therefore the pro-rata payments went up correspondingly. There was outrage in British political and media circles. Even the staunchest pro-Europeans thought the timing of the extra bill for Britain was poor. People forgot Britain had been given an extra £700 million by the EU in the late 1990s to invest in industrial regions which had become desperately poor under the governments of Margaret Thatcher and John Major. Labour MPs outbid Tories and Ukip in denouncing the EU's budget demands.

The business community began to take the idea of Brexit seriously. Three major American banks, the Bank of America, Citibank and Morgan Stanley, revealed they were working on contingency plans to relocate from London to Dublin in the event of a Brexit. For global banks dealing with the 500-million-strong EU market it makes sense to have their European headquarters based inside, not outside, the EU.

But taken as a whole the business community did not sound the alarm about the dangers of a Brexit vote. There was an assumption that the British people could not contemplate voting to quit the EU. Others in the business community began talking of a 'positive' Brexit. This was based on Britain quitting the EU to re-establish some kind of relationship with Europe similar to that which existed prior to 1973. Then the European Economic Community, forerunner of today's EU, was smaller in terms of member states than EFTA, the European Free Trade Association, which Britain belonged to. EFTA had no power to overrule national governments' protectionist measures. It had no single market. There were no enforceable rights in EFTA member states permitting capital, goods and services to move without let or hindrance across national borders. Each EFTA country had its own system of agricultural subsidies and some, as in Switzerland, were far more costly than the EU's Common Agricultural Policy. And EFTA gave no citizen of its member states the right to live freely in other countries, as hundreds of thousands of British citizens have done in Spain since Spain joined the UK in the EU.

No one, however, thought that such a soft Brexit could happen without years of fraught negotiations, as any new treaty between a post-Brexit UK and the rest of the EU would require agreement and ratification by 27 different governments and parliaments.

The voices in favour of the EU, per se, were thin on the ground. The veteran pro-EU Conservative Kenneth Clarke was sacked by David Cameron in a reshuffle in July 2014 which saw the arrival of a new foreign secretary, Philip Hammond, who had said on record he would vote to leave the EU unless the other 27 member states met his Eurosceptic conditions. Mr Hammond went on to tell the Conservative Party's 2014 conference that there had to be 'concrete and irreversible' change in Britain's relationship with its 27 fellow EU member states before he would support continuing membership. Dominic Grieve MP, a French-speaking lawyer, was dismissed as Attorney General. His opposition to defying the European Convention on Human Rights was well known and public. There is no longer a Conservative cabinet minister who is identifiable as pro-European and few Conservative MPs.

If Brexit happens it will be a major turning point in British, indeed European history. Even if a prime minister emerges who refuses an in–out referendum in 2017 he is likely to preside over a weak government without a strong majority, consisting of MPs who have put off thinking about Europe for a decade or more. He will face a political-constitutional wrangle over Scottish MPs voting on laws that apply to England but not Scotland.

In opposition, any conceivable Conservative leadership will be more intensely Eurosceptic. Many Conservatives will demand an arrangement with Ukip, if not a fusion. The anti-EU press will turn up the temperature, increasing its attacks on Brussels, on EU citizens working in Britain and on rulings of the European Court of Human Rights. By the time of the next election in 2020, or earlier, the Brexit question – far from being disposed of by a government disinclined to hold a referendum – will be at the top of Britain's political agenda.

This is not a British–British problem. A Brexit will change the course of history and the contours of European politics. The EU without Britain will be increasingly dominated by Germany – by far the biggest nation, with the strongest economy, which is increasingly integrated with Poland and new EU member states in east and central Europe. European Germany will give way to German

Europe. France will have to accept junior partner status, subordinate to Germany, or seek to create a coalition of dissent with Spain and Italy, a triple alliance of the weakest of the big EU member states.

A new era of British, European and global politics will open. The impact will be far greater than de Gaulle taking France out of NATO or Britain joining with the United States to invade Iraq. The unity of Europe will be shattered. The United States will have to decide where its strategic alliance and interests in Europe lie. Russia and China will have more room for their *divide et impera* tactics. Japan, Brazil, India, South Africa, South Korea and Turkey will see a Europe weak and divided. France will lose its only EU partner which is serious about defence and security policy. Germany, Nordic EU member states and the Netherlands will lose an Atlantic liberal market partner. The EU will lose its financial centre. The only nation that defied Hitler from 1939 and fought from the beginning to the end to defeat Nazism will be cut off.

The losses for Britain will be serious. Either Britain outside the EU seeks the same status as Norway, which has to accept all EU norms and directives, including free movement of EU citizens, or Britain declares itself completely independent of the EU as if it were Canada or India. To be sure, trade and commerce will continue but on terms dictated by the EU. Britain exports half of what it produces to the EU, but the British market amounts to just one tenth of what the EU produces. Britain will lose all say and influence over how the single market works and will be unable to defend core British sectors like financial services and the City. Dubai, Singapore, Hong Kong, Wall Street and Frankfurt will all try and grab some of the business now done in London because London is the EU's global capital and financial hub.

British citizens will lose their automatic right to retire to Spain or France and enjoy access to health care and social rights that come with common European citizenship conferred by existing EU treaties. If Britain seeks to go it alone, there will be years of difficult negotiations over the dense network of rules that allow the single market to work. The 27 remaining EU member states may shrug their shoulders and get on with creating a more integrated, competitive European economy which Britain will only be able to benefit from if London accepts Brussels' rules. Vodafone will have to comply with EU rules if it wants to do business in the rest of the EU. But Vodafone will not be able to talk to British ministers, who today take – jointly with 27 other governments – the decisions that shape EU telecommunications policy. Toyota, Nissan and Tata – Asian automobile companies which have saved the down-and-out British car industry on the grounds that any car made in Britain could be sold anywhere in Europe – will think hard about future investments once their cars lose automatic access to the giant EU market.

A by-product of Brexit is that Europe will lose the ability to laugh at itself: Britain has been confident enough, thanks to its long, if at times complacent history of mocking its rulers and curbing censorship, to laugh and poke fun at princes and potentates, including the new aristocracy of Brussels and Strasbourg.

Alternatively, Britain quitting the EU may unleash other political forces that can be seen in most European countries in favour of national supremacy over European integration. In France, any move to Brexit will encourage Marine Le Pen and the growing voices on the left and right for France to shape a new relationship with Europe. If Brexit happens can Frexit – France exiting the existing EU – be far behind? A vote to leave the EU will be seen as a triumph for the populist nationalist politics of Ukip. The growing populist-nationalist forces elsewhere in Europe will be greatly bolstered. The Swiss anti-Europeans grouped around the Swiss People's Party, the biggest political bloc in the Alpine country, headed by Christophe Blocher, a millionaire and obsessive anti-EU politician, will ramp up their campaign against the EU and the Swiss adhesion to the European Convention on Human Rights. 'England', said Prime Minister William Pitt at the beginning of the nineteenth century, 'will save Europe by her example.' He was talking about Napoleonic hegemony in Europe, but many feel the hegemony of the Brussels institutions has increased, is increasing and must diminish.

So might a Britain loosening its ties with the EU or exiting the EU lead Europe away from the process of integration that began in the 1950s and, with the arrival of a Pole, Donald Tusk, as president of the European Council, continues today? There have always been major political forces opposed to European cooperation, notably the big communist parties of Italy and France, which denounced the European Community as a capitalist, free-market instrument. The French Communist Party by 1980 was demanding an end to the presence of foreign workers in France and denouncing Brussels in much the same language that Ukip uses today. But these anti-European forces never gained sufficient strength to change the line of a major party of government or obtain a referendum on actually leaving Europe. Here Britain is in the lead.

Europe is now centrifugal. The glue that forged first the Steel and Coal Community, then the Common Market, followed by successive enlargement, beginning with Britain joining the six founder states in 1973, the single market, the euro, the idea of common EU citizenship and a host of laws and standards aimed at consolidating an open-market, rule-of-law democracy, social justice, health standards and improved education is slowly dissolving.

Eighteen months after Mr Cameron announced his in–out plebiscite the clamour against Europe grew louder.

- The avowedly Eurosceptic Mayor of London, Boris Johnson, who has cheerfully admitted he can imagine a post-EU future for Britain, was chosen as a candidate in a safe Conservative seat to re-enter the Commons in 2015. This ensured that his party had an alternative leader-in-waiting who had spent 25 years of political activism denouncing the EU with vigour and style. In his biography of Churchill, Johnson described a 'Gestapo-controlled Nazi EU'.

- Ahead of the autumn 2014 Conservative Party conference, the culture secretary, Sajid Javid MP, proclaimed that the UK could benefit economically if it left the EU. 'I think it would open up opportunities. I am not afraid of that at all', he declared.

- His fellow Eurosceptic cabinet colleague, the justice secretary, Chris Grayling MP, sought to raise his anti-European profile in front of Conservative Party activists by pledging that a future Conservative government would pass legislation to block rulings by the European Court of Human Rights, a measure that would lead to Britain quitting the Council of Europe and repudiating the European Convention on Human Rights, adherence to which is expected of all EU member states.

- The foreign secretary, Philip Hammond MP, said that a Brexit referendum would 'light a fire under Europe' – a metaphor appropriate to the nation of Guy Fawkes but worrying to anyone who knows what burning things, books and people means on the continent.
- The defence secretary, Michael Fallon MP, blamed the EU for 'swamping' Britain with immigrants. On Sky TV he said British 'Towns feel under siege, large numbers of migrant workers and people claiming benefits'. He added that British proposals to the EU would try to prevent 'whole communities being swamped by huge numbers of migrants'.

The Brexit centrifuge was visibly working. The British Social Attitudes survey published in September 2013 surveys in depth what Britons think of the country. Sixty-seven per cent said they wanted to leave the EU or only stay in it on condition that there were major reforms. A TNS poll in April 2014 showed 49 per cent declaring they would vote to quit the EU and 41 per cent voting to stay in. The UK was the last of the big western European nations to enter Europe in 1973. Today Britain is preparing to become the first EU member state to leave.

Last in, first out. This is not what Britain's leaders want, or at least it is not what they say they want. The Europe minister, David Lidington MP, told the *Financial Times* in May 2014 that 'some treaty change will be required'. Yet France and other countries committed to having referendums on EU treaties have made clear they cannot envisage rewriting existing EU treaties just to appease Mr Cameron's Euroscepticism and certainly not by 2017, the year of French and German national elections.

Britain's increasing hostility to membership of the EU did not pass unnoticed across the Channel. In an open letter to 'My English friends' published in France's biggest political weekly, the half-million circulation *Nouvel Observateur*, the former French prime minister, Michel Rocard, argued that 'the British have to accept their own logic. Either they should accept the construction of a united Europe or they should leave.' Rocard added: 'Your leaving will be elegant. You will do it with style and thus help to renew a friendship which is waiting to be brought back to life.' A survey by the German Marshall Fund in 2014 found support for Rocard's view: 52 per cent of the French agreed it would better if Britain left the EU.

Rocard's first girl-friend was English. His father was at the side of General de Gaulle in London in the war. Of all the leading French politicians, Rocard is the most Anglophile and speaks the best English. He understands Britain. When he announces we are about to leave Europe it is time to explain how and why. Another French Anglophile is Jacques Lafitte, who was one of the architects of the euro when an official in Brussels. He now runs a Brussels-based firm, Avisa. In a talk in the City for the Centre for the Study of Financial Institutions he stated as a given: 'Virtually all EU officials would prefer the UK to stay, but most assume it will leave, as the referendum appears in Brussels as both unavoidable and impossible to win.'

In her book *Statecraft*, published in 2002, Margaret Thatcher called into question British membership of the EU. She described the EU as 'fundamentally unreformable' and added: ' It is frequently said that it is unthinkable that Britain should leave the EU. But the avoidance of thought about this is a poor substitute for judgement.' Today Prime Minister David Cameron and all his cabinet are Margaret Thatcher's political offspring. They entered politics as disciples of the Iron Lady; they grew under the influence of her ideology and they made her their political model. Britain is now close to the exit door of Europe – Thatcher's legacy. Mr Cameron is both the inheritor and the prisoner of Thatcherism. He cannot claim an economic revolution as she could. There is nothing left to privatize. The unions she broke are weak. He has no partner like Ronald

Reagan in Washington. But he can carry on her campaign against Europe. If Britain leaves Europe following Mr Cameron's referendum, Margaret Thatcher will have won her last posthumous victory.

When Ed Miliband announced in March 2014 that a Labour government would not hold an in–out referendum, it was a brave decision. Labour insiders say that as they talk to people in their homes and when out canvassing, Europe is not a priority issue. Jobs, cost of living, the NHS, affordable housing, cuts to public services are more important. That is true but irrelevant. It confuses democratic *content* – the offer of policies to improve the citizen's life – with democratic *form*, the offer to allow the citizen to decide his or her future directly, not via Parliament.

If you ask voters to rank Europe as an important issue it comes well below immigration, taxation, jobs, utility bills, housing or the NHS. If you ask them whether they should be allowed a vote on Europe the answer is Yes, Yes, Yes. In fact, one opinion poll in October 2013 showed 55 per cent wanting an in–out referendum to be held in 2014. So whatever politicians say, David Cameron, Ed Miliband and Nick Clegg have turned the May 2015 general election into a vote on whether to have an in–out referendum.

Clearly if David Cameron remains prime minister this is a pledge that even with the most liberal smothering of oil or Vaseline cannot be wriggled out of.

Other scenarios are possible. They all place the Europe question at the heart of existential politics in Westminster from 2015 onwards. If, for example, the Conservatives once again emerge as the biggest party but without an overall majority, David Cameron, assuming he stays as prime minister, now has a nod and wink from the Liberal Democrats that they will accept a 2017 Brexit referendum with all the risks it entails.

Alternatively, a minority government – either Conservative or Labour – could limp on a bit towards an early second general election like the one called in October 1974, six months after the one in February 1974 failed to deliver a majority government. There are uncanny similarities between the 1970s and this decade. A lack of a commanding majority government as under Margaret Thatcher and Tony Blair and voters unimpressed with the political leadership on offer. Britain (and much of the rest of Europe) appears to be in a transition decade. The 1970s saw the end of the post-1945 model and the present decade is raising questions about what happens after the three-decade-long era of liberalization and globalization that ended with the crash of 2008. Therefore as in 1974 the need for more than one election to produce a government cannot be excluded.

A Labour government or Labour-dominated non-Conservative administration after 2015 may put off a referendum on Europe but ministers will be hammered day in, day out by the demand for one. Any election after 2015 will almost certainly have the Europe question at its heart.

A radical but unlikely alternative would be an agreement between parties to restore parliamentary supremacy and do away with the plebiscitory decision-making that became established after 1997.

Yet parliament has become less and less important. Many of the MPs who plundered the now-discredited expenses system and made huge personal profits are still in place and have never been sanctioned. Their local voters know who they are, however, and the failure of the profiteering MPs to pay back any of the money they obtained as personal enrichment has further alienated voters. Too many MPs are still employing their wives or children, a practice illegal in most democracies. Despite new rules, every few weeks the media expose some expense fiddle but no action is ever taken against erring politicians. MPs have lost so much status in this century it is hard to see how the Commons can ever again agree to see referendums as 'the devices of dictators and demagogues', as Margaret Thatcher, quoting Clement Attlee, called them.

Whether in 2017 or possibly after the subsequent election an EU referendum will take place within the next political cycle. The rest of Europe, whatever the doubts and difficulties all other member states have over the EU, cannot offer a unique deal to Britain sufficient to meet the demands of citizens hostile to or just unhappy with the EU. And any time spent with voters shows that it is not the narrow issue of EU membership that gives rise to discontent. The losers in the era of globalization feel ignored. They have seen secure working-class industrial jobs disappear. They have seen the mass arrival of outsiders, incomers from other countries who have to be accommodated. In formerly confident, settled industrial regions – in the north especially – the white working-class man and woman on shrinking wages, with no access to social housing for their children and with schools full of chatter in foreign tongues, the years of globalization and the abolition of national controls inherent in EU membership are resented.

All the elites, MPs, MEPs, editors, professionals and business leaders, irrespective of their views on Europe, benefit from the cheap labour that provides a source of low-cost workers as nannies, handymen, mini-cab drivers and those who allow service industries in retail, catering and transport to operate profitably. For many others the open market and open society represented by the EU is to blame for the difficulties they face. Thus the referendum on Europe is not on the benefits or cost of EU membership, but a wider protest about economic and social change which appears inside Britain to produce as many losers as winners.

When making the case for France to vote Yes in a referendum on the Maastricht Treaty in 1992 François Mitterrand said 'Europe is there to protect us'. That is not how millions of losers in the new world and European economic order see the EU. Far from protecting them, the EU seems forever exposing them to a relentless downward pressure on their living standards in the name of market opening competition, privatizations and austerity cuts in social provision to meet criteria on debt and deficit laid down by remote technocrats in Brussels even if the policy decisions are agreed by democratically elected members of the European Council and the Council of Ministers.

A referendum on EU membership will not solve the broader question of the arrival and visible presence in every UK city and town of incomers with different customs, religions or cultures. But when anti-EU forces demand a referendum to restore 'control of

frontiers' they play on fears about immigration that are not necessarily to do with the EU. The clamour for a plebiscite as the cure-all
for concerns that are real but, like anger over rulings of the European
Court of Human Rights, have nothing to do with membership of
the EU and would not be solved by withdrawal from the EU, is now
mainstream politics.

Another factor that is often overlooked is that there is no longer
an automatic sense that being in the EU is good for growth and
wealth creation. Britain is seen as having Europe's best-performing
post-crash economy. The International Monetary Fund hailed Britain
as the fastest-growing G7 economy in its 2014 annual report. Critics
will point to British growth being based on high debt and deficit,
printing money (disguised by the technical term 'quantitative easing'), a housing property bubble with a great deal of employment
based on part-time work, very low wages and zero-hours contracts.
These are true points, but pointless. Britain is on the upward curve
of an economic cycle while the Eurozone economies for the time
being are mired in the austerity economics ordained as a cure for the
crash by the wise men of Brussels and the European Central Bank.

Thus there is no magnetic pull towards European integration
such as generated British enthusiasm for Europe for much of the
second half of the last century. On the contrary, the failure of EU
leaders to grow the Eurozone economies and create jobs and tax revenue is now seen as proof that British detachment from Europe is a
positive.

Of course there are those who see the whole question from the
other end of the telescope. Radek Sirkorski, Poland's foreign minister until September 2014, was a student asylum-seeker from communist repression in Poland in the 1980s. He was a member of the
Oxford University Bullingdon Club with David Cameron and Boris
Johnson in the 1980s. In many newspaper interviews as Poland's foreign minister, Sikorski made it clear that he and everyone in Warsaw
did not want Britain to quit Europe. As he told a London audience in
2013, 'The EU is an English-speaking power. The Single Market was
a British idea. A British commissioner runs our diplomatic service.

You could, if only you wished, lead Europe's defence policy. But if you refuse, please don't expect us to help you wreck or paralyse the EU.' His appeal-cum-warning went unheeded.

The emotions generated by this sense that EU membership is bad for the poor or for workers is not taken into account by commentators who defend Britain's EU membership as a rational, almost common-sense choice. As Le Monde's foreign affairs columnist, Alain Frachon, wrote:

> Why on earth do they want to leave? We know that being original is in the British, especially the English, DNA. But to go from that excellent character trait in the British to actually leaving the European Union is a step that even the least rational of the French finds British, a fact which seems to have escaped the notice of Ukip and the Tories who also want their country to leave the Union.

For Le Monde's writer Europe has rejected the French vision of a 'Europe half social-democratic and half-run by the state'. On the contrary: 'London has won. With an EU of more than 20 members there is no common policy save creating a big single market.' And that thanks to British diplomats. 'An Oxford or Cambridge graduate is worth three French énarques [énarque is the name given to graduates of ENA, the elite training college for top civil servants in France] because they have fashioned Europe according to British conceptions', M. Frachon declared.

Pro-Europeans in Britain know this argument by heart and use it in speeches or articles as they try to persuade their fellow citizens that Europe is not a vast conspiracy against Britain. Usually their efforts are in vain. For the City, the proposal to levy a tiny tax on financial transactions – a minute fraction of Britain's long-established stamp duty – or limit the bonuses paid to the banking elites who destroyed the economy is proof of the existence of a Europe trying to control the British way of life. Allowing Poles or Bulgarians or Romanians (or French, Dutch and Irish) to enter Britain is evidence of the super-state controlled from Brussels that has abolished the frontiers of our island once jealously guarded by the Royal Navy in the Channel. The European Arrest Warrant was proof for many Conservative MPs that Europe now determines policing and extradition in the UK.

During the interminable debates on recent EU treaties since 1998 the Foreign and Commonwealth Office has prepared notes, briefing papers and speeches for ministers using M. Frachon's argument that Europe is more British than Britain is European. This line of argument has had no success in persuading the British to believe in Europe. 'So why therefore do our British friends want to leave "their" Europe?', concludes M. Frachon. The answer is more complex than most debate on Europe, with its reduction to silly knockabout by pro- and anti-European politicians or journalists, ever allows.

Optimists who want Britain to stay in the EU say it can change into a bi-zonal EU with 'two different systems of institutions – one for the seventeen members of the Eurozone and one for all the twenty-eight members of the EU'. Valéry Giscard d'Estaing, the former French president, has written *Europa*, a book which proposes an inner Europe of 12 bigger Eurozone countries plus Poland but excluding Britain and Baltic and Balkan EU member states. David Goodhart, director of the Demos think-tank and a thoughtful outrider from the centre-left on European problems, quotes approvingly Lord (David) Owen's belief that Britain should lead an outer-Europe consisting of Poland and Sweden and other non-Eurozone nations. However, the arrival of Poland's most successful post-communist prime minister, Donald Tusk, as president of the European Council and the defeat of the Swedish prime minister, Fredrik Reinfeldt – a close ally and friend of David Cameron – means that the idea that Poland and Sweden will follow Britain into semi-detached membership of the EU may be held only by some monolingual British politicians. It is not rooted in reality.

Writing in *Le Figaro*, the French historian and international affairs commentator Alexandre Adler argued for a division of the EU.

The European Commission would keep control of harmon-
izing regulations, of defence policy, protecting human rights,
and organizing the single market. The UK [he uses the term
l'Angleterre, as do many in France when writing or talking about
the UK] would not only be a full member of the big union but
one could foresee a British citizen, maybe Peter Mandelson,
being president of the Commission with a reduced role. But
the key decisions on economic and monetary policy as well as
foreign policy would be drawn up separately.

M. Adler is no doubt trying to be helpful but his belief that in the
time between now and Mr Cameron's proposed referendum the
EU can be entirely reconfigured to appease British Eurosceptics is
not realistic. For a start, more countries may join the Eurozone. By
January 2015 Latvia and Lithuania replaced their currencies with
euros. In total, 24 European nation-states use the euro as their official
currency, including Balkan countries like Montenegro and Kosovo,
low-tax Monaco and small UN member states like Andorra and San
Marino. Even the Vatican, an independent state-like entity with a
powerful network of embassies around the world and a voice at the
UN, has adopted the euro as its currency. Alas, such papal endorse-
ment does not appear to have helped the Eurozone in recent years.

In the European Parliament, Conservative MEPs sit with the
Polish Catholic-nationalist PiS (Law and Justice) Party. PiS shares
some hostility to Brussels with British Conservative Eurosceptics.
But Mr Cameron's Polish PiS allies in the European Parliament
want more Common Agricultural Policy subsidies to flow to the
large Polish agro-industry sector. Warsaw vetoes EU energy policy
that threatens its desire to keep using the lignite or brown coal it has
in abundance despite its highly polluting nature. And Poland has
categorically rejected any reform of free movement of workers and
their right to access the same welfare rights (provided they pay tax
and national insurance) that British citizens enjoy.

So hopes that a Polish–British alliance to reshape the EU along
the lines that Mr Cameron and his generation of Eurosceptic

Conservatives have sketched are also unrealistic. Moreover, the Polish economy is now so integrated with Germany. The vision of an EU neatly divided into a Eurozone and non-Eurozone has no takers on the continent. Denmark, for example, does not use the euro but the Danish crown is *de facto* the same currency with the same interest and exchange rate. Ireland does use the euro but the Irish economy is *de facto* part of the British Isles economic space. Musing to his biographer, Janaan Ganeesh of the *Financial Times*, the chancellor, George Osborne MP, said he could envisage Britain leaving the EU as the Eurozone was turned into an EU within an EU. Certainly the closer integration of the countries where the euro is used suggests a neat division. But on closer examination does it make sense? Poland is closer to Germany in terms of economic integration than any other country but has kept the Polish złoty as its currency. Ireland, which uses the euro, is more economically integrated with the rest of the British Isles than are any other two euro-using nations, save perhaps Germany and Austria. Indeed, a Brexit would be a nightmare for Ireland, as Dublin would have to deal with its former colonial master and London would no longer be obliged to treat Ireland on the basis of respect, reciprocity and equal status as a fellow EU member state.

The new European Commission has as vice presidents former prime ministers and others from countries like Estonia and Bulgaria that do not use the euro. So Mr Osborne's idea that only the Eurozone member states matter is a convenient comfort blanket to disguise the core hostility to the EU as a whole, not just Eurozone member states, that is widespread in David Cameron's administration.

France will not surrender sovereign autonomy in foreign and defence policy to Brussels under any imaginable scheme. Nor will a French socialist government or the new Swedish government, whose prime minister was a welder who headed Sweden's main industrial union, Svenska Metall, support any dilution of EU social obligations, a key demand of British businesses and Conservative politicians.

The Dutch government has put forward a plan for a reformed EU with the return of some powers to national governments. But the plan calls for more EU integration on defence and immigration – two policy areas where British Conservatives are in a very different place. And the Dutch proposal rejects a new treaty or a referendum, so the Netherlands is not on the same path as the UK.

Mr Cameron and many of his supporters all put their hands on their hearts and say they do not want Britain to leave the EU. Let us take them at their word. In his latest book, *German Europe*, the late German academic Ulrich Beck, who after Jürgen Habermas is the German intellectual with the most to say on Europe, describes Cameron as a 'vehement Eurosceptic'. This is wrong. 'Vehement' is not an adjective to apply to David Cameron. Mr Cameron was brought up in the relaxed born-to-rule style of the calm, unflappable British ruling class. As Arthur Balfour, Conservative prime minister at the beginning of the twentieth century and like Mr Cameron a product of Eton and Oxford, said of politics: 'Nothing matters very much and few things matter at all.'

The Tories have been winning elections and governing Britain for more than 250 years. Britain has seen the Conservative Party quietly slipping out of agricultural protectionism and into free trade in the nineteenth century, coming to terms with nationalist independent Ireland after 1920 or ditching British imperialism and accepting the mixed economy and welfare state after 1945. It does so by being adaptable.

Personally I have always found David Cameron friendly and courteous. Yet for Mr Cameron all the good manners and easy charm that come from an Eton education, immense personal wealth and a life mapped out as an easy path to the top (though he suffered the personal tragedy of losing a severely handicapped son who died aged six) cannot overcome the dislike of his party and much of the broad Conservative family for the EU.

Cameron's decision to hold a referendum alters the chemistry of politics. The casual way he offered a simple Yes–No referendum to Scotland in 2011 has led to a quasi-insoluble imbroglio over the future of the British constitution. As a result of Mr Cameron's lightly offered Scottish referendum Britain now has to wrestle with the question of whether the House of Commons survives with its MPs having equal voting rights. Voters in England also have to swallow the commitment to enshrine in law more public spending on the Scots than on the English.

It is easy to propose a referendum, but not always easy to guarantee the result. Referendums have their own reasons that have little to do with reason. A plebiscite is about passion, not a calm, disinterested process based on examining the evidence and coming to a mature judgement. The German historian Sebastian Haffner, who witnessed the use of plebiscites in the 1930s in German politics, wrote about the populism of 'the mentality of the crowd' which is 'not the sum total of the mentality of the individuals which form it, but their lowest common denominator: that their intellectual powers are not integrated by contact but bewildered by the interference for their minds – light plus light resulting in darkness'.

Mr Cameron's referendum takes Britain into political *terra incognita*. If the decision is to leave the EU, it will be definitive. There will be no reinterpretation of the result or a swift second vote to stay in Europe. Mr Cameron and other party leaders are walking towards the political cliff of falling out of the EU.

After the initial shock at Mr Cameron's in–out referendum announcement the British elite decided that it was a good idea. The Establishment view was set out by Sir John Major, a former Conservative prime minister, in a speech to the Royal Institute of International Affairs a few weeks after the January 2013 announcement of an in–out referendum.

> As a general principle, I don't like referenda [*sic*] in a parliamentary system. But this referendum could heal many old sores and have a cleansing effect on politics. It will be healthy to let the electorate re-endorse our membership, or pull us out altogether.

Sir John wrote in his memoirs about how much he preferred meetings of the Commonwealth heads of government to meetings of the

European Council because at least with his fellow Commonwealth premiers everyone spoke English. Now with a remarkable insouciance he insists 'it will be healthy to let the electorate […] pull us out altogether'. The idea that Britain withdrawing from the EU 'could heal many old sores and have a cleansing effect on politics' is a return to the isolationism which has tempted British Conservatives in the past. Lord Salisbury, Conservative prime minister at the beginning of the twentieth century, boasted of his policy of 'splendid isolation' a few years before the outbreak of World War I. Sir John's metaphor of a 'cleansing effect', as if a referendum were a kind of political enema that rids the body politic of its toxins, is not backed by experience. Referendums are political civil wars with fratricidal fury unleashed. They harm and do not heal political passions. If Britain does withdraw from the EU it will spark an internal political turmoil and bitterness which will ravage British politics for a generation or longer. If Britain votes to stay in the EU by any margin the British Eurosceptics will not lay down their arms.

All the referendum process will do is mark the opening salvoes in a new Thirty Years War over Europe, which will devour British politics for generations to come. It is not just for the people to vote in a plebiscite, but for political leaders to decide what they believe in and where they want their country to go. Sir John Major and his successors at Downing Street have failed in that task. They – and political leaders from other parties – have let Britain's Europe policy be imposed on them by obsessive anti-Europeans encouraged by newspaper proprietors, sometimes living abroad. Instead of leading they have been followers, appeasing the Europhobe ideology of parties like Ukip.

On what terms might Britain stay in the EU? Sir John gave some indication in his speech when he listed all the changes in Britain's treaty relationship with the other 27 member states of the EU. These are the minimum concessions Britain needs, he said:

- safeguards for the City
- less regulation

- less bureaucracy
- no more social legislation
- enhancement of the single market and more besides
- a full repeal of the Working Time Directive
- changes in other EU policies – Common Agricultural Policy, fisheries, structural funds.

Sir John lies on the pragmatic wing of the Conservative Party and he is not advocating a British withdrawal come what may – in contrast to many in his own party. In November 2014, as Sir John realized that the rest of Europe was not automatically going to grant him his wish list, especially on free movement of EU citizens, he said the chances of Brexit were now 50–50. It was a bleak assessment from the experienced former prime minister. Mr Cameron, in turn, set out in a newspaper article in 2014 broad areas where he wanted EU reform. But these were cast in generalities and were not detailed. Yet in EU decision making all the devil lies in the detail. British voters and the rest of Europe are still waiting for Mr Cameron's specific list of concessions required to enable him to advocate a vote for staying in Europe in his referendum.

For the sake of argument, let us assume Mr Cameron can obtain agreement to a repeal of the EU Working Time Directive thus opening the way to a working week for British workers of 60 hours or more and an end to decent paid holidays. Let us assume a British prime minister can secure a promise that never again will the EU have a word to say about the treatment of vulnerable workers or even dare to hint it is desirable to have social rules across Europe preventing the exploitation of workers anywhere in the EU. Many employers and the anti-trade union press will welcome an end to Social Europe as far as Britain is concerned. But in the subsequent referendum, every British worker, the trade unions, the left and most of the Labour Party would be entitled to call for a No vote to reject a special place for Britain to stay in Europe on terms so inimical to the social interests and workplace rights of the 33 million British citizens in employment. As Glyn

Ford, one of Labour's longest-serving MEPs and a knowledgeable Brussels-based writer on Europe, said:

> If we were being asked to vote to stay in by destroying social rights in Britain with the threat this would set a precedent in future for rightwing governments in other EU countries to demand the same the left should adopt the same selfless heroism Captain 'Titus' Oates did say 'I am just going outside and may be some time' and vote to quit Europe rather than infect it with this toxic Tory virus.

Like the French anti-European leftists in 2005, the tribunes of the workers and those whose argument in favour of Europe is based on the entirety of the EU, including its social provision, would be entitled to say No to the deal Mr Cameron is proposing.

The new president of the European Commission, Jean-Claude Juncker, has made it clear he believes efforts should be made to keep Britain in the EU. He made the obvious point that Britain was not going to join the euro or the passport-free Schengen zone. He accepted that some reforms to welfare benefits paid to EU citizens from poorer countries who migrate to find work in richer ones could be envisaged. Other leaders will also want to help Britain stay in the EU. Let us suppose that, working with British diplomats, they find formulas that appear to offer some concessions to Britain – agreement to a qualifying period before welfare benefits might apply to EU workers, a look at a longer transition period before opening access to labour markets for future EU members, an offer to establish a committee to look at reforming the Common Agricultural Policy, or a pledge that the EU budget will not rise for a decade or that the language about 'an ever-closer union' which has been in all EU treaties since 1957 will be re-examined in any future new treaty.

In fact, the EU budget has been stable at 1 per cent of Europe's Gross National Income (GNI) for some years. But within that overall budget, countries pay or receive different amounts according to how well their economies perform. Today, Britain, with the best-performing European economy since 1995, finds it is paying more than other big EU nations. So even if there is a limit on the overall budget, the British will feel they are paying more than their fair share. The reference to 'ever-closer union of peoples' (for many, including the author, a harmless, generous and worthwhile sentiment) was removed from the EU's Constitutional Treaty after Labour ministers secured a different text. There were no thanks from Eurosceptic Conservatives at the time and in any event the treaty minus the reference to 'ever-closer union' was torpedoed by French and Dutch plebiscites in 2005. In short, the passions of those hostile to the EU are not satiated by new language or concessions. Hence the idea that a British prime minister can negotiate and secure new language that will convert Eurosceptics into supporters of staying in the EU is a dubious proposition.

Mr Cameron may try to persuade voters that such thin promises amount to a major renegotiation of Britain's relationship with Europe. After his final negotiations in Brussels, he returns to Britain to hold the referendum he was obliged to promise in order to win the election in 2015. He will say he is persuaded that the declarations – but no new binding treaty – he has obtained are sufficient to justify a Yes vote to stay in the EU.

He will have the support of some of the Tony Blair generation of Labour politicians, but these are people closer to taking their pensions than to rediscovering the political energy of their youth. In 2017, the 75-year-old Lord (Neil) Kinnock, a passionate Eurosceptic in the 1970s and into the 1980s, but who then converted to a zealous faith in Europe and was a European Commissioner, will speak in favour of staying in Europe. So will Lord (Peter) Mandelson, the Cardinal Mazarin of British politics, now eligible, like Mr Blair, for his old-age Freedom Pass. Lord Hannay, who represented Britain at Brussels between 1985 and 1990, is one of the most respected of the cohort of retired diplomats who speaks in favour of Britain staying an EU member-state. He was born in 1935.

Nick Butler, the influential Labour networker, is a former Number 10 official who moves easily between the private sectors, academia and the think-tank world. In 1996, he wrote a launch pamphlet for the Centre for European Reform in which he described the 'E' – for Europe – generation of those born around 1950 who had incorporated Europe into their thinking and way of seeing Britain.

Twenty years later, the 'E' generation has retired or soon will retire. There is no evidence that a new generation of younger political leaders or opinion-formers infused with belief in Europe or energized to make the case for Europe will emerge between now and 2017 to win a referendum. In fact, the absence of any younger, stylish, witty speakers not frightened to say something positive in favour of Britain being a player instead of a whiner in Europe is a hole waiting to be filled. The pro-Europeans have no Nigel Farage or Boris Johnson, able to make a stylish, persuasive case for the EU in the soundbite and social media era of modern political communication.

Labour and the Liberal Democrats may offer support for a Yes to the EU vote in any referendum, but without enthusiasm for a plebiscite that was devised by Conservatives for internal party political purposes. Once again the Westminster insiders, the despised political elites, will face a sullen, hostile, unhappy electorate living through the lost decade since 2007/8 in which all politicians are blamed for the reduction in the standard of living and public social provision of citizens.

Both Mr Cameron and Mr Miliband, whoever is prime minister after 2015, may hope that their political skills can produce a settlement on Europe. The inevitable cuts in public services, welfare support and a rise in public sector unemployment that will take place after 2015 to control the debt and deficit crisis Britain faces will make any government deeply unpopular, Mr Cameron, but not all his party, hopes to avoid the end result of a process they have themselves initiated or have not been able to avoid – a vote that takes Britain out of Europe. They may be lucky. But Europe and the world should be prepared for a plebiscite that will result in British withdrawal from Europe.

How has this come about? Can anything be done to avoid it? First we must examine Britain's long, tortuous history in Europe.

2

CHURCHILL INVENTS THE UNITED STATES OF EUROPE

The question of Europe tends to be treated as an issue of immediate news. There are headlines but rarely history. Yet in modern British history, beginning with World War II and its aftermath, Europe has always been central. In September 1946 Winston Churchill surprised the world with his appeal for the creation of a 'United States of Europe'. The speech was made in Zürich. It echoed in every city of the war-destroyed continent. It gave rise to the European Movement and the process that led to the creation of the Council of Europe and the European Convention and Court of Human Rights. As early as 1942, Churchill had sent a note to his cabinet colleagues. In it he argued:

> Hard as it is to say now, I trust that the European family may act unitedly as one under a Council of Europe. I look forward to a United States of Europe in which the barriers between the nations will be greatly minimised and unrestricted travel will be possible.

A year later, 1943, in Turkey he dictated what he called 'Early morning thoughts' in which he said Britain should support a Council of Europe as an 'instrument of government'.

As with Shakespeare, Churchill's words can be endlessly glossed and often appear contradictory. In his spirited biography *The*

Churchill Factor: How One Man Made History, Boris Johnson devotes several pages to proving to his own satisfaction that Churchill was never really all that pro-European. Sadly for Mr Johnson, most of the extracts he quotes give the opposite impression. He has to resort to assertions that Churchill 'would have' wanted this, 'would have' wanted that. Of course, what Mr Johnson says Churchill 'would have' wanted – by an unstrange coincidence – appears to match the London mayor's views on European matters. But to be fair, Mr Johnson accurately writes that Churchill 'is claimed by both sides. Europhiles and Eurosceptics: both factions believe in him.'

British anti-Europeans have gone to great efforts in deconstructing the Zürich speech in order to assert that Churchill did not really mean what he said. In 1930, Churchill had written in favour of European unity but qualified his support by adding: 'We are with Europe, but not of it. […] We are interested but not associated.' Looking out on the panorama of European politics in 1930, Churchill could hardly say otherwise. The argument that at Zürich in 1946 Churchill was referring to continental Europe has support from the Belgian socialist politician Paul-Henri Spaak, one of the post-1945 architects of European integration. In his memoirs, he wrote of Churchill's Zürich speech:

> At the time, he appeared to include Great Britain in Europe, but in fact this was not the case. The united Europe which Churchill advocated was a continental Europe, of which France and Germany were to be the joint leaders; Great Britain, the Commonwealth, the United States and, if possible, the USSR, were to befriend and support it. Churchill wanted Britain to promote the creation of a united Europe, but he did not want Britain to be part of it.

Spaak was right. In November 1946, Churchill invited de Gaulle to 'take Germany by the hand and […] rally her to the West and to European civilization'. De Gaulle, like other western European leaders in 1946, was worried that, as after 1918, the United States would withdraw back across the Atlantic and Europe would see the rebirth of a 'unified centralized Reich'. European integration would prevent that, but the General told Churchill that he would support the cause provided that Great Britain became a 'founder-partner' of a European union of states.

In the first stages of European construction Churchill not only took a personal lead, he made sure his key Conservative Party colleagues were actively engaged. To a large extent the European movement that took off in the late 1940s was Churchill's creation. His son-in-law, Duncan Sandys, worked almost exclusively on building it up. Harold Macmillan, a future prime minister, took an active part. So did Robert Boothby, who had been Churchill's parliamentary private secretary before the war and a powerful pro-European voice in the Conservative Party and media of the day. Peter Thorneycroft, later Britain's Chancellor of the Exchequer, was an enthusiastic participant, as were intellectuals like the economist Roy Harrod. Most of Churchill's pro-European acolytes were francophones and Francophiles. London was the centre of activity for many political figures and networkers who sought refuge in Britain after 1939. They were convinced that the way to stop any future war was to construct greater European unity.

The Polish political-diplomatic consigliere Joseph Retinger had an address book covering the continent and knew Churchill and top British politicians as well as younger French figures like Michel Debré and Etienne Giscard d'Estaing. He went to the United States to enrol support for European integration from the Rockefellers and the patrons of big American banks and industrial firms which had emerged from the war rich, powerful and ready to play their part in ensuring that never again would US soldiers have to cross the Atlantic and die in a European war.

Following Churchill's Zürich speech, Duncan Sandys set up the United Europe Movement, while another body, the Union of European Federalists, held its first congress in the summer of 1947 in Amsterdam. US Secretary of State General Marshall's speech to Harvard offering US help for the rebuilding of Europe was a further spur, and in May 1948, the Congress of Europe was held in The Hague, presided over by Churchill.

The wartime leader of the free world was now the opposition leader in the British Parliament. He devoted his time to writing his wartime memoirs, painting and enjoying long Mediterranean holidays. But he spoke consistently in favour of more Europe. He criticized the Labour government for not joining the European Coal and Steel Community in 1950. 'National sovereignty is not inviolable', he told the House of Commons, and may be 'resolutely diminished' because the direction of travel of geo-politics after 1945 'is towards an inter-dependence of nations'. Churchill found time to go to Strasbourg to speak at the first meetings of the Council of Europe. In August 1950, speaking at the Council of Europe, he urged the 'immediate creation of a unified European army'.

On balance, Churchill has to be listed among the great pro-Europeans in British political life. It is perfectly fair to point out that the imperialist, romantic Churchill, who saw Britain as a great power on a par with the USA and USSR, was keener on a continental European economic and political integration with which Britain would be linked but not fully part of. When he was back in power as prime minister in November 1951 he said he had 'never thought Britain should become an integral part of a European federation', but then no more did France or many other European states whose leaders have seen European construction as adding value to national identity and national well-being. Few even of the most ardent pro-Europeans were ready to abolish their parliaments and national democratic control over their people's lives.

The West German Chancellor, Konrad Adenauer, came to see Churchill in Downing Street after his return to power in Britain in 1951. Churchill assured the West German leader that Britain 'would always stand side by side with Europe'. Adenauer replied, 'Mr Prime Minister, you disappoint me. England is part of Europe.' That ambiguity as to whether Britain is part of Europe or exists apart from Europe continues to inform Britain's European debate today.

The question was how and to what extent 'national sovereignty', in Churchill's words, might be 'resolutely diminished'? Churchill wrote of unity among the English-speaking peoples, but from the moment fighting stopped in Europe in 1945, the United States was the strongest supporter of European unity. America had twice sent its sons to die in wars originating in nationalist rivalries in Europe. Integration and unity were the answer, in the eyes of Washington. President Dwight D. Eisenhower said the signing of the Treaty of Rome was 'one of the finest days in the history of the free world, perhaps even more so than winning the war'. The most criticized US president in recent years, George W. Bush, himself told an audience of politicians and ambassadors in London in November 2003: 'My nation welcomes the growing unity of Europe and the world needs America and the European Union to work in common purpose.' In recent years, American mainstream Republicans have always been much more pro-European than British Conservatives.

Today, US State Department officials are publicly warning the British government not to take risks with British membership of the EU. One of the classic continental myths, prevalent especially in Paris, is that Washington uses Britain as a Trojan horse to promote an Anglo-Saxon worldview within the EU. On the contrary, Washington has been closer to Germany or Italy and today Poland than to a Britain with different, discrete interests to defend. Jean Monnet was intimate with key foreign policy officials like the two Dulles brothers, John Foster and Allen, who became respectively secretary of state and director of the CIA, or W. Averell Harriman, the US ambassador to Russia, whose wife, a daughter-in-law of Winston Churchill, was US ambassador in Paris under Bill Clinton. These men decided US policy on Europe after 1945 and in the years thereafter. European unity was essential to Washington's containment policy against the USSR, with the first elements of economic unity arising from the Marshall Plan. For the United States, it was a source of permanent irritation that Britain never joined in the move towards European unity in the 1950s.

Churchill did not have to concern himself as prime minister after 1951 with European construction. The key decisions had been taken by the Labour government and its prime minister between 1945 and 1951, Clement Attlee. While Churchill and his friends inspired Europeans and helped set up the Council of Europe they did so to begin with as political activists, not as government ministers. But the process unleashed by Churchill did not exclude the UK yet did not fully include Britain as a European nation. As he told de Gaulle shortly before D-Day in 1944, every time Britain has to 'decide between Europe and the open sea, it is always the open sea that we shall choose'.

After 1951, Churchill went a step further in the direction of transferring powers to a supranational European body. His home secretary, Sir David Maxwell Fyfe, drafted the European Convention on Human Rights and the Conservative government inaugurated the European Court of Human Rights, which has absolute judicial power in terms of ultimate appeals and rulings over the national courts and parliamentary decisions of its member states. There are two Europes. The first is Jean Monnet's and Robert Schuman's Europe, which gave birth to the Treaty of Rome in 1957 and all subsequent treaties. It is economic and political. Then there is Winston Churchill's Europe based on the treaty setting up the ECHR and its superior powers to uphold democratic and human rights in its 47 member states. Churchill's Europe and the Monnet–Schuman Europe have coexisted for more than six decades. Now, as far as British membership is concerned, there are many ready to repudiate Churchill's Europe with as much vehemence as they repudiate the Monnet–Schuman Europe.

Churchill set the tone and vision for European unity and integration. But the decisions Britain took were not his to make. The 12 years between the end of the war and the Treaty of Rome in 1957 and the 16 years between its adoption and Britain entering the European Community in 1973 were years when the British approach to Europe was determined. The question of Europe was rarely one of party. At different times the Conservatives and Labour have taken different positions on Europe. In opposition, the parties say one thing and in government do another. The big difference today is that it is Mr Cameron as prime minister who has taken the initiative in seeking to occupy Eurosceptic terrain. This is in contrast to the norm of the previous half century, when parties of government chose to be pro-European and parties in opposition often found the populism of anti-Europeanism difficult to resist.

So to understand the deep currents of contemporary British hostility to Europe we must look at how the two main currents of British politics – the left and the right – have dealt with Europe as an ideological and party question.

3

THE FIRST ANTI-EUROPEAN PARTY

The English do not like Europe because they have been told for decades that they should not like Europe. They have transferred to the EU the old enmities they once felt for European powers or belief-systems that seem inimical to England. Mrs Thatcher's favourite minister, Sir Nicholas Ridley, always described the European Community as a 'German racket'. At the beginning of the nineteenth century, Britain's foreign secretary, George Canning, wrote that the French 'have but two rules of action; to thwart us whenever they know our object, and when they know it not, to imagine one for us, and set about thwarting that'. For centuries Protestant England believed the Vatican and Catholic European powers were determined to weaken or destroy English power. A nation does not have a subconscious that a psychoanalyst can explore. But for half a millennium the English have been told that across the Channel lie menace, danger and a threat to the island way of life.

After the creation of Great Britain in the eighteenth century, this generalized English suspicion of the European continent was adopted by the new unitary nation-state. For the first half of the twentieth century Britain stood aloof from the rest of Europe. Once the issue of European integration became significant in British politics after 1945 there were disputes over how much integration was needed or desirable. No one could decide if Britain should join a limited Europe, at best a common market but not a union or accept the full implication of sharing sovereignty. Thus, since 1945, there has never been a moment when leaders of British politics or the formers of public opinion have been calm and settled on Europe. Sometimes they will point to the language of de Gaulle and claim they are with the General's idea of a *Europe des patries*, though de Gaulle said he never used the phrase often attributed to him. British Eurosceptics like de Gaulle's denunciation of Europe as 'this technocratic and antidemocratic thing' which ignored national cultures and languages and instead spoke in 'Esperanto or gobbledegook'. For de Gaulle, 'Europe can only be the Europe of nation-states'.

De Gaulle, however, used that language as head of state of a nation that was fully in Europe as a member of the Coal and Steel Community with its supranational high authority and then after 1957 as a signatory to the Treaty of Rome. De Gaulle's language was not intended to take France out of the process of European integration, but to seek to shape the decisions of Brussels in a manner that benefited France. The most important achievement was to obtain the French cheque – the transfer of money from German taxpayers to French farmers. In exchange, of course, Germany won unfettered access to the French and other EEC markets for their cars, electrical goods, machinery and agricultural equipment. The Common Agricultural Policy stands as a monument to de Gaulle's skilful European tactics – playing on the emotions of nation-state patriotism, scorning the Brussels institutions, but actually making France a full actor in European integration in order to secure generous terms for the modernization of French agricultural and rural life.

British anti-Europeans like to see themselves as Gaullist, yet there is little understanding of the multi-layered complexities of de Gaulle's European strategy. Pro-Europeans in Britain blame de Gaulle's two refusals in 1963 and 1967 to allow Britain to join the Treaty of Rome. They rarely ask themselves if British political leadership at the time was equipped and had the vision to enter the European Economic Community as a wholehearted member. Two Frenchmen – Charles de Gaulle and Jacques Delors – figure large in the demonology of Britain's relationship with Europe. This, however, is transference – the need to find someone else to blame for one's own shortcomings. The real reason for today's dislike and unease about Europe in Britain is that most British political leaders have always found it impossible to situate their idea of their nation and its state fully in the context of Europe.

Today, the hostility to Europe comes from Conservatives. Yet the first and biggest refusal of European integration came under the Labour government elected in 1945. On Europe, the Labour government of 1945–51 (led by Clement Attlee) was without a policy that might have allowed Britain to play a part, indeed even a leading part, in the construction of a new Europe. This is not just a question of history. Parties have memories, a sense of what they believe in and exist for, which can last for decades. Labour's approach to Europe after 1945 ranged from indifference to hostility. The attitudes struck and arguments developed in those formative years resurfaced in the decades after. They are alive today. If it can be said of the French Socialist Party it has never learned how to do social democratic reform it can be said of the Labour Party that it has never learned how to do Europe.

All of Europe's postwar parties have had moments of doubt about or opposition to aspects of European integration. And within broadly pro-European parties there have been individual politicians who have said No to a particular moment of European construction. Jacques Chirac attacked Europe in 1978 as part of his political manoeuvres against his hated rival Valéry Giscard d'Estaing. France's former prime minister, now France's foreign minister, Laurent Fabius, campaigned for a No vote in 2005 against the European constitution. But overall, the main political formations and leaders in France have seen the EU as an accepted part of French existence, just as the British political class and media see NATO as integral to Britain's place in the world. After an initial nationalist distrust in the 1950s at what they saw as a Christian Democratic creation, the German social democrats accepted the EU as part of their political landscape much as they accept NATO membership. In Italy or The Netherlands, in Spain or Ireland, European decisions are often contested but the main political parties agree that member-ship of the European Community and Union are part and parcel of political life.

In Britain, by contrast, one of the two main parties – Conservative or Labour – has usually adopted as its declared policy a critique or opposition to European construction. There are moments of excep-tion, such as the referendum to stay in the European Community in 1975 when both Labour in government and the Conservatives in opposition urged a Yes vote. Even so both the party leaders at the time – Harold Wilson for Labour and the newly elected Margaret Thatcher for the Conservatives – refused to appear on joint platforms with the main Yes campaign organization.

For long periods, one or the other of the two dominant pol-itical formations has preached against Europe. This has been a potent factor in forming public opinion. It is one thing to reject the anti-Europeanism of hard-right or -left politicians or single-issue anti-EU formations like Ukip, but when an entire party capable of forming a government and with thousands of locally elected men and women as well as MPs finds nothing good to say on Europe and every day denounces Europe in terms of contempt and opposition, then it is much harder to create a climate of sympathy for the idea of Europe as part of national political discourse.

After Labour won power in 1945, one of the main architects of the party's rejection of Europe was a young politician called Denis Healey. Healey was a brilliant scholar who had been in the Communist Party at Oxford before 1939. In 1945 he addressed the Labour Party conference wearing his uniform as a war hero. He became the Labour Party's international secretary and provided the words in notes, articles, speeches and pamphlets that shaped the Labour Party response to events and ideas that dominated European politics and decisions between 1945 and 1951.

Later Healey became defence minister in the Labour govern-ment of 1964–70 and Chancellor of the Exchequer, 1974–9. In the 1970s and 1980s, he was Labour's most respected politician, admired as much for his sense of culture and command of German and Italian as for his incisive speeches in the Commons and effective appearances on television attacking Mrs Thatcher. But Healey remained true to his anti-European beliefs. Aged 80 he launched a movement – 'Labour Against the Euro'. During more than half a century Healey remained consistently opposed to most aspects of European integration. At the age of 95 Lord Healey told the *New Statesman* that he would vote in favour of Britain leaving the EU in Mr Cameron's proposed referendum.

In his elegant essay, *The Passage to Europe* (which won the European Book of the Year prize in 2012), the Dutch intellectual and political scientist Luuk van Middelaar, sets out his schema of three Europes: (1) 'The Europe of States'; (2) 'The Europe of Citizens'; and (3) 'The Europe of Offices'. The first is represented by the national governments in the European Council and the other inter-governmental committees. The Council of Europe, for example, is an inter-governmental body where key decisions are taken by ministers or state representatives. The OECD is another.

The second Europe is most visible in the European Parliament, the Council of the Regions and the Economic and Social Committee, but also includes civil society and non-government organizations partly financed by the EU. The third Europe, in Middelaar's schema, consists of the officials who guide the work and shape the decisions of the European Commission and other European institutions set up since 1950, such as the European Court of Justice or the different agencies and high authorities and today the European Central Bank.

For Denis Healey and for Labour ministers and most of their supporting bureaucrats, after 1945 only a limited form of an inter-governmental Europe of nation-states, cooperating but not integrated, was acceptable. Healey, brought up as a sturdy Yorkshire rationalist close to the Methodist traditions of northern England, saw the move to European integration as a Catholic-inspired conspiracy to enshrine capitalism – admittedly a more tolerant capitalism informed by Catholic social teaching but capitalism nonetheless. This he argued would contradict the road map to socialism drawn up by the Labour government. In a key Labour Party policy pamphlet,

European Unity, published in June 1950 on the eve of the Schuman plan's formal adoption by France, Germany, Italy and the Benelux nations, Healey denounced in Labour's name all moves to set up a European structure which might reduce the power of the British government.

> No Socialist Party with the prospect of forming a government could accept a system by which important fields of national policy were surrendered to a supranational European representative authority, since such an authority would have a permanent anti-Socialist majority and would arouse the suspicions of European workers.

With these few words Healey set down more than six decades ago the classic case of the sovereignist left against Europe. By 1950, only a loyal Labour Party apparatchik could believe that the Britain of monarchy, of aristocrats sitting as legislators without election, of private schools, of car firms like Ford and General Motors firmly in foreign private ownership and the nation's defence policy subordinate to Washington's control via NATO, and of growing worker discontent against wage restrictions, was just around the corner from socialism. Indeed, a few months after Healey said Britain should say No to Europe, Britain said No to Labour in 1951 and voted in a Conservative government that stayed in office until 1964.

It is amusing to read Healey today, when the British right reject Europe not because it is anti-Socialist but because the Conservatives and many British business leaders see Europe as being too pro-worker and committed to social policies they oppose. At one level that is just the wheel of history doing its usual turn. What Healey did was set the direction of travel for Labour against European integration, which in one form or another was maintained for four decades between 1950 and 1990 and which still lingers on.

For Labour ministers, it was deeply irritating that European construction after 1945 was so associated with Churchill. In the spirit of 1968 *avant la lettre* the wartime leader even led a march on Downing Street to protest at the Labour government's dilatoriness at setting up the Council of Europe. For Clement Attlee and his foreign secretary, Ernest Bevin, who had battled with Churchill, the anti-trade union Conservative, it was all but intolerable that the old man had emerged from his humiliating election defeat to become the spokesman for a new European order. Joseph Retinger, the exiled Polish diplomat who did much of the networking from London to put together The Hague conference, went to see Ernest Bevin to ask if he would support these moves in favour of the European Movement. Retinger recalled in his memoirs how he

> tried to persuade Bevin to induce the Labour Party to give us their backing, but during this two-hour conversation the only argument he put forward against the Movement was the fact that Churchill was its official leader in Great Britain. Churchill was a political opponent and the Labour Party could not support its political opponent.

The Labour Party instructed its MPs not to attend the founding Congress in The Hague of the European Movement. Some disobeyed and were sanctioned. Others, including young left-wing Labour MPs like Michael Foot, wrote in favour of a federal Europe. But their pro-Europeanism was based on Europe getting closer to the Soviet Union, adopting socialist policies and opting for an anti-American stand. Variations of this third-way politics (as the idea of equidistance between the USA and the USSR was known decades before Tony Blair adopted the term to describe his version of modified capitalism associated with Bill Clinton) were to be found all over Europe after 1945, with Albert Camus as one of its spokesmen.

For Ernest Bevin, who regarded intellectuals as a source of opposition to his idea of what the Labour Party should be, the combination of Churchill and left-wing Labour MPs talking incessantly about a united Europe was maddening. Foot later became leader of the Labour Party when it adopted a policy of leaving the European Community in 1980. He led the party to a bad defeat in the 1983 election when he, along with other Labour MPs like Barbara Castle and Ian Mikardo who had been pro-European after 1945, had become virulently anti-European.

All politicians are entitled to change their minds and positions. But the history of British politics from 1945 until today is full of men and women who have moved from A to Z on the spectrum of attitudes to Europe. For the British people, who like citizens in other countries expect a degree of consistency from their leading politicians on the important issues that face a nation, this constant zigzagging and change of mind and language on Europe is deeply confusing. Some begin as anti-Europeans and become converted to a pro-European position. One such example was Robin Cook MP, appointed foreign secretary by Tony Blair in 1997, who later became a pro-EU zealot and president of the Party of European Socialists. But for many the journey is in the opposite direction. An early enthusiasm for Europe curdles into hostility flattered and encouraged by the anti-European press. In 1981, David Owen, the Labour MP who had been Britain's youngest-ever foreign secretary between 1977 and 1979, left the Labour Party with other pro-European Labour MPs including Roy Jenkins and Shirley Williams and formed the Social Democratic Party. In 1981, Owen was pro-European. By 2012, still with a voice in British politics and a seat in the House of Lords, Lord Owen was opposed to the euro and calling for a referendum which could take Britain out of Europe. This weather-vane approach to Europe runs like a thread in the British left's approach to Europe since 1945. Labour's only consistency has been its inconsistency.

In the 1980s, Jack Straw, later Britain's foreign minister under Tony Blair, was anti-European. As a new leadership took control of the Labour Party in the 1990s Straw became nominally pro-European. He wrote an essay in *The Economist* in October 2002 calling for a constitution for Europe. His enthusiasm did not last six months, as I noted in my diary:

Monday, 29 March 2003

> *Jack is in a very grumpy mood. Blair has come back from Brussels full of breezy gung-ho optimism on the constitution. Jack wishes it*

simply wasn't on the agenda at all. 'This constitution won't fly at all,' he says. He really doesn't like the European Union and that is the top and bottom of it.

Of course Straw moving from being anti-Europe to being pro-Europe and then settling down to just disliking the project or – from an earlier era – the Labour politicians who were pro-European after 1945 but who then became anti-European in the 1970s and 1980s would never admit inconsistency. No politician ever does. But Labour's shifting one way and then the other on Europe is part of the reason why Britain does not like Europe. Many on the left have criticized NATO and the alliance with the United States or called for Britain to renounce nuclear weapons. But both the Conservative and Labour leaderships and their ministers when in government have consistently supported NATO, rebutted criticisms of Atlanticism and supported nuclear weapons. As a result, anti-NATO or anti-American feeling has never become central to British political life. In contrast, Europe has never enjoyed such support. The question of Europe divides British politics as no other issue. And with governing parties and ministers so uncertain, so willing to find fault with Europe, why should the voters be any different?

It was not that Labour was crudely nationalistic. The party simply failed the test of imagination that transforms politics. Ernest Bevin was Labour foreign secretary between 1945 and 1951. Before entering Parliament and the war cabinet simultaneously in 1940 he had been one of the great leaders of the working class as general secretary of Britain's most powerful prewar trade union, the Transport and General Workers' Union. He saw himself as putting postwar Europe on its feet. He helped set up the Marshall Plan, NATO and the OECD and did not veto the Council of Europe. Foreign Office diplomats came from a different world – elite private schools, wealthy families, houses or apartments in the quarters of London reserved for the aristocracy or the very rich. In Ernest Bevin, they confronted a minister who was born illegitimate, who left school at 12 and drove a horse and cart as his first job in rural south-west

England. His rise to power in the land was thanks to the trade union movement. The high officialdom of Whitehall reached for the classic balm of any bureaucracy – flattery and obsequiousness. They bowed to all of Bevin's wishes and agreed with him when he looked to the United States, not Europe, for Britain's future.

They told Bevin – not that he needed much persuading – that all development in Europe should be strictly on an inter-governmental basis. The Council of Europe was left with a parliamentary assembly able to speak, but all decisions were left in its committee of ministers, itself composed of ambassadors and other functionaries with all the suspicion of their caste about radical decisions or allowing anyone who had stood for election to have a real say.

A key cabinet colleague of Bevin and Attlee was Hugh Dalton. He told the Commons in 1950 that the achievements as he saw them of a Labour government could be diluted or put at risk if there was greater integration with governments headed by Catholic centre-right leaders like Adenauer, Schuman or de Gasperi. 'We are determined not to put those gains in peril through allowing vital decisions on great issues of national economic policy to be transferred from the British Parliament at Westminster to some supranational European Assembly', Dalton declared. Ernest Bevin described his opposition to any sharing of power with other European governments in a splendid mixed metaphor: 'Once you open that Pandora's box, you'll find it full of Trojan horses.'

It was no surprise, then, that France's foreign minister, Robert Schuman, and Jean Monnet – the two godfathers of European construction in 1950 – consulted with the Germans, with the US secretary of state and with other continental European colleagues on their proposal to remove the control of coal and steel industries from national governments and create a new High Authority as a supranational body. They did not bother to talk to London, as Labour's opposition to anything that lessened the strict control of national government was well known. Why should Schuman and Monnet waste months trying to persuade the British about what they would never accept? Clement Attlee described the new High Authority for the coal and steel industries as 'an irresponsible body appointed by no one and responsible to no one'. The Conservatives also placed limits on their idea of European construction. Harold Macmillan told the Council of Europe that British people would not hand over to any supranational authority the right to close pits and steelworks.

Labour ministers in London all claimed to speak for the working class at a time when more than a million miners and steelworkers formed the core of the British trade union movement. By 1950, Ernest Bevin was ill and not far from death. Clement Attlee was exhausted after a decade of non-stop work since 1940 as Churchill's deputy and then as prime minister after 1945. The first reaction to the Schuman Plan came from Herbert Morrison, the home secretary and the patron of London Labour. His grandson is Lord Mandelson, one of the most prominent pro-Europeans in the Blair generation of Labour leaders. In 1950, however, his grandfather rejected the chance for his party and country to be one of the midwives of Europe. 'It's no good. We cannot do it. The Durham miners won't wear it.' Durham in north-east England was the centre of coal production. Britain in 1950 produced half of Europe's coal – the oil, gas and nuclear power of its day. In fact, the president of Britain's national miners' union, himself a former Durham miner, was more measured. 'If Mr Schuman or anyone else can prove that his plan will not push back [the wages of British miners], then it is all right, but we want proof', he said.

Tired Labour ministers and a state bureaucracy that still saw Britain as a world power with a different status from the war-ravaged continental countries did not follow the trade unionist's advice. They did not seek talks with the French, German, Italian and Benelux governments so that Britain might have been present at the creation of the first steps to European union. In 1950, Labour thus laid down the foundations for saying No to Europe at the highest level of the party and government.

As Britain now contemplates again saying No to Europe and the rest of Europe seeks to understand why the British seem willing to cut themselves off from Europe, the arguments that raged between

1945 and 1950 resurface – sovereignty, upsetting accepted practice and quarrels between and within parties – and again we see a lack of imagination. British empiricism and pragmatism are rightly famous. In 1940, Churchill and the British people had defied diplomatic logic, imperial self-interest and a detestation of sovietism to risk their all on a war which reduced Britain from a world power to a bankrupt pensioner of American largesse and military protection. In 1940, Churchill summoned up the energy and will to lead the British to a supreme task of imagination and mobilization. By 1950 there was neither energy nor will, still less the creative imagination that might have swept away bureaucratic caution, much as Churchill swept away the appeasement culture of the high British bureaucracy of the 1930s. Labour was offered a golden chance to be a leader in Europe in 1950. But no one would take the risk. The party celebrated its past. It could not seize the future. And so it has remained.

4

LABOUR SAYS *NON, MERCI* TO EUROPE

The 1950s saw Labour in opposition and taking little interest in Europe. In 1960, Labour abstained in a Commons vote organized by the Conservative government that called for 'political and economic unity in Europe'. As Britain made its first application to join the Common Market in July 1961, Labour opposed the bid in a Commons vote that was defeated. At one level it was little more than the duty of an opposition to oppose what the government proposes. Richard Crossman, one of Labour's senior political figures and a leading intellectual, noted in his diary that the Common Market was already dividing the party. At a meeting of Labour's national executive committee, Crossman said that if Britain joined the Common Market, 'we would have to become federalists and see our Socialism in terms of strengthening a federal state'. Crossman also insisted that before entering the Common Market there should be an election on the issue. 'The whole future of British democracy and sovereignty' was at stake, he wrote.

In 1962, this extravagant language was trumped by the party leader, Hugh Gaitskell, who committed Labour to outright opposition to Europe. Already Labour MPs had formed an 'Anti-Common Market Committee' that led to the creation of a pro-European faction of younger MPs headed by Roy Jenkins. At the party conference in 1962 Gaitskell spat out a philippic against Europe. It contained many of the arguments that are used today by anti-EU British politicians. Gaitskell said entering the EEC would mean the end of control over the economy, over agriculture, perhaps over foreign policy. To thus link Britain with Europe would 'mean the end of Britain as an independent nation-state. It would mean an end of a thousand years of history. It does mean the end of the Commonwealth [...] if the mother country is a province of Europe.' The Labour leader pointed out that Switzerland was doing very well without signing the Treaty of Rome. European growth was not very impressive: Asia and Africa held out better economic prospects. The language mirrors today's Eurosceptics, who say the future lies in Asia (despite stalling growth in China), in Africa, anywhere except across the Channel.

The paradox was that Gaitskell was seen as leading the efforts to modernize the Labour Party and align it more closely with continental social democracy and away from traditional national-statist Labourism representing mainly the interests of unionized workers. But on Europe, Gaitskell defined a sovereignist ideology for Labour that overwhelmed the party for 25 years after 1962 and which has not been eradicated today.

De Gaulle closed the debate by rejecting Britain's first bid to join the EEC in 1963 and Gaitskell himself died early in 1963. His successor as party leader, Harold Wilson, had joined in the applause for Gaitskell's anti-Europeanism. However, once Wilson became prime minister in 1964 Labour's weather-vane turned once again and Britain applied to join the EEC. De Gaulle said *Non* again in 1967. For today's older generation of British voters the two snubs by France and especially by the man Britain saved in 1940 and who then became leader of France still rankle.

States do not owe each other gratitude. France's rejection of British attempts to join Europe in the 1960s meant a further decade's wait. The British never treated Europe as a natural part of their country's life and future. De Gaulle's haughty dismissal of Britain did nothing to make the British pro-European. Some today would like to prove the General right and show that Britain does not need France and the EU to have a twenty-first-century future. The General's death and the arrival of the unequivocally pro-European Edward Heath as prime minister in 1970 again spun Labour's wheel. Labour cabinet ministers discussed the forthcoming election in April 1970 and the question of Europe came up. Tony Benn noted in his diary that European integration was a project Labour should support:

> If we have to have some sort of organisation to control inter-national companies, the Common Market is probably the right one. I think that decision-making is on the move and some decisions have to be taken in Europe, some in London, and an awful lot more at regional and local level.

Benn's cautious pro-Europeanism did not last long. In government, 1964–70, the Labour Party had sought to join Europe. In opposition after 1970 the party rejected this course.

As the curious decade of the 1970s got under way, Labour drifted into the embrace of anti-Europeanism. The Labour Party's special conference on Europe in 1971 was an orgy of Europhobia. Anyone who was there, as I was, can recall the roaring hate against Europe from the platform. The finest orators in left politics queued up to denounce Europe. Just as Labour ministers after 1945 refused to support a project they associated with Winston Churchill, so too was it easy for Labour in opposition to oppose what a Conservative government under the disliked Edward Heath adopted as its core policy. Heath was determined to take Britain into Europe. That decision and its successful conclusion stand as his monument. He won the support of 69 Labour MPs who voted in the Commons with Conservative MPs to enter the European Community. Heath also had anti-European Conservative MPs who would not sup-port him. They repeatedly made the point that Britain would lose a degree of absolute independence and political sovereignty by signing the Treaty of Rome and accepting, among other political changes, the authority of the European Court of Justice over Britain. One of the oddest myths in today's debates is when people say they supported EEC entry in the 1970s as an economic project without any polit-ical implications. On the contrary, the Conservative MPs who voted

against EEC entry made very clear that they rejected the political
implications of entering Europe. Professor Philip Norton, one of our
senior politics academics and today a Conservative peer, points out
in an article on the European Communities Act 1972 in the journal
Parliamentary History that the Act had 'important consequences for
the UK constitution, including creating a juridical dimension unpar-
alleled since before the Glorious Revolution of 1688. Parliament has
provided for its own legislation to be subordinate to that of the EC.'
It is a comfort blanket for those who supported Europe in the 1970s
but now are Eurosceptic to say they voted to enter a free-trade area
without political consequences. They simply have not read the many
debates of the 1960s and 1970s when many Conservative MPs, peers
and jurists spelled out the political consequences. But what remains
true is that without Labour's support the law to ratify the Accession
Treaty would have failed. The Labour pro-Europeans were led by Roy
Jenkins and included a future leader and deputy leader of the Labour
Party, John Smith and Roy Hattersley.

The vote took place against a background of growing social discontent in Britain. Heath had introduced laws to weaken trade
unions. Thus it was possible to portray Europe and Heath's enthusiasm for joining Europe as part of a right-wing Conservative move
to vitiate the British left. Once Britain entered in 1973, Labour
Eurosceptics refused to accept the decision of the Commons. Instead
they claimed Heath had reneged on his pledge to join the EEC only
with the 'full-hearted consent of the British people'. Heath never
spelled out what he meant by this choice of words, but for Labour
anti-Europeans it was translated into the need for a referendum.
The proposal to hold a referendum was actually put forward by a
Conservative MP, Neil Marten, but was seized upon by Labour as a
mechanism to embarrass the Heath government.

So again we see Europe transforming British politics, as a
mode of deciding law alien to the British tradition of representative democracy with all decisions routed through and taken
by the Commons made its way into the British political system.
The paradox of Labour anti-Europeans turning to a continental

European mode of decision-making – the referendum – in order
to obtain their wished-for exit from Europe caused little concern.
It was more a mechanism for maintaining party unity than a permanent shift to plebiscitory politics. At the time the referendum
pledge was accepted by both pro- and anti-Europeans. Labour's
anti-European wing believed their own rhetoric that Europe was
an unacceptable conspiracy to promote free-market economics
and that the British people would certainly vote No to such a
Europe given a chance. Labour's pro-Europeans, who had risked
their future with their local party activists by voting with Edward
Heath, were wiser, as they looked at the balance of forces likely to
campaign for a vote in favour of Europe in a putative referendum.
These included the press, four out of five MPs, the TUC and 99
per cent of businesses. After initial protests, including the resignation of Roy Jenkins as Labour's deputy leader, the pro-Europe
Labour MPs swallowed their dislike of replacing parliamentary
democracy with a plebiscite but one that would confirm a decision taken by Parliament. Thus the Labour Party stayed uneasily
united, with both pro- and anti-European MPs putting off a final
day of reckoning by accepting a referendum.

Labour also indulged traditional British Francophobia when James
Callaghan, a future prime minister, told an audience in 1971 that
to enter Europe was to exchange America and the Commonwealth
for 'an aroma of continental claustrophobia' which meant 'a complete
rupture of our identity'. The reason was that on the continent people
spoke foreign languages, especially the French, who spoke French. 'The
language of Chaucer, Milton and Shakespeare' would be challenged:

> If we have to prove our Europeanism by accepting that French
> is the dominant language in the Community, then my answer
> is quite clear, and I will say it in French in order to prevent
> misunderstanding: 'Non, merci beaucoup!'.

It was a shock to hear on BBC television news the bluff,
anti-intellectual, non-literary Callaghan invoking the poet John

Milton, whose year spent in France and Italy in 1638–9 helped make him one of England's greatest poets and one of Europe's first champions of press freedom. And to hear Callaghan speak French to insult the French on BBC television news seemed to sum up all that was petty, provincial and in poor taste of the average British politician talking about Britain and Europe.

Labour was back in government in 1974 and held a referendum in 1975 on whether Britain would accept the results of a so-called renegotiation. It was not the in–out referendum David Cameron has promised, but a simple Yes–No to the very small changes that Britain obtained as a present from Valéry Giscard d'Estaing and Helmut Schmidt. Harold Wilson and the government announced they were in favour. So did the Conservative Party, now headed by Margaret Thatcher. A survey of 419 company chairmen produced 415 saying Yes to staying in Europe. The national trade union leadership was in favour. Most important – and in contrast to today – the press, including a newly arrived proprietor, Rupert Murdoch, also campaigned strongly for a Yes vote.

Yet when the terms of Labour's cosmetic renegotiation were voted on in the Commons, 145 Labour MPs voted against accepting them, with only 137 following the lead of Harold Wilson to endorse Britain staying in Europe. At a special Labour Party congress in 1975 delegates voted two to one in favour of quitting Europe. The West German Chancellor, Helmut Schmidt, in fluent, humorous English, sought to explain why a Labour Britain and a Social Democratic Germany should cooperate in shaping Europe. It made no difference. Labour Party activists did not want Europe. The Yes vote of 1975 disguised the fact that the majority of Labour MPs and party members remained opposed to Europe.

Their language was loud and metaphors lurid. Michael Foot, who had been an advocate of a federal Europe after 1945, now urged Britain to withdraw. He was Labour's best orator and a man of culture whose books on such heroes of English literature as Jonathan Swift are still read. But on Europe he was implacable: 'The British parliamentary system has been made farcical and unworkable by the superimposition of the EEC apparatus. It is as if we had set fire to the place [i.e. the Commons] as Hitler did with the Reichstag.' At the time, the 67 per cent vote in the 1975 referendum in favour of staying in Europe was thought to settle the question. But the great lie about referendums is that they are definitive. Labour supporters of the No campaign went away and began organizing to overturn the referendum result and commit their party to full withdrawal from the European Community.

In 1976, Britain faced an economic crisis similar to those experienced recently by weaker Eurozone economies like Greece, Spain and Ireland. British debt could not be serviced. It was necessary to call in the International Monetary Fund (IMF) to provide a special loan. IMF officials flew to London in 1976. In a similar manner officials of the IMF, the European Central Bank and the European Commission have gone in recent years to Athens to dictate Greece's tax and spending policies. The result was a cut in government spending and wage freezes for workers. Two conclusions were drawn from the IMF having to come in to dictate the government's management of the British economy. For many Conservatives and for Labour's pro-European wing, it was proof that Britain needed to integrate with and fashion its economic future along European lines. The post-1945 British mixed economy welfare state model with ultra-adversarial relations between employers and trade unions was doing too much economic damage.

An opposite analysis came from the left. It was that external powers – the IMF and the EEC – were now dictating the terms of Britain's future. Washington and Brussels were preventing the adoption of policies – never fully explained – that would restore economic health and bring in higher pay and more measures of social justice. The Labour Party remained divided between its revisionist and statist wings. The Labour revisionists or reformists confronted those who wanted more state control and planning. For the former, an integrated Europe allowed a response to the globalization that all could sense was on its way. For the statists, Europe represented a neo-liberal surrender to supranational capitalism. The use of the

word 'globalization' did not become widespread until the 1980s, but
for many on the left the European Community seemed more on
the side of post-national capital than on the side of workers who
depend on a strong national sense of solidarity and shared community and identity. In the name of efficiency or economies of scale
Europe removed power from the national level to the supranational
European Commission or European Court of Justice.

From 1980 onwards Labour became as anti-European as the
Conservatives are today. In fact, unlike Prime Minister Cameron,
who is offering an in–out referendum while professing a desire to
stay in a Europe reconfigured to suit British Eurosceptic ideology,
Labour in 1980 voted to adopt as official party policy a call to quit
the European Community. This decision led to a major split in
Labour as a group of prominent pro-European Labour MPs formed
the Social Democratic Party (SDP), as mentioned earlier. In the
1983 election, the Social Democratic Party (in alliance with the
Liberal Party) won 25 per cent of the votes cast, nearly as many as
Labour. The Labour Party's call for Britain to leave the European
Community helped the Conservatives to a bigger victory than in
1979. Labour's anti-European policy saw the party with 3 million
fewer votes in 1983 than in 1979.

Slowly Labour turned away from its anti-European course.
A new generation of younger Labour MPs and officials represented
by Tony Blair and Gordon Brown, both elected in 1983, and Peter
Mandelson, who became Labour's press officer in 1985, nudged
Labour away from Euroscepticism. In 1985 the Fabian Society
published a pamphlet called *French Lessons for Labour* (authored by
me) which argued in the context of victory of the socialist François
Mitterrand in France that Labour should drop its anti-European
stand and learn from other parties in Europe like the Nordic social
democrats, the Spanish socialists under Felipe Gonzalez and, indeed,
Mitterrand's nominally socialist presidency in France.

Jacques Delors came and made a major speech to the TUC in
1988 that was interpreted as strongly in favour of trade union rights
and this helped to move the Labour Party-linked unions away from

the hostility many had to European construction. The Friedrich Ebert Foundation, Germany's influential and well-funded Social Democratic international network, opened an office in London and encouraged the Blair-Brown-Mandelson generation to attend conferences in Europe and pick up the best of applied social democratic thinking and policy. The direct elections to the European Parliament also worked to Labour's advantage. Labour won 37 per cent of the votes in the 1989 election to the Strasbourg assembly. Forty-five new Labour MEPs with their local offices, allowances and staff appeared on the political scene, showing that European politics could help strengthen Labour.

In 1992, after its fourth successive election defeat, the new Labour leader was John Smith, who as a young MP had voted in 1972 with Edward Heath and against his party in favour of Britain entering the European Community. He promoted other pro-Europeans to leading positions in Labour, notably Tony Blair and a cohort of pro-EU Scottish MPs like Gordon Brown and George Robertson. Eurosceptic Labour MPs of the 1980s like the future ministers Robin Cook and Jack Straw changed their stance and decided to see more virtue in a Europe that the post-Thatcher Conservatives were increasingly unhappy with. British trade unions have a strong influence in the Labour Party, sitting on its national executive committee and speaking or voting at its policy conferences. The unions were now converts to the European cause. The Conservative government under John Major (1990–7) was more and more ill at ease with Europe. Major himself had trouble with MPs who refused to back the new Maastricht Treaty. He faced Margaret Thatcher, now in the House of Lords, who said she 'could never have signed' the Maastricht Treaty, which was 'a recipe for national suicide'. Major negotiated an opt-out from the social provisions of Maastricht which angered the unions still further. As inequality and poverty grew, there was more and more support for the idea of Social Europe. It was clear that the Conservative Party was growing increasingly anti-European.

The election of Tony Blair as Labour leader in June 1994 appeared to complete the metamorphosis of Labour into a pro-European party. Or did it? As we keep looking for the reasons to explain why the British do not like Europe and may be happy to exit the EU, a closer examination of the pro-European credentials of Blair will be required. However, the main hostility to Europe today comes from the right, not the left, so we need also to look at why the British right became increasingly opposed to European integration.

5

THE TORIES BECAME THE PARTY OF EUROPE, OR DID THEY?

Between 1950 and 1990 Labour and much of the left drifted into a Sargasso Sea of, at best, indifference to Europe, but more often nationalist rejection. It was the Conservative Party and British business that made most of the running on British efforts to enter the European Community. They were not helped by British state officialdom, which carries on the administration of the state seamlessly even as the political complexion of government changes. The permanent state establishment exists in a parallel universe to the institutions of democracy – Parliament, cabinet, ministers. Whitehall officials do what ministers ask. But when ministers do not know what to do, or worse, what to think, power stays with officials, who follow the maxim of de La Rochefoucauld: 'What annoys us about negotiators is that they give up the interests of achieving what they should get and instead just become interested in whether the negotiation is concluded. They get more satisfaction from being good at negotiating than achieving anything.'

Too much of the history of Britain and Europe since 1945 is taken from the notes, records and later memories of the negotiators. The negotiations over Europe took place as much inside the state administration in Whitehall as it did between British and different European representatives. British officialdom was divided. Often from an elite and academically well-trained background, the mandarins of the British state tended to be recruited at the age of 21 or 22 directly from Oxford or Cambridge. They were sent to learn French, usually as exchange students or with a French family, but there was not the automatic training in one or more other European languages that became the norm for the administrative cadres in France, Germany, Italy or The Netherlands.

This lack of cultural feel for other European nations contributed to poor judgement on the part of British negotiators. Churchill's successor as prime minister was Sir Anthony Eden. He was another cultivated Old Etonian and Oxford classicist, one who spoke Persian. His French was good, but his sense of where Europe was going in 1955 when he became prime minister was poor. He was invited to take part on Britain's behalf in the Messina conference early in 1956 that negotiated the outlines of the Treaty of Rome. Eden thought the Messina conference was below his rank and dignity. Instead he sent a civil servant, not from the high-status ministries like the Treasury or Foreign Office but from the Board of Trade. This official is reported to have told the delegates at Messina, including the Belgian prime minister, Paul-Henri Spaak: 'Gentlemen, you are trying to negotiate something you will never be able to negotiate. But if negotiated, it will not be ratified. And if ratified it will not work.' The words were elegant and it was thought were written by Eden himself. They represent the disdain for Europe that led Britain to refuse to be a signatory to the Treaty of Rome. A Labour government had said No to the Coal and Steel Community Treaty in 1950. Seven years later a Conservative government said No to the Treaty of Rome.

Just after this rejection of Europe at Messina, Britain was launched into a defining adventure of the European geo-politics in the 1950s. The secret agreement with France and Israel to invade Egypt turned into disaster as the United States refused to support the armed attack on Nasser and threatened to cut off oil supplies and start selling the pound unless Britain withdrew. It was the last time before Vietnam, Iraq and Afghanistan that Washington under the leadership of a man who knew what war meant – Eisenhower – showed restraint in neo-imperialist militarism. France and Britain drew different conclusions from the Suez debacle. For France, soon to be led by de Gaulle, America's failure to back Suez meant that Washington was not be relied on. France would have to make its peace with Germany and build a European destiny. For Britain, it proved the world was now dominated by the United States and Britain therefore should align herself with the new imperial centre.

Harold Macmillan, Eden's successor as prime minister between 1957 and 1963, said that Britain should play Greece to America's Rome. He too was an Old Etonian who had studied classics at Oxford. The fantasy that Roman Washington was ready to be tutored by Athenian London remained ever present in the minds of British prime ministers. They liked to use the term 'special relationship', as if America and Britain shared something more than a common language. The phrase was often heard in London, rarely in Washington. American disdain for British pretensions to be a world power but remain outside the process of European integration was summed up by the former US secretary of state, Dean Acheson, in a speech to the West Point military academy in 1962 when he said 'Britain had lost an empire but not yet found a role'.

For some British politicians a new role could be found in Europe, but a Europe on British terms. Macmillan was a cultured Francophile and francophone who had collaborated with General de Gaulle as Churchill's minister in North Africa during the war. He had a sense of history, writing in a private letter to his foreign secretary in 1959 that:

> For the first time since the Napoleonic era the major continental powers are united in a positive economic grouping with considerable political aspects, which though not specifically directed against the United Kingdon, may have the effect of excluding us both from European markets and from consultation of European policy.

Macmillan made the first application by UK to join the EEC in 1961, only to be humiliated by General de Gaulle. The British insisted that any entry into the Common Market would have to include continued access to Britain for agricultural imports from the Commonwealth countries – wheat from Canada, butter and lamb from New Zealand, fruit from Australia or even potatoes and sickly-sweet sherry from Cyprus. There seemed to be little realization in London that the Common Market could only work if it had external tariffs, just as the United States was ruthlessly protectionist for its agro-industrial sector. Nor did Britain realize it was no longer the accepted world power it had been 1945. Britain had decided to link its nuclear weapons programme to the United States, adopting the Polaris missiles on its submarines. De Gaulle had finally pulled France out of its Algerian nightmare. With his strong franc policy and his increasing disdain for American foreign policy, de Gaulle's idea of France left no room for a financially weak Britain content to be a subordinate satellite of the United States.

The British put together a top team of negotiators, headed by a rising young Conservative minister, Edward Heath. Summit meetings were held with Adenauer and de Gaulle and the British really thought they were making progress and could persuade France to accept a free-trade Europe in which Commonwealth nations would sell freely their agricultural products. In fact, the European Economic Community Britain thought it wanted to join in 1961 was not unlike the one David Cameron thinks Britain could stay in today. De Gaulle thought differently. The Commonwealth countries were not willing to abolish their various trade policies and tariffs to allow free movement of goods or capital from the EEC, so why should Brussels agree to a one-sided British adhesion based on old imperial trading patterns? Macmillan was bitter and disconsolate. 'French duplicity has defeated us all. All our policies at home and abroad are in ruins', he wrote in his diary. It was the end for Macmillan, who stood down as prime minister in 1963, the first of many whose careers were broken on the Europe question.

The next Conservative prime minister was Edward Heath (1970–4). He was a convinced European who had visited Nazi Germany as an Oxford student in 1938, heard Hitler speak and had shaken hands with Himmler. In his first speech in the House of Commons in 1951 Heath spoke in favour of reconciliation between

Britain and Germany. For the next half century Heath continued to make pro-European speeches in the Commons. Heath has entered history as the prime minister who took his country into Europe. But as we have seen, he did so at a price. His party was split and Heath needed opposition Labour votes to win a majority in the Commons. Britain's entry into the ECC in 1973 coincided with a weakening economy, and national emergencies such as energy shortages or strikes stopped Britain from working normally.

Britain's first year in the EEC coincided with the triple impact of the oil shock and the first great energy crisis, inflation of up to 25 per cent in prices and turmoil on currency markets following the end of the Bretton Woods system. It was not the fault of the European Community, of course, that these external shocks left the British economy fragile and Whitehall frightened. Nor did the rise of widespread trade union strikes powered by the '1968' generation of militant syndicalists have any connection with British entry into Europe. Across the Channel more intelligent trade unions structures in Germany, Denmark or The Netherlands showed that social partnership concepts derived from Teuto-nordic traditions could deal with major economic dislocation without the bitter labour-market confrontations of the Heath administration, which lasted just 40 months in office.

Considered alongside Labour's opportunistic call for a referendum and rhetorical denunciation of Europe, Britain's first period of full participation in Europe after 1973 was not happy. The most dominant and popular Conservative politician of the era was Enoch Powell. He was a charismatic, intellectually brilliant populist who in 1968 had made a major speech denouncing immigration into Britain and calling for the repatriation of non-white immigrants to Africa, India, Pakistan and the Caribbean. He said he foresaw a river 'foaming with much blood' unless steps were taken to halt and reverse immigration and settlement by people with a different-coloured skin. The quotation came from the Roman author Virgil but was seen at the time as predicting violent conflict as a result of immigrants arriving in Britain. The leader of the Conservative Party, Edward Heath, dismissed Powell from the shadow cabinet because of the extremism of his language. Powell's speech was the forced entry into British politics of xenophobic themes not from an extremist, quasi-fascist party but from a respected senior Conservative politician who had held important ministerial posts and had been a Professor of Greek at a young age. Powell was considered a leading parliamentarian and dressed up his 'anti-foreigner' appeal in classical language as a defence of the essence of the nation. Powell maintained a highly publicized campaign against immigration and against Europe during the Conservative government 1970–4.

Early in 1974, Heath called an election in the middle of a strike by miners. Europe entered the election campaign because Powell announced he would vote Labour. He argued that only the Labour Party offered a referendum and the possibility of withdrawing from the EEC, thus making himself a hero to many in Britain, not just Conservative Association members but large numbers of white working-class voters.

There is no doubt that the swing to Labour of white working-class votes in 1974 was helped by Powell's declaration that only a Labour vote would produce a referendum that in his view would lead to a rejection of Europe. Many voters heeded Powell's call by voting Heath out and Labour's Harold Wilson in. Just as Harold Macmillan felt his political career had been destroyed by the European question – de Gaulle's *Non* in 1963 – so a dozen years later Edward Heath's premiership came to an early end as voters chose the party that at least offered them the chance to say No to Europe.

Another Conservative prime minister had been swallowed up by Europe. Heath found his dismissal hard to take and it was made worse by the challenge of his ambitious education minister, Margaret Thatcher. She defied the deep patriarchy of the Conservative Party and humiliated the pro-European Heath with her successful challenge to become party leader in 1975 and then prime minister in 1979. Until his retirement in 2001, Heath stayed in Parliament. He openly criticized Mrs Thatcher on many different aspects of her conduct of government. Above all, on Europe he sat like a male Medusa in the Commons, spitting venom at his successor.

6

JACQUES DELORS LAUNCHES BRITISH EUROSCEPTICISM

As we have seen, Britain first applied to join the EEC in 1961. For the next three decades, the European party in British politics was the Conservative Party. Labour was generally anti-European. In the 1983 general election Labour called for an immediate withdrawal of Britain from Europe. It is arguable that 1983 was the worst year in Labour's history. The party had split on the European question. Some of the most clever modernizing politicians of the left could not stay in a Labour Party that was so crudely anti-European. The result was an open field for the Thatcher revolution. Mrs Thatcher was easily re-elected in 1983 and 1987.

And then in 1988, thanks to one of the most disastrous and counter-productive speeches in postwar British political history, Jacques Delors began the process of changing the Conservative Party into an anti-European Party. That was not his intention. In his memoirs Valéry Giscard d'Estaing, president of France between 1974 and 1981, describes 'the ultra-conservative Margaret Thatcher, who believed in the idea of a free trade Europe, nothing more, and was determined to achieve her ends'. The former French president was writing in 2006, when Lady Thatcher's anti-European views were clear. But in 1983 she was re-elected as a pro-European British leader against the Eurosceptic Labour Party, which called for a mandate to take Britain out of Europe.

For most of her 11 years in office (1979–90) she worked constructively with other European leaders. She supported the appointment of Jacques Delors as Commission president. She made a major speech at the Fontainebleau European Council in 1984 calling for Europe to have a common foreign and security policy. She supported the Single European Act, which still to this day entails the biggest sharing of sovereignty between the nation-states of Europe.

Many of the symbols of Europeanism – the common passport cover or the directly elected European Parliament – were instituted under Mrs Thatcher, as was the final coupling of Britain and the continent with the Channel Tunnel and Eurostar. Although she secured agreement for a rebalancing of how Britain helped fund the European Community (the famous rebate), Mrs Thatcher actually increased UK contributions to the EC by 400 per cent. The British contribution to the common European budget administered from Brussels rose from £656 million in 1984 to £2.54 billion in 1990. So for someone always depicted as an anti-European, waving her handbag and demanding her money back, Mrs Thatcher loosened Britain's purse strings more than any other British prime minister. She slapped down Eurosceptic MPs such as Labour's future foreign secretary, Jack Straw, who at the time protested that British taxpayers' money should not go via Brussels to new member states like Greece, Spain and Portugal. On the contrary, Mrs Thatcher told MPs, it was important to help the poorer economies of southern Europe integrate with the richer north. She was far more generous to new, poorer EU member states than Europe's next major female head of government, Germany's Angela Merkel.

It is therefore wrong to depict Mrs Thatcher, during most of her years in office, as a simple free trader opposed to European construction. She supported political Europe, foreign policy Europe, a Europe generous to poorer states and a Europe based on a significant transfer and sharing of national sovereignty implicit in the Single European Act that she enthusiastically enacted in 1985. It may be argued that her enthusiasm for a Europe with a foreign policy, redistributive measures in favour of poorer regions and a major increase in majority voting in place of unanimity which meant she and other heads of government lost their right to veto any policy or directive they disliked was not properly understood and somehow became policy and practice behind her back.

This is rather condescending to a woman who was a legend for being on top of details in her dossiers and who worked harder than most to master the implications of policy she supported. Instead we must look for other reasons for the Iron Lady's metamorphosis into an out-and-out Europhobe. What was the catalyst that made this happen? For good or ill, one man has to take a large share of responsibility – Jacques Delors.

The alpha and omega of Mrs Thatcher's premiership was her attack on the syndicalist militancy of British trade unions, culminating in the epic struggle between her and British coal miners in the great strike 1984–5. This was similar to the French communist-inspired assault on the Marshall Plan with strikes and protests in 1947–9, including violent attacks and derailing of trains that led to deaths. Three people were killed in the British miners' strike – two men on picket duty and a taxi driver taking a strike-breaking miner to work. The violence, police attacks on miners and the bitterness between the men who stayed on strike and those who returned to work remain unhealed wounds in the all-but-extinct mining communities of industrial Britain.

The British trade union movement was nominally a unitary one, with just one trade union central organization – the TUC (Trades Union Congress). But this hid the reality of a very strong communist presence. The British Communist Party, unlike the postwar French or Italian communist parties, never achieved any significant numbers of elected posts as MPs or councillors. But it had an effective policy of entryism into individual trade unions, especially in the mining and metal industries. In the 1970s, communist and other left networks inspired by a new '1968' generation of university-educated militant organizers, were able to conduct strikes that turned Britain into the playground of militant workers and post-1968 leftist militancy. Their strikes and go-slows helped bring about the defeat of the Conservative government in 1974.

Mrs Thatcher had been education minister (1970–4) and observed with impotent fury as a handful of trade union leaders appeared to have brought down the democratically elected government by strikes and protests. She watched with concern as elected Labour ministers between 1974 and her arrival in power in 1979 spent hours each day negotiating with trade union leaders who sought to dictate policy to the Labour government.

During the Labour government of 1974–9, which attempted to deal with the inflation produced by the first oil shock and the end of Bretton Woods currency stability, the strike movement became more energetic. Not yet 30, I had been elected president of the British journalists' union in 1978. Three years before, at a young age, I organized a strike of BBC journalists that took BBC home and overseas news off-air. What Hitler had failed to do – silence the BBC – a handful of young militant organizers achieved. It made me feel cocky then. I am ashamed now at my infantile leftism. In the 1970s, the classic social democratic reformism of northern Europe had little purchase on the British left. The Labour government collapsed as Britain's postwar mixed economy settlement came to an end with uncollected stinking rubbish bags forming 5-metre-high mountains in the tourist and theatre areas of London. Municipal cemetery workers went on strike, leaving the dead unburied.

The workers, or at least their spokesmen, felt their claims for more pay or shorter working hours were justified. But the public turned away in horror from a trade union movement that seemed keener to attack the public than capitalism, or refused any of the labour–capital compromise politics to be seen in social democratic Germany or Scandinavia.

The heart of the platform on which Mrs Thatcher won the election in 1979 and again in 1983 and 1987 was her pledge to change trade union practices and reduce syndicalist militant power in British workplaces. After her military victory in the Falkland Islands in 1982 she described the unions as 'the enemy within'. Trade union leaders and militants protested, but voters were with Mrs Thatcher, not with union leaders or left-wing activists. The miners' strike of 1984–5 was crushed with a brutality never seen before in Britain. The Labour Party began to distance itself from too close an identification with militant trade union activity. But in 1987, Mrs Thatcher's hate of and assault on unions seemed to have been vindicated with her third successive election victory – a political achievement not won by any previous prime minister in the century.

And then came Jacques Delors with his speech to the annual congress of the trade unions in September 1988. The speech was a closely argued explanation of the 1992 single market project. Delivered in Delors's English with a thick French accent the speech sounded neither radical nor was there any attack on the British government. Listening to his speech at the time it seemed to be a standard defence of Delors's 1992 project for the greater integration of European capitalism. The references to trade unions were moderate and echoed the Catholic *Rerum novarum* labour tradition based on social partnership, compromise and support for market economics. It was light years away from the socialist rhetoric of the confrontational trade unionism that Mrs Thatcher had crushed.

Delors invited the trade unions to join him and other 'architects' in constructing Europe. In a challenge to the British prime minister, Delors said Europe required a social dimension based on:

> The establishment of a platform of guaranteed workers' rights, containing general principles, such as every worker's right to be covered by a collective agreement, and more specific measures concerning, for example, the status of temporary work.
>
> The creation of a Statute for European Companies, which would include the participation of workers or their representatives.
>
> The extension to all workers of the right to lifelong education.

In themselves these were commonplace generalizations little different from the conventions of the International Labour Organization and broadly accepted in western democracies. But for the British trade unions, Jacques Delors was received like a Joan of Arc saving the British worker and trade unions from the crushing tyranny of Mrs Thatcher. They cheered Delors as no visiting speaker had been cheered before. They spontaneously burst into song chanting *Frère Jacques* or singing the striking miners' hymn 'Here We Go' to the tune of the French revolutionary song *Ça ira*. Both the left and the right of the trade unions welcomed this hero from across the Channel who put the banned 'Social' back into the vocabulary of British politics.

Among French trade unions Jacques Delors was no favourite of the communist Confédération Générale du Travail trade union or the Trotskyist-influenced Force Ouvrière union. But as the British trade unions rose as one to clap and cheer him, tears could be seen in his eyes as finally trade union militants were in love with President Delors!

Mrs Thatcher took the Delors speech as a personal insult. To her it was an onslaught on her decade-long campaign to reduce the power of British trade unions. In fact, she and Delors had much in common. Both came from modest backgrounds and powered their way to the top through relentless hard work. Neither was a socializer: both were disciplined and austere in their personal lives and demanding of colleagues. Delors told journalists that the difference between him and Mrs Thatcher was that she was a Protestant and he was a Catholic. She in turn explained her difficulties with Delors thus: 'He's a socialist and from the extreme wing of socialism.' Nothing was less true. Delors had been a functionary in the Banque de France and had been attacked by many on the French left when he worked for the centrist right-wing prime minister, Jacques Chaban-Delmas. Delors was active in the Catholic trade union movement. He was an open political foe of the French Communist Party, which was a dominant force on the French left throughout Delors's life before he became a minister in 1981.

Far from being an extreme socialist, Delors had fashioned the turn away from leftist state control in 1983 when he helped persuade French president François Mitterrand to bow to the rules of open-market economics and globalization. That is why Delors was acceptable to the majority of centre-right European leaders in 1984 as European Commission president, including Mrs Thatcher. She also supported his appointment as chairman of the committee set up in June 1988 after the Evian European Council meeting to examine the possibility of introducing economic and monetary union (EMU) for the European Community.

The Bundesbank president, Karl Otto Pohl, was deeply sceptical about monetary union and disliked the creation of the new group. If EMU really came about then the monetary and economic power that the Bundesbank had gathered to itself would be diluted. Yet Mrs Thatcher, combined with Chancellor Kohl and President Mitterrand, set up the group and installed Jacques Delors at its head. Pohl complained that 'She fell for the idea of setting up a group with Delors as the chairman. She must have known it would have a political dimension.' Between June and September 1988, Mrs Thatcher's relations with Delors were transformed as the Commission president entered into British political consciousness in a way no European political leader had done since General de Gaulle.

In content, Delors's TUC speech could have been made by Conservative ministers in the 1970s as they tried to bring law into workplace relations – the norm in many continental countries. Mrs Thatcher had outlawed the closed shop – the system used by British trade unions to insist that without a union membership card it was impossible to get a job in industries like printing or industrial manufacturing. But the closed shop contradicted European legislation and had long disappeared in Europe. Mrs Thatcher's other trade union reforms included secret ballots ahead of strike action. These were standard in many unions across the Channel. If Jacques Delors had thought more carefully about the impact of his speeches in the summer of 1988 and if Margaret Thatcher had patronized Delors for giving moderate and useful advice to British trade unions, perhaps history would have been different.

But the role of Delors in sowing the seeds of British Euroscepticism in 1988 cannot be underestimated. Already in July 1988 Delors had told the European Parliament that in a decade's time 80 per cent of economic, social and possibly even tax legislation would be made at the European level. His then *chef du cabinet*, Pascal Lamy, who wrote all of the major Delors speeches, said that the line about 80 per cent of legislation being decided at a European level was added by Delors spontaneously while he was making the speech. 'I buried my head in my hands as I heard Delors make this claim. I knew just what a disaster it would be around the national capitals of Europe to be told that the work of their governments and parliaments in passing legislation would disappear to be replaced by European law-making', Lamy told me.

Delors's claim turned out to be inaccurate exaggeration. A quarter of a century later, it is still the national parliaments of Europe that decide most of the key laws that affect their peoples, save on trade policy, where the EU has competence and where the World Trade Organization determines many of the rules of economic exchange. Whatever his intention in making his boast (and it is true that speakers to the European Parliament often seek to stroke MEPs with flattering if fallacious assertions that ever-more Europe is on its way), Delors's assertion that the House of Commons would soon fade into irrelevance as law-making was transferred to Brussels and Strasbourg caused intense irritation in London.

The whole of British political history, indeed national history, is based on the concept of parliament being supreme. Some of this was myth but not all. It was the Commons that made Churchill prime minister in 1940 while French parliamentary democracy crumbled as French deputies handed power to Pétain. American hopes in 1982 that Britain might negotiate a peace deal with Argentina over the Falklands came to nothing as the Commons rose with fury against the Argentinian junta with its record of torture, disappearances and anti-Semitism and called for military action to throw the invading troops out of the tiny British possession in the southern Atlantic. It was in the Commons that Margaret Thatcher saw her political life come to an end as her own MPs and former ministers turned publicly against her in 1990.

It was the Commons, not the then prime minister, Edward Heath, who took Britain into the European Economic Community in 1972 when 62 Labour MPs voted against their party and supported British entry. Later it was the Commons, and not Tony Blair, who decided British participation in the Iraq war in 2003. After a bitter two-day debate, 417 British MPs endorsed the invasion. When the debate began no one could be certain that the final vote would be for war and in the Foreign and Commonwealth Office ministers were ready to resign if the vote had gone against the government. For good or ill, it was Britain's MPs in the House of Commons who decided on the war with Iraq. Again it was the Commons who rejected, in August 2013, Prime Minister David Cameron's hasty rush to seek approval for launching a cruise missile strike against Syria – an unprecedented and humiliating rebuff for the head of government on a question of war and peace.

It is not that the Commons makes for better legislation or exercises more control over the executive than other parliaments such as the US Congress, the German Bundestag or France's National Assembly. It is simply woven into the idea of what Britain is. To belittle or lessen the importance of the Commons as the only source for law in Britain by suggesting that soon eight out of ten laws would be decided outside its frontiers was to attack the very democratic foundations of the island's history.

Delors, of course, did not have any of these ideas running through his head in 1988 as he said law-making would be transferred from the British Parliament to Europe, any more than he thought he was attacking Mrs Thatcher with his friendly words to the trade union delegates. He had also given an interview to *Le Monde* that summer in which he said that the European Commission was the beginning of a European government. This claim, like the picture of most laws being made at a European level, was not taken particularly seriously, but when combined with Delors's TUC speech provoked Mrs Thatcher into a full-scale attack on the Commission president.

Ten days after Delors spoke to the British unions, Britain's prime minister went to Bruges. There she made a speech as significant for

Britain's relationship with Europe as Churchill's 'United States of Europe' speech in Zürich four decades before.

Mrs Thatcher's 1988 Bruges address has entered the British political canon as one of the defining speeches of Britain's relationship with Europe. In it, Mrs Thatcher implied a comparison between the European Community and the by-then dying Soviet Union. The speech had been discussed, written and rewritten several times by the best brains at the heart of Downing Street and the Foreign and Commonwealth Office. As ever, there were nice words about Europe just as there were in David Cameron's speech of January 2013 announcing his Brexit referendum. But the core message, accepted and sharpened by Mrs Thatcher, was a repudiation of all that Jacques Delors had said to the European Parliament and the TUC. She did not quite compare Delors to a Soviet leader but she did argue that:

> Just when those countries such as the Soviet Union, which have tried to run everything from the centre, are learning that success depends on dispersing power and decisions away from the centre, there are some in the Community who seem to want to move in the opposite direction.

The Bruges speech coincided with the opening of the US presidential election to choose Ronald Reagan's successor in the autumn of 1988. 'Maggie and Ronnie' had been the double act of the 1980s. They both claimed to have lessened the role of the state and dismantled the post-1945 model of a mixed economy with an accepted role for trade unions. Now in a clear attack on Delors's TUC speech Thatcher proclaimed: 'We have not successfully rolled back the frontiers of the state in Britain, only to see them re-imposed at a European level with a European super-state exercising a new dominance from Brussels.'

Thus the metaphor of Europe as a 'super-state' entered British political discourse. Even the lip service she paid to a stronger Europe came with a warning about the role of national parliaments: 'Certainly we want to see Europe more united and with a greater sense of common purpose. But it must be in a way which preserves the different traditions, parliamentary powers and sense of national pride in one's own country; for these have been the source of Europe's vitality through the centuries.'

With some understatement, the Margaret Thatcher Foundation says of her Bruges attack on Delors, 'The speech began the transition by which the Conservatives ceased to be "the party of Europe" in British politics, moving fitfully by lurches, lunges and sidesteps, to a position now known as "Euroscepticism". The term itself was invented in the process.'

It seemed, however, that Delors would have the last laugh. Despite Mrs Thatcher's dislike of European integration it proceeded apace, driven by the need to harmonize standards and rules to create the single market. Mrs Thatcher, like today's Conservatives, set great store by a single market. But no market place operates without rules, including rules protecting consumers from harmful products and usually some rights for employees to be fairly treated. Whenever a crisis emerges, for instance over horse meat being sold as beef or the faulty PIP breast implants, the cry goes up for stronger regulation, stricter inspection and punishment for those who abuse the market by not abiding by its common regulations.

Absolute national sovereignty and common rules applied across borders are not compatible. The Germans had to surrender their five-centuries-old rule that beer should be brewed in a special way not used by brewers in France or Britain. The French had to accept that British beef was safe after the initial outbreak of mad cow disease was dealt with. When the scandal over horse meat in lasagne and other processed meat products exploded in 2013, the cry in Britain was to ban imports from the continent. British meat eaters may say No to imports from Europe, but British farmers export lamb and horse meat worth hundreds of millions of euros to the continent. British sheep farming would collapse overnight if there were no enforceable common rules to keep the meat market open beyond national frontiers.

The British are never taught logic and formal reasoning at school so appear to believe that a single market can exist without common

rules regulating market activity. British thinking confuses free trade
with a single market. The former exists, as in the form of trade
between the United States and most countries that allows the USA
firstly to deny market access if Congress so decides and secondly
to give subsidies to favoured industries that distort competition.
A single market prevents such favouritism or protectionism. The
USA bans the import of British beef on spurious health grounds
and limits Mexican lorry drivers travelling with their trucks through
America to deliver Corona beer. Even though under NAFTA, the
North American Free Trade Agreement, lorries are meant freely to
cross the US–Mexican border, there has been such opposition from
the US Congress and trade unions that 20 years after NAFTA was
signed there is one small pilot programme allowing just 14 Mexican
trucks into America! The Buy America Act means that federal and
state authorities in the United States cannot buy from European
manufacturers and must buy products from domestic American
producers. In contrast, the EU expressly bans such protectionism
by EU governments or regional governments, which are obliged to
tender for the cheapest product irrespective of where it comes from.
President George W. Bush placed a temporary ban on steel imports
into the USA from Europe in order to win votes from the steelworker
communities of Pennsylvania. The US steel unions applauded this
measure. British steelworkers and their unions were horrified at such
naked protectionism, which damaged their jobs and incomes.

Free trade allows each nation to decide the terms of its trade.
A single market that obliges every European consumer to be allowed
to buy British beef if so desired and allows British lorries carrying
Marmite and English muffins to go freely to every shop from Poland
to Portugal requires some supranational supervision and enforce-
ment mechanism. Many European nations with strong lobbies
against animal cruelty, for example, would like to ban the sale of foie
gras on the grounds that force-feeding the geese is cruel. The EU
stops such barriers to trade, with the task of defending the open, liberal market undertaken by the European Commission and enforce-
ment by the European Court of Justice. If you want a single market

you must have a strong supranational Europe to enforce it. And the more single market you want, the more Europe you need. Both Margaret Thatcher and Jacques Delors pushed hard for the single market. If either had had better consiglieri or different personalities, perhaps they could have become partners in European construction.

But that was not to be. Jacques Delors was turned by Margaret Thatcher into a monster from Brussels seeking to impose a domineering Europe on British democracy. In 1979 and in subsequent elections in 1983 and 1987, Mrs Thatcher had been an eloquent defender of Europe. She had used her considerable political skills and force to push through the Single European Act. But she and her ministers fell out over the establishment of the European Exchange Rate Mechanism. Her two chief lieutenants, the Chancellor of the Exchequer, Nigel Lawson and her foreign secretary, Sir Geoffrey Howe, resigned because she would not accept their view that Britain should work constructively in Europe. The resignation speech by Howe in the Commons was a devastating attack on her growing hostility to Europe and precipitated the political crisis that led to her resignation in November 1990. (See the next chapter for more on this.)

In her last speech in the House of Commons before she was forced to resign as previously loyal Conservative MPs voted against her, she attacked Delors:

> The President of the Commission, Monsieur Delors, said at a press conference the other day that he wanted the European Parliament to be the democratic body of the Community, he wanted the Commission to be the Executive and he wanted the Council of Ministers to be the Senate. No! No! No!

This cry of 'No! No! No!' was the emotional appeal of a British prime minister against Europe. When Lady Thatcher died in April 2013, her attacks on Delors and her 'No! No! No!' to Europe were shown endlessly on television. For the last 23 years of her life her main political interventions were against Europe. Delors's 1988

TUC speech triggered a profound genetic change in what hitherto had been her pragmatic, if unenthusiastic pro-Europeanism. Shortly afterwards, Rupert Murdoch's *Sun* newspaper (with 12 million readers) attacked Delors's ideas for a new treaty to set up a single currency and a European Central Bank. The *Sun* front page was filled with a headline 'UP YOURS DELORS!', which the paper turned into a personalized anti-Delors hate campaign with T-shirts bearing the slogan available to its readers. Delors was turned into a hate figure by the offshore-owned press for the remainder of his term of office as Commission president and thereafter whenever he made pro-European interventions after stepping down as president in 1995.

In his memoirs, Delors skates over the 1988 crisis of relations with Mrs Thatcher. He insists that he sought to cooperate with her and went readily to London to meet her when required. In 1988 he was getting into his stride as the Commission president, whereas the glory days of Mrs Thatcher were already behind her. In 1986 at a press conference in London Mrs Thatcher refused to allow him to speak. The British political class had always regarded European Commissioners as officials and the president of the Commission as the head of the European civil service. In Britain it is elected politicians who speak and are the public face of political decision-making and administration. The civil servants are silent in public until they go into the Lords and never stop talking. But in office they exercise their power behind closed doors. When asked why M. Delors was saying nothing, Mrs Thatcher sneered that he was 'the strong silent type'.

Delors went on to become Europe's most prominent figure, strong but never silent. His influence over Europe's public and political life continued after 1995, with many on the left in France hoping he would run for president of France. Mrs Thatcher became more and more anti-European. She was worshipped by many Conservatives as the last great prime minister Britain had. Her funeral was turned into a major state occasion, even though for many in the north of England and in Scotland she was a divisive and disliked figure. At the time of her death she was still memory and not yet history. But in the extremes of her hostility to any development in European construction and integration after 1990 she appeared obsessed, bad-tempered and unable to come to terms with the end of her political career, which had been her life since 1950. For those who revered her, the hostility to Europe she showed in the 1990s helped generate the Conservative opposition to the EU that is now deeply embedded in the party's psyche.

The sadness of her final years of illness, captured by the American actor, Meryl Streep, removed her from public discourse as she coped with what de Gaulle called the shipwreck of old age. In contrast, Jacques Delors, in December 2012, at the European Book of the Year award ceremony in the European Parliament in Brussels, debated with Helmut Schmidt for two hours over the way forward in Europe. Delors was born, like Mrs Thatcher, in 1925 but over the nearly two decades after his retirement he continued to be a reference point in the unfolding of European politics. This irritates Eurosceptic Conservatives in London. They watched sadly as their heroine declined into a sad shadow of her former self until her death alone in a hotel room in the Ritz in April 2013. In the meantime her nemesis was still active and still as strong an advocate of European construction as he was in 1988.

It would be too simplistic to blame British Euroscepticism on the Delors interventions of 1988. When Mrs Thatcher left office in November 1990, Europe had never been more popular, at least according to Eurobarometer polling, which showed 53 per cent finding UK membership of the European Community to be a good thing compared to just 16 per cent who thought Europe was bad for Britain. So the turn to Euroscepticism did not suddenly arise following Delors's 1988 speeches. But they have lingered in British political consciousness and Mrs Thatcher's reaction in her Bruges speech is now rightly seen as a defining moment. Had Delors been more guarded in his boast that Europe would replace national government and parliaments as the source of law and if he had not been able to find a free day his diary to make that TUC speech but instead gone to speak to British employers on the importance of the single market, including polite words about Social Europe, then the fury of Mrs Thatcher would not have been unleashed. Politics is about *paroles* – the words that define where we want to go and who we want to be. Delors's words in 1988 helped fertilize an incipient British hostility to the EU he was bringing into being. At times, to say nothing is best.

7

FROM MAGGIE TO MAJOR: THE DRIFT TO CONSERVATIVE EUROSCEPTICISM

If Jacques Delors's 1988 intervention was the moment when the turn to anti-EU hostility started to infect the Conservative Party, this was not immediately evident at the time. To begin with, once installed at Downing Street in 1979 Mrs Thatcher continued Heath's pro-European line. The Single European Act of 1985 transferred more power and sovereignty to Brussels than the Treaty of Rome. But as we have seen, by the end of her first decade as prime minister, Mrs Thatcher had become hostile to Brussels and especially Jacques Delors. As she came out against Europe her predecessor Edward Heath's pro-European beliefs curdled into a personal venom against Mrs Thatcher, which he never hid from the public. For the new generation of young, ambitious Conservatives who left Oxbridge in the 1980s to make their entry into political life – men like David Cameron, Boris Johnson, George Osborne and the journalist Charles Moore, who became editor of the *Spectator* and *Daily Telegraph* – Margaret Thatcher was the heroine to be followed and Edward Heath, the man who presided over a disastrous and losing Conservative government in the 1970s, a failure to be despised.

Heath's friends, like his former aide, Douglas Hurd, who was home secretary under Mrs Thatcher and then became foreign minister under John Major, tried to build bridges. Hurd was a committed pro-European who wrote positively in his memoirs: 'To our vigorous member of the most hopeful organization Europe has ever seen I felt and feel a robust commitment which comes from the brain and the heart.' Another Heath aide was the lawyer Sir Geoffrey Howe MP, who resigned as a minister from Mrs Thatcher's government in November 1990 in protest at her increasingly strident hostility to Europe.

Howe had been a careful, cautious, mild-mannered Chancellor of the Exchequer and foreign secretary. But in a speech in the autumn of 1990 that electrified the House of Commons, he urged Conservative ministers to join his rebellion against the now openly anti-European Mrs Thatcher. Another senior Conservative politician and also a strong pro-European and protégé of Edward Heath was Michael Heseltine MP. He announced he would challenge Mrs Thatcher in an election for a new party leader and hence prime minister. In some of the most dramatic days in British parliamentary history, Europe rose up like an avenging force and ended Mrs Thatcher's career. Although the pro-European Heseltine did not win more votes than Mrs Thatcher, he won enough to show that she had lost the confidence of her party. Edward Heath celebrated her downfall, as did other pro-European Conservatives and many on the continent who had become fed up with her increasingly strident anti-European language. They opened the champagne too early. Far from Mrs Thatcher's exit from Downing Street with tears in her eyes marking the end of anti-European politics in the Conservative Party, it was only the beginning.

If Mrs Thatcher's career ended because of Europe, her successor, John Major, saw his seven years as prime minister (1990–7) turned into misery by the question of Europe. While Jacques Delors, helped by Helmut Kohl and François Mitterrand, kept pushing forward European integration initiatives, Mr Major found himself under the triple challenge of first, a growing anti-European grouping inside his party; second, the open embrace of crude, often-sensationalist anti-European campaigning by important sections of the press; and third, the rise of well-funded campaigns, movements and new political parties all dedicated to the proposition that the EU was inimical to British national interests. The steps towards greater European integration represented by the change of title from European Community to European Union, the Maastricht Treaty and the launch of the process to monetary union left Mr Major isolated. The Maastricht Treaty of 1992 took the process of European integration several significant steps forward. The most important decision was to begin the process of Economic and Monetary Union, with the goal of creating a completely new currency – the euro. This required setting up a European Central Bank to issue money and decide interest rates. The so-called Maastricht criteria governing how EU member states should handle their internal budgets in terms of debt and deficit were a major new development in obliging finance ministers to accept rules set at a European, not a national level.

Elected in 1990 as Conservative Party leader and thus prime minister as a relatively unknown compromise candidate, Mr Major had been in the Commons only 11 years and was not known to have strong opinions on anything. He was intimately friendly with Edwina Currie MP, an outspoken pro-European, and many of John Major's political friends, such as Chris Patten MP, later a European Commissioner, or Kenneth Clarke MP, who became his Chancellor of the Exchequer, were also known to be strongly in favour of Europe. Thus it was no surprise that one of his first statements on becoming prime minister in 1990 was that he wanted 'to restore Britain to the heart of Europe'. His ambition failed. Europe became his political Calvary.

A new generation of Conservative MPs who entered the Commons in 1992 refused to back the Maastricht Treaty and formed an aggressive Eurosceptic grouping as they put up spokesmen like Iain Duncan Smith MP, a future Conservative Party leader, to attack Mr Major. Within his own cabinet he faced pressure from Eurosceptic ministers whom he described as 'bastards'. The future Conservative leader Michael Howard MP, the employment secretary, threatened to resign unless Mr Major obtained an exemption for Britain from Europe's social policy. Foreign and Commonwealth

Office diplomats invented the concept of 'opt-outs' so that Britain was not bound by the Maastricht Treaty's Social Chapter. However, this obsessive hostility to core employee rights, which did not appear to bother other employers in Europe, came at the price of restoring some of the discredited status of trade unions, who were now fully converted to the virtues of the EU.

Britain's expulsion from the Exchange Rate Mechanism (ERM) in 1992 added to Mr Major's unhappiness. ERM had been set up to try and link permanently the different currencies of EU member states. Clearly, it was hard to have a fully open single market if countries could unilaterally devalue their currencies, thus making their exports more competitive in relation to their neighbours. After volatile and inflationary movements of the pound sterling during the Thatcher years, it was decided to enter the ERM. But the pound entered at too high a rate and could not withstand global market movements as speculators decided to bet against the pound. In consequence, the pound was forced out of the ERM and the Chancellor of the Exchequer, Norman Lamont MP, was forced to resign in humiliating circumstances. His previous pro-Europeanism curdled into an unforgiving hostility to the EU which continues to this day.

The volatility of the pound sterling and an erratic interest-rate policy which was still decided by ministers, not an independent central bank, precluded Britain taking part in euro preparations. But there was no need for Mr Major gratuitously to describe the idea of a single currency as being 'as quaint as a rain dance'.

The one area where Britain thought it was strong and Europe weak was that of foreign policy. But Mr Major's government handled the rise of fascistic nationalist militarism in the Balkans, culminating in the siege of Sarajevo and the Katyn-style massacres at Srebrenica, with all the finesse of Britain's pre-war Conservatives appeasing Hitler, Mussolini and Franco.

As Marx noted, history repeats itself: first as tragedy, then as farce. Having done nothing to mobilize Europe to stop the tragic genocidal massacres in the Balkans, Mr Major decided to get tough and show leadership. As mad cow disease sent Britain into a panic in which no one wanted to eat British beef and every Commonwealth country, including the British-controlled colony of Hong Kong, banned the import of British beef, Mr Major insisted that French, German and other European meat eaters should keep serving up the good old roast beef of England. Not unreasonably, most European countries, under pressure from consumers, wanted to suspend imports of British beef until all health fears had been allayed. Angry at this attack on the temporarily deranged British cow, Mr Major retaliated by saying Britain would send no more ministers to European Council meetings in order to stop progress on all dossiers where unanimous agreement was required.

This bizarre version of General de Gaulle's empty-chair tactics three decades previously produced no more than a puzzled shrug of the shoulders from the rest of Europe. The '12' were now '15', with Sweden, Finland and Austria bringing a strong tradition of social democratic fairness into the EU. The rest of Europe just assumed that Mr Major had been eating too much raw steak and had gone a little mad if he thought Europe would be forced to sit down and eat British beef given the fears of infection of the animals' brains and spinal columns.

Finally, Mr Major became so angry with his anti-European MPs he resigned. Not as prime minister but as leader of the Conservative Party. Months ahead of a general election he was re-elected, but not before one of the cleverest intellectuals in his government, John Redwood MP, quit as a minister to stand on an anti-European platform against his party leader. Mr Redwood lost. A former fellow of All Souls, he spent the next two decades using his status, his energetic writing gifts and his undoubted intellect to devote himself to relentless criticism of Europe. Mr Redwood's place as a minister was taken by the rising young star William Hague MP. Mr Major thought he had removed one Europhobe but in fact replaced him with another. By the end of Mr Major's government in 1997, his party was increasingly Eurosceptic.

8

TONY BLAIR: WAS HE PRO-EUROPEAN?

Sunday, 11 May 1997

> *Martin Walker, an old friend and the* Guardian's *correspond-*
> *ent in Washington, came round for dinner tonight. He told me*
> *that he had lunched with Peter Stothard, editor of* The Times,
> *who remains resolutely anti-single currency. On the other hand,*
> *Martin said he had had a conversation with Bill Clinton in which*
> *Clinton made clear his support for Britain playing a full part in*
> *Europe and entering a single currency. So far the Government*
> *line on Europe has been energetic and engaged and as a result*
> *a great deal of the Euro tension that existed prior to the election*
> *has simply faded away. But the big decisions on a single currency*
> *and some greater institutional pooling of sovereignty remain to*
> *be taken.*

Together with Margaret Thatcher, Tony Blair was the dominant peacetime prime minister in postwar Britain. There is a standard history which sees her Euroscepticism in contrast with Blair's passion for Europe. This rendering of history needs revision. It confuses form or style with content or substance. When Margaret Thatcher left office after 11 years in 1990 she had a substantial record of European construction to her name, even if she finished as a devout Eurosceptic. In her decade of leadership Spain, Portugal and Greece entered Europe.

Europe in the 1980s enjoyed a reasonable decade of prosperity, growth and innovation. Workers in Germany obtained the 35-hour week. The Single European Act with its important sharing of power and pooling of national sovereignty came into operation. The foundation stones of the single currency were laid. Europe was at peace. Communism and with it non-democratic rule crumbled in Eastern Europe. Mrs Thatcher began the 1980s as pro-European. Yet by 1990 she was hostile to European construction.

Tony Blair, by contrast, remains as much a pro-European today as when he became prime minister in 1997. But like his predecessors as prime minister, Harold Macmillan or Harold Wilson, he was unable to lead Britain into the heart of European integration, by replacing the erratic pound sterling with the euro. He kept Britain out of the Schengen area so British citizens have to queue up to show passports to cross a British frontier, just as their parents and grandparents had done in the years when Britain was not in the European Community. While Britain agreed in 1997 to adopt the provisions of the EU's Social Chapter – in contrast to the previous Conservative government's demand for Britain to be excluded from its provisions – Blair refused to implement two important social policy directives on working time and to end employers' abuse of workers from other EU member states or workers provided by employment agencies.

The two EU treaties signed by Blair – Amsterdam and Nice – were both minimalist in contrast to the Single European Act (1985) or Maastricht (1992). Blair was the first European leader to announce a referendum in 2004 on the European constitution. This forced the hand of Jacques Chirac and played into the hands of Eurosceptics in France who destroyed Europe's hopes of a final settlement to the constitutional questions that plagued the EU after its enlargements in 1995 and 2004.

Europe was broken in half over the Iraq war and Blair's alignment with George W. Bush. Success in 1999 in stopping the genocidal tendencies of Slobodan Milosevic or the hand extended to Turkey despite the Islamophobic hostility of conservative politicians in France, Germany and Austria could not offset the convulsions and divisions over Iraq, which left the idea of a common European foreign and defence policy in shreds.

As the Labour government began work in May 1997, Tony Blair sent me to the Foreign and Commonwealth Office to try and promote his pro-European vision and values. But there was no consistency. Altogether there were ten Europe ministers in Labour's 13 years in power. Blair's three Foreign Secretaries had spent the first half of their political lives in the 1970s and 1980s supporting anti-European positions. They had made speeches and written articles hostile to Europe, even if like most of Labour they had come round to a sullen acceptance of British membership of the EU. Blair had other enthusiastic pro-European Labour MPs to choose from to become ministers. However, he gave little thought to ensuring that his administration would be dominated by unambiguous and enthusiastic supporters of Europe.

Under the umbrella of the European Policy Institute, Robin Cook, Blair's first foreign secretary, had criticized in 1996 the move towards monetary union which other EU member states had committed to. In a conversation early in 1997 with Peter Hain MP, later one of Blair's Europe ministers, I told him I thought that the future of the EU was now inextricably bound up with the single currency. 'You're full of shit', was his reply. We were and remain friends, and as someone who uses robust language himself I had no problems with his rejoinder. But it worried me that one of Labour's better politicians was so out of touch with what was happening across the Channel.

I decided to keep a detailed daily diary to record from within what the Labour government, its ministers and deputies were doing and saying. Today as I reread my daily record I can see that Blair never completely imposed the European policy we talked of privately. Before becoming prime minister he had promised a referendum on any British entry into the euro. But to win a referendum there had to be enthusiasm and belief in the utility of the pound being replaced by the euro. This was lacking. Instead, from the first confusion on Europe's next development was everywhere. Soon after

the Labour government was formed, I met the general secretary of
the TUC, John Monks, and his deputy, David Lea. I noted:

Tuesday, 15 July 1997

> *David Lea told me that he and John Monks [General Secretary of
> the TUC] had met with Gordon Brown for breakfast this morn-
> ing and Gordon was pushing them to be supportive for an entry
> into EMU. Yet when I went back to the Commons I found Don
> Touhig [a Welsh MP who was Gordon Brown's PPS] after me to
> stop my tabling a parliamentary motion which had been signed
> by other MPs which was critical of the high value of sterling and
> positive about the 'next stages of European construction' which
> is a euphemism for EMU. Once again the left hand and right
> hand doesn't know what it's doing. What Gordon says at a TUC
> breakfast in the morning is contradicted by his chief aide a few
> hours later.*

In effect, Labour came to power with no clear ambition for where the
party wanted Britain to go on the question of Europe. Ministers contradicted one another in private meetings on whether joining the euro
was possible politics. If Gordon Brown met the strongly pro-European
leaders of the TUC then he smiled and agreed with their enthusiasm.
But later the same day his office prevented me from putting down a
motion for debate in the Commons in favour of the single currency.
The British state is more than its elected ministers and unelected
officials. It has its own unwritten culture and *Weltanschauung* which
influences the direction that Britain will take.

It was clear that enthusiasm for Europe was waning, as I noted in
my diary later in 1997.

Monday, 1 December 1997

> *I went across to the Foreign Office for some kind of Christmas
> party for the media. I had a brief chat with Tim Garton Ash
> who is fretting and worrying about Europe and trying to work
> out where he'll want to be in ten to twenty years time. I had a go*

at him for his hostility to EMU which he resents but he is backed
up by Sir Nigel Broomfield the ex-cavalry officer who was our
Ambassador to Germany whom I met in Manchester and who is
still locked into a Conservative critique of Europe.

It is too easy to blame British Euroscepticism on populist, often
xenophobic loud-mouths. Suspicion or hostility towards Brussels is
common in the cultivated, ruling elites.

Wednesday, 3 December 1997

A dash to the City to have lunch with Lord Simon, Sir Christopher
Mallaby [a former ambassador in Paris] to discuss the Anglo-French
colloque. As I was waiting to go in to the BP offices at Finsbury
Circus there was a small dapper chap who looked like Mr Anybody
who turned out to be the boss of St Gobain, Jean-Louis Beffa. The
Frenchman was passionate about the Euro and EMU but warned
of great restructuring which is the big business code for factories
being shut down. He was very sharp about [Lady] Sylvia Jay, the
nice wife of our Ambassador in Paris, Michael Jay. 'I had dinner
with her the other night and she was very sceptical and went on
about losing identity and sovereignty to Brussels.' This is interest-
ing as Michael, of course, is meant to reflect the new Government's
pro-European line but so deeply engrained is Euroscepticism in the
very fibres of the class from which Sylvia comes that her hostility
remains unstoppable. It is fascinating how something as banal as
a little conversation at dinner gets reported and circulated around
and around and around.

In the Commons, Blair spoke confidently about Europe and mocked
the obsessive Euroscepticism of the new Conservative Party leader,
William Hague, who was seeking to become the champion of
anti-Europeanism, which he thought would attract voters to the
Conservative Party. Yet what was Blair's ambition in Europe? As the
first months of his government went by there was certainly an excitement and energy in political life. Much of it was a contrast to the

exhaustion of the defeated Conservative government. Blair proposed a new parliament for Scotland and a regional assembly for Wales, thus beginning a process of devolution. There was the beginning of the end to the 30 years of quarrels, terrorism and sectarian strife in Northern Ireland. He formed a partnership based on personal chemistry with Bill Clinton, and together they launched a global campaign to win support for their third-way politics – a claim that a modernized social democracy could coexist with globalized capitalism. This was endorsed by Gerhard Schröder in Germany, but rejected by Lionel Jospin in France. The three-way tension between the new leaders from the left of Britain, France and Germany persisted and was never resolved. Blair encouraged me to network in Europe and try to forge a progressive alliance consisting of a dense network of centre-left leaders, ministers, MPs and opinion-makers.

Tuesday, 21 July 1998

> *I go to St. James' Hotel to have dinner with Günter Verheugen. He is Schröder's European spokesman and pumped out the message that Schröder wanted to work closely with Blair and Britain at the expense of a uniquely Franco-German axis. I will write a little note on this to send to the usual key people. He was taken with my idea that European Ministers should meet informally on a party political basis every two or three months just to exchange views and get things off their chest before they become inter-governmental or EU points of contention. This is the effective networking that needs to be done. The flying visits by ministers and MPs and Number Ten aides are useful but it is not a systematic development of contacts and it is that that we really now need.*

In the end, however, domestic politics always trumped European policy. Schröder had inherited 4 million unemployed from the outgoing Christian Democratic Chancellor, Helmut Kohl. He was willing to take big risks with reforms of the German labour market, which Jospin was too nervous to embrace in order to modernize France. Blair painted a more social and humane face on the British economy, which had gone through the wrenching brutal reforms of the Thatcher–Major era. He continued a policy of easing credit and encouraging personal debt to buy homes, cars or holidays. Subsidies in the form of a negative income tax were provided so that employers could take on employees at very low wages whose income was then increased with a payment from the state. Growth was strong and unemployment fell. A big programme of improving schools and hospitals began. More teachers, doctors, nurses and policemen were employed. Blair brought in new social policies to help poorer people. The government was a popular success and for the first time in its history Labour looked like winning two full mandates to govern.

On Europe, however, where was Blair heading? What did he want? What strategic ambition did he have for Britain's role in Europe? The 1997 EU Amsterdam Treaty was accepted by the Commons, but already the enthusiasm for Europe inside Labour was dwindling. By December 1997, Labour MPs were already bored by Europe.

Thursday, 4 December 1997

> *Yet another European debate. It was a general adjournment debate and Robin Cook opened it. He arrived with his usual handwritten speech all in his red felt tip pen and as usual it was a very good. There was only one problem. No one was there to hear it. Everybody had gone home. After a couple of minutes of this I went into the tea room and tapped anybody and everybody on the shoulder. 'The Foreign Secretary is facing up to Michael Howard [the shadow Foreign Secretary and future leader of the Conservatives] and there is no one there to listen to him. Please come in and sit behind him, even for ten minutes or till the end of his speech', I begged.*

I worked for Blair, trying to encourage more interest in Europe. I developed a network of Labour MPs who would go and build links with the growing number of social democratic or socialist governments on the continent. A special committee was set up to bring together ministers from every ministry to discuss how to work and cooperate in Europe. But these efforts fell foul of the opposition within the permanent state bureaucracy in London, which did not want any outside elected politicians trying to steer what the Labour government was doing on Europe.

In the background was the shadowy figure of Rupert Murdoch. The Faustian pact between Blair and Murdoch has never been properly examined and probably never will be, as the discussions between the two men were private. According to Professor David McKnight, like Murdoch an Australian, in his book *Murdoch's Politics*, 'From the very start of Murdoch's support of Blair, in 1997, he was explicit that he wanted assurances that a Labour government would not favour further integration into Europe.' Blair wrote an article for Murdoch's *Sun* newspaper, which at the time had 10 million readers. 'Let me make my position on Europe absolutely clear. I will have no truck with a European super state. If there are moves to create that dragon I will slay it.'

But this chest-puffing language did not satisfy Murdoch. He obtained a more important promise from Blair, argues Professor McKnight:

> The key device by which Murdoch blocked any British move into Europe was his insistence on a commitment from Blair that he would call a referendum before joining European Monetary Union. This would mean fighting out the issue in a public campaign in which Murdoch's popular newspapers would be at their loudest and most influential.

Blair tried to create some counter-pressure against the overwhelming media hostility to Europe and the money put up to campaign against Europe by rich right-wing businessmen who had amassed fortunes in the Thatcher era. In 1999, he launched 'Britain in Europe' with senior Conservatives like Michael Heseltine and Kenneth Clarke, who still clung to the pro-European beliefs of Edward Heath's Conservative Party, along with more youthful Liberal Democrats like Charles Kennedy and Danny Alexander. Britain always had a

European movement but it relied on voluntary donations and its age profile steadily got older as the enthusiasm for Europe as an idea generated in the decades after 1945 dwindled.

The leaders of British business who had been the strongest supporters of Britain being fully engaged in the European Community before the 1990s had now changed their line. For many it was a question of party ideology. As the Conservative Party and the business community's heroine, Margaret Thatcher, spoke out more and more frequently against Brussels, it was normal for business leaders, whose natural political affiliation is to the right, to fall in with the new Eurosceptic ideology that was taking over the Conservative Party. Slowly, the strongly pro-European business voices became silent.

Businesses also need to keep on the right side of any elected government, so it would be wrong to attribute the decline of pro-Europeanism among business simply to political affinities. A more important reason was that mainland Europe had lost its attraction as a source of growth, economic energy and new entrepreneurial innovation. Between 1950 and 1973, British growth averaged 2.9 per cent each year. Over the same period Germany had grown by an annual average of 6 per cent, France by 5.1 per cent and Italy 5.1 per cent. Between 1973 and 1995, Britain still lagged behind, with annual average growth of 2.4 per cent, below Germany and France (both 2.7 per cent) and Italy (2.5 per cent). Post-Maastricht, British growth surged past its EU partners. Between 1993 and 1997 UK growth was 3.14 per cent annually, compared to France's 1.36 per cent, Germany's 1.14 per cent and Italy's 1.24 per cent.

Despite being outside the EMU and the Schengen zone Britain was out-performing its main European rivals. Unlike the 1960s, the 1970s and the 1980s, when British business leaders looked with admiration on their more vigorous, successful European counterparts, now it was Britain that was heading league tables for economic performance and adapting to a new world economic order. Under Tony Blair, Britain's growth figures remained impressive. Between 1998 and 2002 Britain's growth each year averaged 3.24 per cent compared to 1.68 per cent in Germany, 1.8 per cent in Italy and 2.62 per cent in France.

In other words, Britain, having been the weak man of Europe for nearly half a century after the war, was now racing past its principal rivals to become the EU's economic champion. Moreover, Britain looked to the United States for economic inspiration, not Europe. Across the Atlantic, new products from Apple or Microsoft or new services powered by the internet, such as Google and Amazon, combined with a fast-expanding and ever-wealthier privately funded university system appeared to be creating a new economic model. Financial engineering as much as industrial engineering became the model of wealth creation. More than 30 million legal immigrants were living in America in 2000, with nearly as many illegal migrants. Compared to the hysteria in Europe at the arrival of Polish workers in Britain, the United States model of a country open to foreigners ready to work hard and realize the American dream was attractive to British companies. While Europe still boasted about the 40-year-old Airbus, North America was churning out iPhones and BlackBerries. In short, Britain looked west to the United States, or east to Asia, but the economic model in Europe lost the magnetic appeal it had had up to 1990.

As we sat in Number 10 in the first years of the twenty-first century discussing the EU, or as I went out to speak at meetings on Europe as his minister for Europe, Blair could no longer look to Europe for economic inspiration or point to the Eurozone countries as evidence that they had better economies as a result of the single currency. Of course there were external reasons, notably the huge burden of West Germany having to absorb the bankrupt third-world economy of corruption, cheating and lies of communist East Germany and pay all the new citizens West German salaries and benefits. I tried to persuade friends in Paris who were in Lionel Jospin's cabinet that 'flexibility' was not a swear-word and that allowing a few more taxi drivers to operate in Paris was not the end of the world or that cheap aspirins might be sold in autoroute service stations instead of by the protectionist oligopolies of high-priced pharmacies. It was a waste of time. France does revolutions. It finds reform much harder.

For Blair, a pro-European, it became much more difficult than in the era of Harold Macmillan or Harold Wilson or Edward Heath or even the early Margaret Thatcher to sell Europe to the British. The British prefer practice to theory. They want empirical proof before they will believe anything. Certainly the introduction of the euro was a major technical success. Jean-Claude Trichet, head of the European Central Bank, claimed that the low inflation of the Eurozone was a tribute to the single currency's success. But in the first decade in the twenty-first century there was low inflation everywhere in the world, including in Britain. Europe had many attributes, but Blair could no longer use Europe as an example of superior economic performance.

The organization Britain in Europe was set up in 1999 with one specific goal – abolition of the pound and entry into the euro. But it was immediately countered by Blair's rival, Gordon Brown, the Chancellor of the Exchequer, who announced that Britain would create a special committee to examine five economic tests which would have to be passed before Britain could contemplate entering the euro. The tests were jotted down on the back of an envelope in a taxi by Brown's chief aide, the Eurosceptic Ed Balls. I gave Ed Balls and David Miliband a lift in my ministerial car once to a British–French forum. Ed Balls joked to us that he could never actually remember what the five economic tests were.

So while Britain in Europe, urged on by the prime minister, was seeking to make the case for British entry into the euro, the second most powerful Labour minister was making sure this was unlikely to happen. Brown was careful always to keep the door open to a possible entry into the euro, especially if he was talking to audiences in countries that had decided to use the euro. But everyone in politics knew of Ed Balls regularly briefing against the euro at his lunches with economics journalists, who obediently conveyed the hostility of the Brown camp to European economic integration. Civil servants, consultants they hired to do their work and academic economists busied themselves with producing papers about Brown's five economic tests. It allowed the fiction that Britain was serious about joining the euro, but only once there had been a full examination of the economic benefits or disadvantages.

More important were two insurmountable objections which did not feature in the Brown–Balls economic tests. The first was the strength of the pound as a currency. In the 1980s and 1990s, the pound had been Europe's most unstable currency, going up and down against the main European currencies. One year the pound would buy 13 French francs and the next year it would buy only eight. In the nine months before Blair became prime minister in May 1997, the pound had risen by more than 25 per cent against the currencies in Europe about to form the euro. The high-value pound did great damage to Britain's industrial economy and to exports. It helped control inflation by keeping low the import price of raw materials, energy and food. The high-value pound made British citizens feel good on holiday in France or Spain. But for the pound to have entered the euro at such an overvalued rate would have produced unbearable tensions for the British economy.

This hindrance to Blair's ambition to enter the euro and thus align Britain with the next major stage of European construction stood alongside a more formidable barrier. This was the obligation to hold a referendum on euro entry, designed to appease Eurosceptic opinion before the 1997 election. The Conservatives under John Major announced there would be no euro entry without a referendum. Blair did not want to leave the Conservatives as the only party offering a plebiscite, so matched John Major's offer. It turned into a plebiscite prison for Blair. He dared not risk a referendum on euro entry. He knew that nearly all the press would campaign for a No. Even the *Guardian*, broadly supportive of Europe from a liberal-left position, was hostile to the euro. When taxed about holding a referendum on the euro early in his premiership when his popularity and authority were at their highest, Blair would respond bitterly: 'I am not going down in fucking history as the prime minister who took Britain out of Europe.'

Blair was right. His referendum pledge on entering the euro meant the gamble of chancing a vote was too risky. The Conservative Party, down and demoralized after its 1997 defeat, would have come back to life as it united against the euro. The new populist parties of the right – Ukip and the British National Party – were beginning to make an impact, especially on white working-class voters hostile to immigration and asylum seekers as well as distrustful of Blair's embrace of globalization. A euro referendum would have allowed them to mobilize and unite to defeat Blair and reject Europe, much as the French *souverainistes* of left and right did in France's 2005 referendum on Europe. The press would have campaigned against the euro. Labour itself would have split, as there were many Eurosceptic Labour MPs after 1997 who simply kept quiet in the interests of party unity but who would urge a No vote against euro entry. Blair's closest ally and friend in European social democracy was the Swedish prime minister, Goran Persson. He organized a referendum on Sweden joining the euro in 2003, confident that the Swedes would say Yes. They said No. His government never recovered, opening the way to the arrival of a conservative government in Sweden (2006–14).

Wednesday, 24 January 2001

> *On to a dinner for Joschka Fischer, the German Foreign Minister. Fischer made a brilliant speech, essentially pleading for more integration while accepting the centrality of the nation state as a source of democratic legitimacy and attachment of peoples in Europe. It was beautifully done. I slipped a note to Nick Butler who was sat beside David Miliband saying 'Who on earth could do this in our political system and in a foreign language' and Nick scribbled back that he had made exactly the same point to Miliband. We have great power as a rich leading country but we have no politicians who are fully capable of shaping the European argument other than Blair himself and he doesn't want to get engaged.*

So if entering the euro was not possible politics, what was left of Blair's European policy? He had signed a statement with Jacques

Chirac at Saint-Malo in 1998 which called for a 'common defence policy' and declared 'the Union must have the capacity for autonomous action, backed up by credible military forces, the means to decide to use them and a readiness to do so, in order to respond to international crises'. The Saint-Malo statement was meant to show a new Franco-British dimension to European integration based on defence. It came to nothing. In 2001, the new Republican administration in Washington lobbied hard against European defence on the basis it meant the European and North American wings of NATO being pulled apart. Where some progress might have been made – in creating more integrated European defence industry firms along the lines of Airbus Industrie – nothing happened. The attraction to short-sighted British arms firms of doing business in the United States and getting some crumbs from the Pentagon's groaning table as well as the appeal of well-remunerated jobs in the defence industry for retired generals and ex-officials in the Defence Ministry was more agreeable than creating a Schuman Plan for Europe's Balkanized and ineffective defence procurement policies.

The division over the invasion in Iraq effectively buried Saint-Malo. The proposed EU constitution also produced more division than unity. The Conservative Party and right-wing, anti-EU editors attacked Blair for his insistence that any new EU treaty arising from the constitutional convention should be ratified by Parliament as had every previous European treaty, indeed all treaties in British history. The call for a referendum awoke the dormant Euroscepticism in Labour's ranks. In meetings with the foreign secretary, Jack Straw, and other political ministers in the Foreign and Commonwealth Office I was isolated in refusing to surrender to the popular clamour for a plebiscite.

Monday, 29 March 2004

> *Jack Straw is again dismissive of the EU. The other three Foreign Office ministers in the Commons are all calling for a referendum on the constitution. This is rank defeatism. It is giving in to the current tabloid and Tory pressure. Once we have surrendered on*

this they will move on to something else that they demand we deliver on Europe. And then when the referendum comes – and when should it come, before or after a general election? – we will face a horrendous divided party. All Labour's latent hostility to Europe bubbles up with the referendum call.

Labour faced a major loss of seats in the June 2004 European Parliament election. Ukip was by now the main political vehicle for channelling the votes of those opposed to the EU. It was poised to make its breakthrough, and made clear its message – still current today – the need for a referendum to reject the EU. Labour candidates were nervous, and every time I went on the radio to discuss Europe the only call from listeners was for a referendum. In the end, the nominally pro-European Liberal Democrats, whose status had risen on the left because they were the only major party to oppose the Iraq war, announced they would vote with the Conservatives in the Commons in favour of a referendum. This forced Blair's hand, and in April 2004 he announced a referendum on the EU constitutional treaty. The referendum never took place, because in June 2005 the French and Dutch said No to the proposed EU constitution.

Blair won re-election in May 2005, but the European adventure was over for him. In his memoirs, *A Journey* (2010), the former prime minister has relatively little to say about Europe. He boasts about how he 'had organized opposition to the French-German demand that the Belgian prime minister, Guy Verhofstadt, become president of the Commission. This was the first time the twin-engine motor of Europe had been stalled in respect of such a big issue.' It seems odd that the highpoint of Blair's role in Europe was to stop something happening, a negative rather than any claim to having moved Europe forward, to having achieved a positive that the rest of Europe might remember him by. As it happened, Verhofstadt was unelectable as Commission president in 2004. Other governments were queuing up to veto him and José Manuel Barroso, the Commission president 2004–14, had the support of all the socialist or centre-left prime ministers in Europe. Blair also claims to have launched the so-called Lisbon process that was meant to make the EU a world-competitive economic power by 2010 and the Saint-Malo statement. A decade and a half later Europe has no common defence policy and its economy is in deep trouble.

Blair as head of government did the best for Britain in terms of economic improvement, social fairness, investment in collective public provision and cultural openness of any national leader in my lifetime. In his memoirs he described his pro-Europeanism thus:

> In general terms, for me, Europe was a simple issue. It was to do with the modern world. I supported the European idea, but even if I hadn't, it was utterly straightforward in a world of new emerging powers. Britain needed Europe in order to exert influence and advance its interests. It wasn't complicated. It wasn't a psychiatric issue. It was a question of realpolitik.

Maybe. But one does not have to be a Freudian to find it curious that Blair seeks for the mid-nineteenth-century Prussian concept of *Realpolitik* to explain his approach to Europe. To some extent, he is right. At European Councils I watched prime ministers and presidents defend their country's national interest like miniature Bismarcks. The nineteenth-century unifier of Germany under Prussian rule declared that the 'great decisions of the day are not decided by majority votes or speeches but by blood and iron'. The time of imposing unity by blood and iron had run its course in 1945. And without majority decisions, there would be no Europe and certainly no hope of a more liberalized economy, which Blair always supported. Blair seemed to miss this fundamental truth, namely that if Europe was going to have a true internal market or some foreign policy weight in the world this required, as in 1950 and subsequent stages of sharing sovereignty, more, not less integration. Instead he wrote: 'Europe had its own delusion that the way to make Europe stronger was simply to integrate its decision-making process.' Blair spoke French and had always engaged with European politics from the moment he entered the Commons as a young MP in 1983. But

did he understand Europe? His most trusted adviser on European
affairs, a senior official and dedicated European, Sir Stephen Wall,
expressed his concerns to me.

Thursday, 22 February 2001

> *'The Prime Minister has given me the job of trying to bring the*
> *Germans round from their integrationist view towards our more*
> *intergovernmental position and I wonder if you can help', Wall*
> *said. Apparently Blair had met Schröder recently and had been*
> *quite shocked how in private conversation Schröder had insisted*
> *that he supported a more integrationist view of Europe than Blair's*
> *Europe of nation states cooperating together. 'Perhaps in private*
> *I might be a bit closer to your view Tony, but as Chancellor of*
> *Germany it is the integrationist route that I will support and*
> *express publicly as my position', he told Blair. Wall said that Blair*
> *was shocked by this but I found that baffling since the absolutely*
> *central core of German policy is not for Germany to express itself*
> *aggressively and openly as a unilateral nation state with inde-*
> *pendent, nationally decided economic, monetary, trade, immigra-*
> *tion or defence policy. Surely Blair understood that core aspect of*
> *modern history? I wonder if Blair had got a more serious blind*
> *spot on Europe than I would have thought.*

Inside Downing Street there was a jokey mockery about European
affairs, which were seen as irritating intrusions in making a success
of domestic politics and working in alliance, first with Bill Clinton
then with George W. Bush, with the White House. Blair's press chief,
Alistair Campbell, although he spoke French and some German
and had a home in Provence, would rarely find time for Blair to do
interviews with European news correspondents and regarded EU
news stories as almost inevitably negative and requiring constant
news management to limit damage. France's foreign and then prime
minister, Dominique de Villepin, was called 'Vile Pen' in a childish
word-play on his name. Blair stuck close to this coterie of advisers
with their mocking superiority about the EU.

Blair loved solving problems and used his charm and undoubted commitment to Europe to help untie European knots. He was ready to take risks and make concessions. Despite predictable abuse from Eurosceptics, he supported an increase in the EU budget in 2005 to help support EU investment in the new member states. He also opened Britain to workers from Poland, Slovakia and the Baltic states and did not hide behind a transition period like France, with its fear of Polish plumbers. The French, like the Germans, quickly dropped their transition-period limits for Eastern Europeans working in France and Germany. But the bolder British decision which ensured that all the new EU member state workers paid tax and national insurance and thus helped grow the UK economy produced years of ugly press criticism of Blair for such generosity to Eastern European workers. It was actually in Britain's self-interest. Fruit that previously rotted as no British worker could be found to pick it could now be harvested. Many small firms that might have relocated abroad stayed in Britain thanks to hard-working European labour. The decision to allow citizens of new EU member states the right to work in Britain certainly made Blair popular in Eastern Europe. But it also fitted in with his idea of a British economy based on low wages and flexible workforces after the model of the Reagan–Clinton US labour market. An alternative would have been to oblige employers to invest in apprenticeships, to enforce EU rules preventing the abuse of employment agencies to provide cheap labour and insisting on trade union rights in every workplace to prevent any exploitation. But that would have required a different form of social democracy in Britain, closer to the north European model.

Blair was not convinced, probably rightly, that British employers would accept this or that British trade unions could move from adversarial modes of operation to the permanent acceptance of employment flexibility, capital accumulation and free trade, including relocation of firms to emerging economies that the Nordic and Dutch unions accepted.

Blair brought to power a Labour Party that had shed or relegated much of its Euroscepticism. Many of the 1997 intake of MPs used positive language about Europe. But Blair did not build on this. He made excellent speeches about Europe but he made them in Paris or Warsaw, in Aix-la-Chapelle or Strasbourg. He was fervently pro-European in the Commons when it was a question of boxing-ring exchanges with Eurosceptic Conservatives. But to the rest of Britain he had little to say on Europe. And to Rupert Murdoch he had nothing to say at all.

Blair arrived in Downing Street at an unhappy time for European foreign policy. Europe's failure in the Balkans and, after 9/11, bitter divisions over Iraq and crude hostility to George W. Bush left Europe rudderless in terms of world policy. Blair did not know which French leader – the president, Jacques Chirac, or the prime minister, Lionel Jospin – to work with in the first five years of his premiership. The hostility of the French Socialist Party to any common reformist, modernized social democratic ideology left the dominant centre-left parties in power in 2000 in most EU member states without a common vision or purpose. It was not that Blair was right and Jospin wrong or vice versa, but the failure to create a Paris-London-Berlin (plus Stockholm, Rome, Lisbon, Amsterdam and other nations whose governments were dominated by parties affiliated to the Party of European Socialists) axis of progressive modern left theory and practice meant that each nation prioritized its national objectives. No one was able to fashion an idea of Europe that, as in the years between 1950 and the early 1990s, was broadly accepted as adding value to each nation's separate efforts.

The miserable economic growth in too many EU member states, notably Germany, which was the sick man of Europe for most of Blair's period in office, meant it was too easy for the British Eurosceptic press to paint Europe as going nowhere. No one had (or has today) an idea of how to relate to the rising economic giant of China, which in this period became the world's factory, producing the MacBooks and iPhones and a million and one other goods that filled Europe's shops, both high-end luxury stores in Knightsbridge and Bond Street as well as the Primarks, Poundlands, Decathalons and Currys. Some European leaders were not up to the task. In many countries in Europe a politics of nationalist identity that was often racist and usually xenophobic was coming into being.

The mass movements of people from the Balkans, from Africa and from the Middle East seemed to be out of control. The opening of the EU to eight new members from Eastern Europe in 2004 (plus Cyprus and Malta) appeared to require that every French plumber or British carpenter should make way for a Pole or Lithuanian willing to work longer hours for much less pay.

It was a big task to keep talking up Europe and keep finding reasons to persuade people to like it. Blair made little effort to enthuse people about Europe or try and reverse the steadily increasing Euroscepticism in political and public life. He had a handful of convinced, sometime passionate, pro-European officials in Downing Street. But this bureaucracy lived in its own self-referring and self-reinforcing world. Blair did little to promote convinced pro-Europeans to ministerial posts, and a weary cynicism about Europe pervaded his administration at the end of the Blair decade.

Thursday, 12 February 2004

> *I work on an article for the Italian paper,* Riformista. *The Italians are very tetchy about the meeting of Blair, Chirac and Schroeder in Berlin next week. I want to put a case explaining why we are doing it and why it is neither a new* Directoire *nor a replacement for functioning institutions in Brussels. 2003 was the annus horribilis for Europe. Divisions over Iraq; no agreement on the constitution and no movement on the Eurozone economy. Someone has to get things going. I am not sure these now quite badly wounded and weakened leaders are the people to do it.*
>
> *Of course once I put my article up for clearance the little maggots at Number 10 come in and say it shouldn't be published. This is insane. If we don't explain why we are doing things then people will always assume the worst. It really is fairly pathetic the level of defensiveness and insecurity that now pervades Number 10 on European issues.*

So my efforts to speak for Europe were not welcome. Bit by bit Britain's ruling Labour Party adopted the policy of the three wise monkeys and saw, said and heard as little about Europe as possible. Blair appeared not to realize the gap between his personal pro-European commitment and the gradual disappearance of any equivalent pro-Europeanism among his ministers and many Labour MPs. On becoming foreign secretary, Jack Straw closed down an inter-ministerial coordination committee on the EU set up on Blair's instructions after 1997 which tried to get ministers thinking more about Europe in their ministerial silos. Imperceptibly during the years following the first Blair government (1997–2001), pro-Europeanism withered on the vine. And if ministers and MPs are not enthusiastic for a pro-European policy, why should the public be convinced of the benefits of European integration? In countless cabinet committee meetings Europe was seen as a problem, never a solution. If that is what the nation's political leadership said behind closed doors in Whitehall, why should they expect the public to be in a different place?

Blair's successor as prime minister, Gordon Brown, did even less to put the case for a positive engagement in Europe. He did bravely reject the incessant demands from the anti-European press for a referendum on the Lisbon Treaty and worked with the new French president, Nicolas Sarkozy, to firefight the fall-out from the banking collapse of 2008, even though both he and Sarkozy, as finance ministers, had allowed the growth of banking practices that turned out to be disastrous. He told the Labour Party conference that he would promote 'British jobs for British workers'. Unfortunately this was a slogan of the BNP – the racist and antisemitic party of the extreme right. Brown's language appeared to validate their campaign and in the 2009 elections to the European Parliament the BNP won two seats – the first time British fascism had ever won a parliamentary election. Labour MEPs shrank to a tiny group of just 13, the same number as the anti-EU Ukip.

Brown turned up late to sign the Lisbon Treaty, hours after the official ceremony. It symbolized the growing detachment of Britain from mainstream Europe. Britain had a last card to play given the decision to create new posts for a president of the Council and a new EU foreign affairs supremo, to be called a High Representative. Blair campaigned arduously behind the scene to get the nomination for president of the European Council. He failed to realize how unpopular he had become in Europe as the aftermath of the Iraq conflict brought endless bloodshed. There was also widespread press criticism for the millions he made travelling around the world as an apostle for neo-liberal globalization or working with authoritarian governments. His impressive charity work and his efforts to help support Palestinian economic development counted for little against the continuing images of death from Iraq or what his critics saw as his continuous money-making.

Blair's candidature was stopped dead by one of those typical little corridor deals which give the Brussels–Strasbourg political world such a bad reputation. Without consulting national governments or parties, a handful of Brussels insiders agreed that the centre-right European People's Party grouping of parties including Angela Merkel's CDU and Nicolas Sarkozy's UMP would have the presidency of the Council and the centre-left Party of European Socialists that grouped Labour, Spanish socialists and sister parties would have the post of EU High Representative for foreign policy. Thus were excluded qualified and more impressive candidates like Joschka Fischer, a Green, or the Liberal, Guy Verhofstadt. The Socialists arrogantly thought they could offer the foreign policy post to David Miliband MP, a Blair protégé and Britain's young foreign secretary. In November 2009, Miliband refused the offer as he expected to become leader of the Labour Party after the forthcoming election defeat for Gordon Brown. At that time no one expected his younger, less-experienced brother, Ed, to seek the Labour leadership.

Instead, Brown offered the post to Lady (Catherine) Ashton, a competent Labour functionary who had never been elected to Parliament. She was unfairly mocked by the French media in particular, but worked away on negotiating with Iran or persuading the Serbs and Kosovans to come to an agreement that allowed Kosovo to exercise control over all its territory. But as Europe became mired in the economic misery of its recession and successive euro crises, there was little room for innovative pan-European international policy initiatives. As with the president of the European Council, Herman van Rumpuy, the new posts created under the Lisbon Treaty failed to live up to hopes.

Labour lost power in 2010. A key theme in the election was the Conservative promise of a referendum on the Lisbon Treaty. They also accused Labour of allowing a tsunami of immigrants into Britain from the new EU member states. Immigration, that most toxic of populist political issues since the 1960s, was being fused into anti-EU discourse. Brown was permanently on the defensive. His policy of keeping Britain out of the euro and of rejecting EU directives that would have increased social justice had made little impression. Labour had not reverted to the anti-Europeanism of the early 1980s, but it had lost all the enthusiasm for Europe that had arrived with Blair in 1997.

Ed Miliband was elected Labour leader in 2010. His brother, David, emigrated to New York in 2013. The generation of Labour politicians who had turned around the party and made it into a pro-European party 25 years ago have died, retired or, like Peter Mandelson, passed into the netherworld of the House of Lords. Ed Miliband has pro-Europeans working for him in his private office. One or two possible next-generation Labour ministers, such as the young MP Emma Reynolds, have worked in Brussels, speak French and still see Europe in positive terms. But Labour cannot escape the deep pessimism and hostility about Europe that pervades Britain. Two diary entries from November 2011 sum up the mood.

Tuesday, 8 November 2011

> *Bill Cash has a Ten-Minute Rule Bill calling for Parliament to take back all control over all aspects of Europe. It's his usual refrain and I get up and make a spontaneous speech just pointing out that fewer than 7% of our laws actually originate in Europe and the total EU budget is only 1% of EU GDP most of which comes back to national governments as agricultural and regional investment subsidies. Quite a lot of Eurosceptic Tories who had*

been in there to support Cash stay on and listen to me and shake their heads. It matters little but you just keep having to tell the truth in the face of all these lies.

Then to a debate on the EU budget. Again I have to get up and make the point that Poland is the fourth biggest contributor to the UK rebate and that in the 1980s Mrs Thatcher had been very generous in increasing the UK contribution to the then EC budget and why were we so mean today.

In the office, Axelle [Axelle Lemaire, my parliamentary assistant elected as a French socialist MP in June 2012 and named Minister for the Digital Economy in 2014] says that she was in Brussels recently with the Party of European Socialists and they all lament my loss. 'When Denis was there at least he was committed to building a political relationship with us but now the Labour guys come and just say, "We don't want to be associated. Take our name off this document. You can pass what you like but it has got nothing to do with us."' It really is going to be the lost decade.

Ed Miliband made one clear and principled decision, namely to reject the 2017 Brexit referendum proposed by David Cameron. He was criticized publicly by senior Labour MPs like Keith Vaz and Frank Field and other Labour MPs always ready with advice for their leader. Labour shadow cabinet members sought to deflect the political storms whipped by the Conservative–Ukip hostility to workers from the EU holding down jobs in Britain by saying that Labour would support 'fair' immigration policies without ever defining what 'fair' meant. Labour made modest advances in the 2014 European Parliament election but fell well short of the number of Ukip MEPs. There was no strong, confident, high-profile voice from within Labour's ranks ready to make the case for Europe. Adjectives like 'hard-headed' or 'pragmatic' or 'realist' were used and Labour vied with Conservatives to criticize the EU budget increases that Britain's increased wealth obliged it to pay. Labour in 2014 had certainly not reverted to the Euroscepticism of the 1980s, but equally it had lost all the enthusiasm for Europe that marked New Labour's arrival in 1997.

9

WILLIAM HAGUE AND DAVID CAMERON HELP CREATE UKIP

Politics is about transforming a nation into something different – economically vibrant for the right, more socially just for the left. However, as politicians embark on a process by which they seek to transform their country they sometimes find that the policies they espouse start to transform them. When William Hague became leader of the Conservative Party and began to indulge the increasingly Eurosceptic views of the rump of MPs who survived the Labour landslide of 1997, he could not have imagined that within less than two decades this process would have turned his party into a solidly Eurosceptic political organism.

Nor could it have been his intention that as he sought to harass Tony Blair's pro-European line more and more voters would come to believe in such politics and turn to a new party, Ukip, and a new political leader, Nigel Farage, who seemed more authentic and sincere in following William Hague's Euroscepticism to its logical end – an exit from the EU. The Conservatives since 1997 have undoubtedly helped transform Britain into a more Eurosceptic nation. But at the same time they have transformed British politics by opening the space to new political forces which in turn transform the Conservatives into a party which sees the EU as a problem that is unlikely to be solved.

Thursday, 27 January 2000

> *On BBC I am all over the place with Bill Cash [leader of the Eurosceptic Tories]. He is actually becoming a moderate within the Conservative Party, which has been taken over by hard-faced men who know only one thing – that they really hate Europe.*

David Cameron is in a steady line of anti-European Conservative Party leaders since 1997. Each has contributed in his own way to creating today's culture of hostility to Europe. After John Major's defeat, William Hague led the Conservatives firmly into the Eurosceptic camp. Hague was the leader of the Conservative Party between 1997 and 2001 and foreign secretary between May 2010 and July 2014, when he announced that he would leave politics. William Hague is a fascinating study of failure in politics. That may read counterintuitively, as he has risen to the leadership of his party and held the high office of foreign secretary for four years. But he could not lead the Conservatives to victory and his stewardship of the Foreign and Commonwealth Office has been marked by increasing British loss of influence globally and a serious alienation of the UK from Europe and a distancing from the United States. Having helped create the deeply Europe-hostile Conservative Party of the twenty-first century, William Hague is standing down as a Conservative MP just as his party faces the crucial test of retaining power and the historic issue of deciding whether to lead Britain out of Europe or fight with principle and purpose to keep it in the EU.

Unlike most in David Cameron's cabinet, who come from wealthy backgrounds in the richest region of Britain – London and the Home Counties – and who were educated in elite private schools, Hague comes from the mining and steel region of South Yorkshire. His father ran a small business and supported the Conservative Party in a town which is working class and solidly Labour. William Hague won national fame when he spoke at the Conservative Party conference aged only 16 in 1977. He was then and is today a very effective orator. Unlike the youthful Conservatives from elite schools with their refined voices, here was an authentic voice of northern England speaking with the raw vowels normally heard from proletarian trade union leaders.

Hague had the best state education Britain could offer at a West Yorkshire grammar school that Mrs Thatcher turned into a comprehensive. He went quickly to Magdalen College, Oxford, became a management consultant and then entered parliament before he was 30. He was chosen as Conservative leader aged 36. He made hostility to Europe the *Leitmotif* of his party leadership. This culminated in 2001 with Hague playing a crude nationalist card, telling voters: 'Let me take you on a journey to a foreign land – to Britain after a second term of Tony Blair. The Royal Mint melting down pound coins as the euro notes start to circulate. Our currency and our ability to set our own interest rates gone forever. The Chancellor returning from Brussels carrying instructions to raise taxes still further.'

The idea that a pro-European Tony Blair – who to any half-awake observer was as robust in defending British national interests in the EU as any of his predecessors – was going to turn Britain into a 'foreign land' was populist language, closer to the metaphors used later by Ukip or continental anti-European rabble-rousers than previous Conservative leaders.

Hague enjoyed making speeches with plenty of jibes about Europe. His status as a former party leader and then after 2005 the party spokesman on foreign affairs meant that his mockery of other European nations was taken seriously even though they were presented as jokes. On one television comedy show in 2005 Hague discussed the 200th anniversary of the Battle of Trafalgar and how it was being re-enacted for a television programme. Hague told viewers that in order to avoid upsetting the French the recreation of the decisive naval battle would be fought between a red fleet and a blue fleet. 'Just a little tip if you want to put a bet on it', he added. 'The cheese-eating surrender monkeys are in red this time.' The phrase 'cheese-eating surrender moneys' to describe the French was used by neo-Conservative propagandists in the Washington of George W. Bush in their fury at President Chirac's refusal to join the invasion of Iraq. For Hague the use of red and blue fleets instead of ships flying the colours of Britain and France was 'like teaching people about World War II and not mentioning that the Germans were on the other side'.

Asked about the results of a survey which suggested that Germans were not relaxed when on holiday abroad, 'I'm not so sure', Britain's future foreign minister said. 'If anyone's got a history of making themselves feel at home in other people's countries, it's the Germans.' Commenting on news that France's population was increasing, he wrote: 'Maybe drinking lots of wine and being totally unreasonable is good for your sex life after all.' That column was in one of Rupert Murdoch's newspapers. Mr Murdoch paid his favourite Eurosceptic politician £250,000 a year to denounce Europe. Since entering government in 2010, William Hague has conformed fully to Mr Murdoch's wishes, making clear Britain's increasing distance from the EU. What were unfunny jokes about the French and Germans a few years ago became part of Britain's ruling political philosophy.

Hague was succeeded after he crashed to defeat in the 2001 election by Iain Duncan Smith, commonly known by his initials, IDS. This former army officer had entered the Commons in 1992 and at once placed himself at the head of the anti-European faction. He is a pleasant, courteous man and his social Catholicism generates unfeigned compassion about the plight of the poor, even if like many right-wingers he believes that the way to help poor people is to reduce support for them. Newly elected in 1992 he used his military training to organize rebellions and votes against the Maastricht Treaty signed by his own leader and prime minister. Neither a good speaker nor gifted with any noted political intelligence, IDS was known only as a leading Eurosceptic. By 2001, the Conservatives had moved so far in this direction that his only qualification for political prominence – his hostility to the EU – was enough to get him made party leader. By now the parliamentary Conservative Party had lost most of its former pro-European MPs. Their replacements were to a man and woman cut from the same anti-European cloth as William Hague and IDS.

Yet this obsession with Europe was not enough, and IDS's poor performance in the Commons and on television against a confident Tony Blair did little to help the Conservatives. They dumped him and in November 2003 elected as their third party leader in six years, Michael Howard. His claim to fame, other than being a home secretary obsessed with increasing the prison population, was that he had led the group in the cabinet in 1992 in opposition to John Major signing the Maastricht Treaty if it included a social clause. Major, or rather his clever diplomats, found a way over Howard's objections, by inventing a special British opt-out from EU social obligations. This satisfied Howard's anti-EU hostility in 1992, but he wallowed in anti-Europeanism as shadow foreign secretary after 1997. This helped him to be elected party leader after IDS was removed, as Conservatives would accept only a proven Eurosceptic to lead them.

Howard also failed to stop Blair being re-elected for a third time in 2005. By now the Conservative Party was captured by Eurosceptics. Pro-European former ministers of an earlier era like Chris Patten, Douglas Hurd or Michael Heseltine had disappeared to the House of Lords or like Kenneth Clarke now in opposition had gone off to devote time to earning money in the private sector while remaining an MP. Conservative MPs and MEPs started publishing books with titles like *The Death of Britain* (John Redwood MP) or *A Positive Vision of an Independent Britain outside the EU* (David Campbell Bannerman MEP).

In the summer of 2005 I talked to David Cameron in the changing-room of the House of Commons after Labour's third election victory. I was having a shower after a game of tennis and Cameron was towelling himself dry after an energetic bike ride to Westminster from his fashionable Notting Hill home. I said to him that he should run for leader of the Conservative Party.

'You are the closest the Conservatives have to Tony Blair. Even if you lose the fact of being a candidate will give you high national profile so you will be one of the top three or four people of the next generation of Conservative leaders.'

He nodded with interest as he kept towelling himself dry. I assumed he had long since worked out the obvious political points I was making to him.

I then added: 'But you know Dave, if you do become leader, which I think is likely, you will have to do what all big leaders of major parties do when they take over and that is sacrifice a sacred cow or bury a shibboleth the party believes in.'

I cited Tony Blair removing Clause 4 in the Labour Party constitution or similar moves by Willy Brandt in Germany, Felipe Gonzalez in Spain or François Mitterrand in France when they became leaders of their parties and showed that the new leader was firmly in charge and setting the party on a new course even if it upset veteran militants. When she became Conservative leader Margaret Thatcher famously repudiated the postwar settlement with a role for trade unions accepted by such predecessors as Harold Macmillan and Edward Heath.

I said to Cameron: 'For you it would be to drop the manic Euroscepticism that now ravages the Conservatives. The British state, the City, the inward investors, and Washington do not want and will not allow Britain to quit the EU. You can show you are leading instead of following your party by speaking out against the crude Euroscepticism is it now linked with.'

He looked at me with a quiet, friendly smile – Cameron is one of the most polite senior political leaders I have dealt with – and said: 'Thanks, Denis. But I am much more Eurosceptic than you imagine.'

It was a sincere declaration of faith. Nothing Cameron has done since becoming leader of the Conservative Party in December 2005 and then prime minister after May 2010 contradicts the view that Britain has a prime minister who is firmly against further European integration or construction.

The contest six months after our changing room chat between the two candidates to lead the Conservatives – David Cameron and a former Europe minister, David Davis – was a fight in which Europe was not an issue that divided them. Both men were seen as Eurosceptic. If anything, David Davis, the older, apparently stronger, more experienced politician, had a longer record of being critical of the EU, drawing upon his time in government. In the first ballot the two Davids tied. Forty Conservative MPs had voted for a third candidate, the Thatcherite Liam Fox. Their votes would decide who was the next Conservative leader.

This bloc of Conservative MPs asked both Mr Cameron and Mr Davis for a pledge of commitment to a clear anti-European line. They asked that the Conservative Party withdraw from the European People's Party (EPP) – the centre-right federation of parties including France's UMP, the CDU in Germany and the Partido Popular in Spain. Mr Davis refused the offer. He told me later that even though he was profoundly Eurosceptic, a serious Conservative Party could not break all links with its fellow parties of the right who formed governments in Europe. 'I made clear to them we have to work with these sister parties even if we do not share their views on Europe', he confided to me.

Mr Cameron took a different line. He said he had no problem in rupturing party links with his fellow centre-right politicians in Europe and if he was elected leader of the Conservatives he would indeed pull the British Conservative Party out of the EPP, the majority party bloc in the European Parliament. That promise of withdrawal from political Europe was enough to win him the election for party leader. It was a taste of what was to come under Mr Cameron's leadership. Like his referendum pledge eight years later, the promise to divorce the Conservative Party from all their traditional allies and friends in Europe was taken quickly in order to score a domestic intra-party political point. But it ensured that Cameron had to commit himself to a steady stream of anti-European political initiatives.

The most important of these was to insist on the primacy of a referendum in European politics. Cameron, his shadow foreign secretary, William Hague, and other Conservative MPs constantly attacked first Blair and then, after 2007, Gordon Brown for not holding a referendum on the Lisbon Treaty. In 2007, Cameron offered a 'cast-iron guarantee' that if elected prime minister he would offer a referendum on the Lisbon Treaty. After 2010, he reneged on that promise, but has now brought it to life with his offer of a referendum not on a treaty but to give voters the possibility of taking Britain out of Europe.

Mr Cameron sent out a constant stream of Eurosceptic signals between his election as party leader in December 2005 and his entry into Downing Street that he wanted the Conservatives to develop their anti-European profile. He promoted as shadow cabinet ministers two former party leaders, William Hague and Iain Duncan Smith, who were high-profile Eurosceptics. Others favoured by Cameron and today in his cabinet were also anti-European. No pro-European, other than the septuagenarian Kenneth Clarke, found favour and he was removed from the cabinet in 2014 as the prime minister shaped what the BBC called a Brexit government. In the selection of candidates to contest seats in the 2010 election, Mr Cameron and the party machine encouraged future Conservative MPs to toe his Eurosceptic line. Middle-of-the-road Conservatives open to Europe say sadly in private that it was impossible to win selection in seats likely to elect a Conservative MP except on the basis of telling local party activists they were opposed to Europe.

As the new party leader, Mr Cameron constantly opposed every decision made by the Labour government on Europe. The Conservatives criticized the arrival of workers from new member states. They never criticized the large number of American, Australian or white South African citizens working in Britain. The biggest group of non-British EU workers employed on the 2012 London Olympic site came from the Republic of Ireland. Catholic workers from an EU member state to the west of Britain were welcome, but not Catholic workers from an EU member state further to the east.

The generation of anti-foreigner and anti-immigrant passions did more to help first the extreme right-wing, racist and antisemitic BNP, which won a number of local council seats after 2004, and then Ukip. The BNP focused on a crude denunciation of British Muslim citizens and their religion. Ukip constantly attacked the presence of European workers in the British labour market, but some of its candidates were unpleasantly Islamophobic. Ukip is now denounced as 'racist' by its founder, Alan Sked, a London School of Economics lecturer, who in late in 2014 told the *New York Times* that the party he created had 'grown into this hideous, racist, populist, xenophobic, Islamophobic thing'. Both the BNP and Ukip made significant gains in the European Parliament election of 2009.

After the European Parliament election in 2009 David Cameron fulfilled the pledge made when he was elected Conservative Party leader by pulling out of the EPP. Nicholas Sarkozy in France, Angela Merkel in Germany, Fredrik Reinfeldt in Sweden, Donald Tusk in Poland and other ruling conservative parties were aghast at Cameron's initiative of breaking Conservative Party links with other centre-right parties in Europe. The dominant centre-right leader in Europe, the German chancellor, Angela Merkel, attaches particular importance to the EPP. She helps consolidate it with financial support and a network of offices in all EU capitals under the Konrad Adenauer Foundation. She was particularly upset at Cameron's decision to appease his anti-EU MPs by quitting it.

But the Conservative leader had little regard for his natural European allies. A leader of the Conservative MEPs, Edward McMillan-Scott, resigned his Conservative Party membership in protest and joined the Liberal Democrats. In Britain, such was the disdain for all EU institutions that no one in the new party Mr Cameron was fashioning really noticed. Cameron decided to create a new group in the European Parliament consisting of more robust nationalist parties, mainly from Eastern Europe, including Poland's PiS (Law and Justice Party) headed by the Kaczynski twins, Lech and Jaroslaw. There was negative publicity when it was revealed that some of the Conservative Party's new Polish allies had made anti-Jewish statements, while a Latvian party now linked to the Conservatives had excused Nazi crimes during World War II.

The economic misery unleashed by the bankers' crisis of 2007–8 that turned into the wider economic recession further alienated British public opinion from the EU, which seemed unable to come up with any response other than demanding years of austerity from the citizens of Europe. After the dominance of the British political scene by Tony Blair, the Gordon Brown years appeared unhappy and unconvincing. But the Conservatives' hostility to Europe was growing.

Tuesday, 20 October 2009

> *Lunch with the French Ambassador and the National Assembly's Europe Committee, headed by Pierre Leguiller. They were all shocked at the Conservatives' approach to Europe. Pierre exclaimed that is would be impossible to have a modern government in the EU with the kind of anti-European obsessions that Cameron and Hague were manifesting.*

M. Leguiller was wrong. A few months later David Cameron became prime minister in a coalition government. He failed to achieve what his Conservative predecessors had always managed – a majority of seats in the House of Commons. In the 2010 election campaign the Liberal Democrat leader, Nick Clegg, had accused Mr Cameron in a television debate of entering into an alliance with 'nutters, anti-Semites and homophobes' in the European Parliament. Mr Clegg has impeccable European credentials. A Dutch mother, private wealth, holiday homes in the south of France and Davos, a Spanish wife, study at the College of Europe, work in the European Commission followed by five years as an MEP (which he combined with working for a Brussels lobbying company) and entry into the House of Commons in 2005. Within two years he was leader of the Liberal Democratic Party and three years later he became deputy prime minister as junior coalition partner under David Cameron.

Any hopes that on becoming deputy prime minister the pro-European Clegg would slow down the growth of Euroscepticism as the organizing principle of the new governing coalition evaporated. Very quickly 100 Conservative MPs, a third of the total number of Mr Cameron's colleagues in the Commons, identified themselves as supporting a referendum with the aim of withdrawing from the EU. They played parliamentary games, organizing votes to embarrass Mr Cameron. He responded by using a veto to block an attempt to find a solution to the Eurozone crisis in December 2011. Other EU leaders simply ignored this petulance and moved ahead with what they wanted to do.

In 2011, a new law was enacted which required that a referendum would be held if any new EU treaty meant a 'significant' transfer of power from Britain to be shared with EU partners. The Liberal Democrats, whose profile for decades had been as the most pro-European party in British politics, went along with the increasingly Eurosceptic tone of Mr Cameron and his ministers. They tried to assert that without the presence of Nick Clegg as deputy prime minister, the British government would be even more hostile to Europe. No one could find any evidence of this Liberal-Democratic hand restraining Mr Cameron's gestures in the direction of Eurosceptic politics.

On the contrary, the Eurosceptic press and many Conservative MPs kept attacking any sign of the government cooperating positively in EU affairs. A new front was opened against the European Court of Human Rights (ECHR) that Conservative MPs blamed for preventing the immediate deportation of Islamist extremists to countries where they might be tortured. The ECHR also urged Britain to allow some prisoners to vote, which is commonplace in Switzerland, France and other modern European states. This provoked further outrage, joined in by the Labour Party, which put up the former foreign secretary, Jack Straw, a devout Eurosceptic in the 1970s and 1980s, to make common cause with the Eurosceptic Conservatives in attacking the Strasbourg court.

Experts knew the difference between the EU and the ECHR but all the public heard was that Europe was inimical to British interests. The ECHR also suggested that long-sentence prisoners who had shown over 20 or 30 years an impeccable record in prison might be considered for parole. The *Daily Telegraph* attacked the idea with a front-page headline: 'Europe Backs Murderers'. After nearly three years of being chipped at by his anti-Europe MPs and party activists, and with more and more evidence that Conservative voters were deserting to Ukip, Mr Cameron made his promise of an in–out referendum in January 2013 in the hope that it would settle the matter and quieten down the anti-EU fervour which he had whipped up during his period as opposition leader.

Alas for his hopes, anti-Europeanism is an appetite that grows with feeding. More and more of his own party came out in favour of either an immediate referendum, before the 2015 election, or simply a decision to leave Europe. In the words of Douglas Carswell, a Conservative MP with a high profile who later defected to Ukip, Britain's EU membership was like 'being shackled to a corpse'. Ukip, as we have seen, outperformed the Conservatives in the elections to the European Parliament in 2014 and added to the scores of councillors in the important municipal elections held in cities and big towns.

After swallowing humiliating defeat at the European Parliament polls David Cameron then launched himself like Don Quixote at the broad agreement in the EU that the next president of the Commission should be the veteran former Luxembourg prime minister, Jean-Claude Juncker. In the last EU treaty signed in Lisbon in 2007, it was stipulated that the 28 EU heads of government should appoint future presidents of the Commission taking into account the votes cast in the European Parliament elections.

The centre-right EPP grouping, which included the governing chiefs in Germany, Spain, Poland, Sweden, Ireland, The Netherlands, Greece and elsewhere, had nominated Juncker as their man for Brussels at the EPP convention held in Dublin in March 2014.

He was a compromise choice agreed without much enthusiasm. No one in British politics or the media paid any attention at the time of his nomination. Yet when his name was put forward three months later to be president of the Commission it came as a surprise to the London political-media establishment

While the rest of Europe, including social democrats and liberals in the European Parliament, accepted without enthusiasm the arrival of Juncker as Commission president, the British government decided at all costs he had to be stopped. The media was briefed and a venomous campaign in the British press against Juncker was launched. He was accused of being a drunk, a manic federalist and an opponent of Britain. British officials in barely confidential briefings in Brussels briefed that Juncker's arrival as EU Commission president would hasten Brexit.

In fact, Juncker's nomination was a sign of the Commission's growing weakness. Power in the EU resided with national governments and more and more in Berlin. Juncker was only in place because Angela Merkel rejected a French alternative candidate. The European Parliament was also enjoying a power creep conferred under the Lisbon Treaty. Four presidents of the EU – the Commission, the Council, the Parliament and the Eurogroup – would all be appointed. Juncker was at best *primus inter pares* – first among equals.

None of this mattered to David Cameron. The prime minister spent the month after the May 2014 European elections telling everyone that Juncker should not be appointed. He climbed into a boat for a row on a lake in Sweden with his fellow centre-right leaders from Sweden, Germany and The Netherlands. They did not quite push the British prime minister overboard, but they closed their ears to his entreaties. The conservative leaders in Europe, bar the ultra-nationalist and illiberal Hungarian, Victor Orban, all voted for Juncker, as did 26 of the 28 EU heads of government, including those on the left like President François Hollande of France and Prime Minister Matteo Renzi of Italy.

The whole of Europe scratched its head in wonderment at Cameron's obsession with Juncker, all the more so as the Luxembourg veteran had made clear he would do all to help keep Britain in the EU. But as Cameron's opposition to Juncker commanded weeks of headlines, the Conservative Party forgot its defeat at the hands of Nigel Farage's Ukip in the European Parliament and municipal elections. Indeed, for a brief period, the Ukip leader did not dominate the airwaves, as the prime minister sounded like an honorary member of Ukip in his hyperbolic denunciation of the proposed Commission president.

It is not as if the British prime minister proposed anyone else. It was a vision of the EU in which London just had to say No and everyone would fall into line. The European Union Council meeting of heads of government at the end of June 2014 confirmed Jean-Claude Juncker as the next president of the European Commission. The British prime minister spluttered and fulminated against the choice of his fellow EU leaders as he met the media after the decision was taken. The British people took note. They had a prime minister and a government and a press that did not like Europe. In an opinion poll published in July 2014 by the *Mail on Sunday*, 47 per cent said they would vote to quit Europe and 31 per cent to stay in the EU.

In the past the Foreign and Commonwealth Office was the centre of pro-Europeanism at the heart of the British state. Not any longer. The foreign secretary, William Hague, had made hostility to Europe the organizing and policy theme of his leadership of the Conservative Party after 1997. According to the *Telegraph*'s experienced political editor, Ben Brogan, Hague told Cameron in 2011: 'If it's a choice between keeping the euro together or keeping the Conservative Party together, it's in the national interest to keep the Conservative Party together.' A senior British official working in a British embassy in Asia won a £100,000 prize in April 2014 for an essay explaining how Britain could quit the EU and prosper. Hague's successor as foreign secretary, Philip Hammond, had never bothered to hide his dislike of the EU since his arrival as an MP in 1997. He told the BBC he would vote in any referendum to leave the EU unless there were substantial changes in the way the EU operated.

The Conservative government tried to send out signals that it was keeping a distance from Europe. Some of these bordered on the farcical. In 2014, a junior minister was ordered not to attend a signing ceremony to promote an EU Statement Against Homophobia in case it upset Conservative Party members and voters opposed to Europe and gay marriage in equal measure. A Whitehall spokesman told the *Sunday Times*, 'The Conservatives have made clear that anything that involves gay rights and Europe is not something they are touching with a barge pole'.

Boris Johnson, the main rival to David Cameron for the leadership of the Conservative Party, announced that leaving the EU 'would not be the end of the world'. The days when a Conservative could find warm words for Europe were long over.

Other Eurosceptic Conservatives demanded a double referendum – one to vote on whether Mr Cameron should begin negotiating a major repatriation of powers from Brussels to London followed by a second plebiscite to endorse or reject the renegotiation. This was mocked by Margaret Thatcher's chancellor, Nigel Lawson. He wrote an article for Rupert Murdoch's *The Times* in May 2013 saying that any so-called renegotiation would produce only 'cosmetic results' and it was better for Britain's economic future to leave the EU.

So in three decades British Conservatives had moved from the Single Act and the Maastricht Treaty to a politics of calling for a plebiscite with the hope and intention of many that the outcome would be a Britain outside the EU. Endless scenarios were discussed in newspaper columns about a new relationship with the EU. But all were predicated on a willingness of all or a majority of other states accepting a position for Britain that allowed full access to the single market but where Britain could rewrite the rules of Europe to discriminate against other EU citizens, ignore social obligations accepted everywhere else in the EU and win EU support for Britain tearing up the European Convention on Human Rights. The Europe minister, David Lidington, insisted there had to be treaty change, but no other EU member state was remotely interested in opening up the lengthy quarrelsome process of trying to negotiate and ratify a brand-new treaty just to please British anti-Europeans. Some argued that the announcement of a plebiscite would produce a willing acceptance in Brussels that Mr Cameron is right and all necessary concessions must be made to his position. There is no evidence that this is true. The EU institutions and most member states certainly want Britain to stay in the EU but cannot offer more than what Nigel Lawson accurately calls 'cosmetic changes' to existing EU treaties, law and practice. And the EU has no power over the ECHR, which many Conservatives want to quit.

Mr Cameron hopes that a referendum announcement followed by some form of renegotiation of Britain's membership of the EU can be controlled and steered to the political profit of the Conservative Party. Perhaps indeed Britain will have its cake and eat it. A new EU will come to existence that fits perfectly with British needs and prejudices by 2017. But if not, then the wise European and sad Englishman needs also to understand that a rupture between Britain and Europe will be the legacy by which Mr Cameron – assuming he stays as prime minister – is remembered in history books.

The anger and disarray in Conservative ranks worsened after Ukip won the by-elections of Clacton and Rochester and Strood late in 2014. The turn to anti-EU language after 1997 seemed not to be profiting the Conservative Party but Ukip. Senior figures in the party quarrelled with one another. After Sir John Major had said the other 27 member states should allow Britain the right to turn away European citizens coming to work in Britain, his former colleague, ex-chancellor Kenneth Clarke, attacked him and the manner in which so many Conservatives seemed to be agreeing with Ukip. Interviewed by Michael White on his life in politics, he said:

> If you all start saying how wise Mr Farage was and how we must persuade everybody to let us tackle this problem [of immigration] it is not surprising, angry, disappointed, protesting people go out and vote for Mr Farage. I would have hoped that John would have avoided that trap. I expected him to do so.

Clarke also attacked the prime minister as he spoke on Sky TV News after Ukip won its second by-election victory. He said the Conservatives had 'gifted them two by-elections', and added that measures being considered by David Cameron to limit migrant access to welfare were 'totally discriminatory'.

The Conservative Party has been crucial to many of the major turning points in British history. It was Tories led by William Pitt who organized the resistance to Napoleonic military domination of Europe. It was Robert Peel who split the Conservatives over free trade. It was the Conservative Party which resisted Irish home rule, leading to the Irish taking the path of IRA violence and the shame of Britain executing, in cold blood, the leaders of Irish independence after the Easter 1916 movement for freedom. It was a Conservative home secretary who wrote the European Convention on Human Rights and it was a Conservative prime minister who took Britain into Europe.

So at any major turning point in the constitutional-political changes in the story of Britain, the Conservative Party and its leadership have been at the heart of history. David Cameron also stands at the cusp of history. He says he does not want the UK to quit the EU. Yet his own leadership and that of the senior Conservatives he appointed to the shadow and after 2010 the governing cabinet have been unequivocally hostile to European integration and many of the values and decisions accepted by other EU member states. He has done nothing to control, let alone sanction, senior Conservatives who talk openly of Britain leaving Europe. It is hard to see the Conservative Party ever again being the party of Europe.

And the man who turned the Conservative Party in the direction of Euroscepticism, William Hague, will no longer be in the Commons after May 2015. Reports suggested that Hague was unhappy with the rupture with the EPP. As he grew into the task of being shadow and then, after 2010, the actual foreign secretary, his speeches became more measured. He sought to work with other EU foreign ministers as he realized that a go-it-alone Britain had little clout in modern global affairs and ended up punching below its weight. He sought to inject more mercantilism into the Foreign and Commonwealth Office with instructions to ambassadors to focus on trade. Alas, the UK's balance of trade deficit grew with almost every country Hague visited as foreign secretary. He cooperated with Paris in bombing Libya and ousting Colonel Gaddafi, but that turned into ashes as Libya descended into warlord factionalism and became a turntable and armoury for jihadi killers in the region. He worked hard with the EU High Representative for Foreign Affairs, Lady Ashton, in promoting dialogue and a lessening of tension in the Balkans and there, at least, where Hague engaged positively with the EU's new European External Action Service (EEAS) and Lady Ashton, some important progress was made in the troubled western Balkan region.

By 2014, his earlier, often crude Euroscepticism had vanished from his speeches. Did he realize that the ideology he and his generation of Eurosceptics had helped promote was turning into something destructive and dangerous for both his party and his country? William Hague has written major historical studies of two great British Conservatives – William Wilberforce and William Pitt. After May 2015 William Hague will be free of party political passions. Might he be the man who, no longer burdened by leadership or high office, can guide the Conservative Party out of the anti-European cul-de-sac which he led it into after 1997?

10

WHERE'S THE VISION THING?
ASK FRIEDRICH HAYEK

The British are good at prejudice, better at pragmatism, best at mocking their rulers, but at vision, well, even the biggest fan of Britain and its people would struggle to define the British as a visionary people. The idea or ideal of Europe has never entered into the consciousness of the British people or even its political class in the way it has across the Channel. Most British citizens cringed when Helmut Kohl said European construction was a question of 'war or peace'. The photograph of François Mitterrand and Helmut Kohl holding hands at Verdun as a symbol of Franco-German reconciliation appeared mawkish in the eyes of most in Britain.

When the German Chancellor Angela Merkel said in 2011, 'If the euro fails, Europe fails', the reaction in London was a mixture of puzzlement and scorn at what was seen as hyperbole. Britain sees itself as the hero of two world wars, the bringer of freedom to a continent that had fallen into bad hands. When the then Polish foreign minister, the Oxford-educated Radek Sikorski, and the then German foreign minister, Guido Westerwelle, published their joint article under the headline 'New Vision of Europe' in September 2012, the *New York Times* gave them star billing on the paper's comment pages. The idea of a British foreign secretary writing in visionary terms about Europe is unthinkable.

Europe, as this book has sought to argue, has never entered the consciousness of the British people. Even today many refer to the

'Common Market', the choice of words reflecting the subconscious view that Europe is just about buying and selling goods, a Poundland, perhaps a Euroland, writ large where the Brits may buy and sell but not much else. There are many learned books on Europe, some partisan or polemical, many technical academic or legal studies, but no writer has produced a work that might inspire citizens to see Europe other than in the 50 shades of darkish-grey painted daily in the press or uttered by politicians.

The default setting is always to mock and scorn Europe. When the EU was awarded the Nobel Peace Prize in 2011, the political and journalistic elites in London could not hide their scorn. The former Chancellor, Norman Lamont, spluttered that the 'decision seems preposterous and absurd. It would require a heart of stone not to die of laughter. It is the most ridiculous decision since the committee gave the peace prize to Barack Obama when he had been US president for two minutes.' *The Economist* joined in the rubbishing: 'Today many might ask themselves why it has been awarded to an institution whose most ambitious project, the euro, is failing so badly.'

The *Telegraph*'s resident Euroscorn commentator, Daniel Hannan, an MEP, dipped his pen in sarcasm and wrote:

> Does anyone seriously suppose that, but for the EU, the Grand Duchy of Luxembourg might annex the Belgian province of the same name? Or that, unconstrained by Brussels, the Italians would re-occupy Nice? Does anyone imagine, these days, that the right-on, pacifist Germans, who can barely be persuaded to join NATO peacekeeping operations, are secretly itching to send tank divisions into Silesia and Pomerania? It is terrifically offensive to the peoples of Europe – in particular Germans, who are often singled out – to suggest that they need to be saved from themselves.

Yet Guy Hands, the head of Terra Firma, one of the UK's leading investment funds, declared: 'The concept of another European war is inconceivable while the EU is together, so to tear that up and go back to nation states would be very dangerous.' His was a voice in the wilderness. To be fair, one or two British commentators gently pointed out that the EU was brokering peace in the Balkans, which European national foreign ministries had allowed to descend into the charnel house of the 1990s. Asserting that the EU was responsible for peace and for war not breaking out was like proving a negative. For every pro-European who talked of Erasmus programmes and free movement of people, others like David Goodhart, the prominent commentator and director of the centre-left think-tank Demos, criticized the arrival of so many European workers in Britain.

The same was true in past decades when the Irish came to do low-skilled jobs, in the 1950s when Britain imported Afro-Caribbeans to work in public transport, hospitals and car factories or in the 1960s and early 1970s when scores of thousands of Pakistanis, Indians and Bangladeshis came to do poorly paid work spurned by Britain's white working class. Goodhart describes himself as 'social democratic', but he is typical of many on the left as well as most on the right in seeing Europe as an unending source of problems for Britain. Seeing and describing Europe always as a problem and never as a solution means it is nearly impossible to persuade British citizens that there is a wider role and meaning to European construction than simple market-opening measures.

So when an in–out referendum comes there will be little hope of finding commanding, vivid voices in Britain offering a positive vision of Europe. In July 2013, the veteran Conservative Kenneth Clarke and the veteran Labour politician Lord Mandelson produced a pro-European manifesto. It called for an end to the reference in EU treaties to 'ever-closer union' and argued that the EU should cut costs and have less waste and fraud. It is hard to see how painting the EU in such negative terms and accepting much of the Eurosceptic case – why is closer union between peoples such a bad thing? – will change many minds. Fraud and waste are endemic in British public administration, as endless reports by the House of Commons Public Accounts Committee demonstrate. Highlighting the bad use of the

EU's budget – only about 0.15 per cent of Europe's gross national income is actually spent directly under the control of Brussels – is unlikely to persuade voters of the merits of being fully engaged in Europe. If the British left represented by David Goodhart, a former *Financial Times* correspondent in Europe, and Lord Mandelson, a former EU Commissioner, find it hard to use unequivocally pro-European language, why should voters be enthused to vote Yes?

The pragmatism of British political culture does not lend itself to vision. The exception is at a moment of upheaval such as war. In the crucible of the politics immediately after 1945, when war forced through revolutionary changes in thinking about the economy and society, there is some visionary language about Europe. The most obvious example remains Churchill's United States of Europe appeal in Zürich in 1946. From the social democratic left came another vision from George Orwell. Writing in the *Partisan Review* in 1947, Orwell complained that 'there are also active malignant forces working against European unity'. For Orwell, European unity would have to tilt to the left. But ranged against his idea of a united socialist Europe were formidable forces that he listed as:

1. Russian hostility. The Russians cannot but be hostile to any European union not under their own control.

2. American hostility. American pressure is an important factor because it can be exerted most easily on Britain, the one country in Europe which is outside the Russian orbit. Since 1940 Britain has kept its feet against the European dictators at the expense of becoming almost a dependency of the USA. Indeed, Britain can only get free of America by dropping the attempt to be an extra-European power.

3. Imperialism. The European peoples, and especially the British, have long owed their high standard of life to direct or indirect exploitation of the coloured peoples. The British worker, instead of being told that, by world standards, he is living above his income, has been taught to think of himself as an overworked down-trodden slave.

To the masses everywhere 'Socialism' means, or at least is
associated with, higher wages, shorter hours, better houses
and all-round social insurance. But it is by no means certain that we can afford these things if we throw away the
advantages we derive from colonial exploitation. However
evenly the national income is divided up, if the income as
a whole falls, the working-class standard of living must fall
with it. [...]

It may be that Europe is finished and that in the long
run some better form of society will arise in India or
China. But I believe that it is only in Europe, if anywhere,
that democratic Socialism could be made a reality.

Seven decades later neither Churchill's United State of Europe nor
Orwell's Socialist European Union has ever been close to being
realized. But at least Churchill and Orwell had a vision. Today no
one writing in English can offer a vision that inspires. Indeed, even
pro-Europeans, as we have seen, fret as they moan about the EU of
500 million free citizens as a mess of problems, not an achievement
of hope. For Churchill and Orwell, the idea of Europe was worth
their engagement and enthusiasm. Today, Britain's insular intelligentsia and opinion formers are like woodpeckers, chip, chip, chip-
ping at the European tree. There are no eagles able to soar and see a
bigger picture.

Another intellectual writing in the 1940s also saw the advantages of European political union. Friedrich Hayek's short book *The
Road to Serfdom*, published in 1944, is often hailed as the founding
charter of postwar economic liberalism. It was seen as an assault
on the collectivist, statist, social democratic and socialist ideas that
were emerging as the response to both Nazism and communism.
Margaret Thatcher venerated the Austrian-born economist and gave
him one of Britain's top honours in 1984. The Mont Pélerin Society
was founded in Switzerland to give voice to his ideas. Hayek became
an icon for the right, especially the anti-European right. Yet a study
of *The Road to Serfdom* shows a man who seems to be promoting the

very federalist ideas, as well as endorsing a strong political Europe, that his disciples on the British right find anathema.

Hayek quotes approvingly Lord Acton, the greatest of England's nineteenth-century historians: 'Of all the checks on democracy, federation has been the most efficacious and the most congenial [...] The federal system limits and restrains the sovereign. It is the only method of curbing not only the majority but the power of the whole people.' For Hayek, as he contemplated the organization of the postwar world, the nation was the source of problems. 'There is little hope of lasting peace so long as every country is free to employ whatever measures it thinks desirable in its own immediate interest', Hayek wrote. The individual citizen or firm, not the nation must be at the heart of the post-Nazi, non-communist world order. 'If international economic relations, instead of being relations between individuals become increasingly relations between whole nations organized as trading bodies, they inevitably become the source of friction and envy between whole nations.'

These insights are contained in the last chapter of Hayek's book. It is probable that Mrs Thatcher and all the other Hayekians did not bother to examine closely the arguments advanced in its final pages. Hayek, however, makes a better case for the EU as it has developed than many a more overt Europhile. As he wrote: 'We cannot hope for order or lasting peace after this war if states, large and small, regain unfettered sovereignty in the economic sphere.' Contrary to the present British belief that the EU should simply be a free trade economic sphere Hayek argued that:

> Far from its being true that, as is now widely believed, we need an international economic authority while the states can at the same time retain their unrestricted political sovereignty, almost exactly the opposite is the case. What we need is [...] a superior political power which can hold the economic interests in check and in the conflict between them can truly hold the scales.

Hayek advocates 'the form of international government under which certain strictly defined powers are transferred to an international authority, while in all other respects the individual countries remain responsible for their internal affairs', and concludes that the name of this form of governance is 'federation', which should be 'neither an omnipotent super-state, not a loose association of "free nations" but a community of nations'. Did Hayek have premonitions of the shape of European construction to come? It is uncanny to think of this Austrian intellectual, later a Nobel economic laureate, sitting in cold, dark, rationed, wartime London and describing much of what became first the EEC and then the EU. He dismisses the dreamers like the nineteenth-century poet Tennyson, who called for a global federation:

> For I dipt into the future, far as human eye could see,
> Saw the Vision of the world, and all the wonder that
>   would be;
> Heard the heavens fill with shouting, and there rain'd a
>   ghastly dew
> From the nations' airy navies grappling in the central blue;
> Till the war-drum throbb'd no longer, and the battle flags
>   were furl'd
> In the Parliament of Man, the Federation of the world.

Hayek was more modest and precise in his geography. 'The comparatively close association which a Federal Union represents will not at first be practicable beyond perhaps even as narrow a region as part of Western Europe, though it may be possible gradually to extend it', he wrote.

Like Churchill with his call for a Council of Europe in 1942, there were men in London ready to go beyond the confines of conventional thinking. Hayek is a hero to the British Eurosceptics who now appear to want to return to the narrow national sovereignisms of pre-1939 Europe that Hayek warned against. He offered a blueprint for a federal Europe not as super-state but as a community of nations. It is shame that Hayek the European is not as widely read as Hayek the liberal economist.

In Britain, Hayek's most devoted admirer was Margaret Thatcher. She admired his neo-liberal economic theory. But did she understand his argument that to make a fully open or liberal economy work in Europe some federal or political direction was required? For Mrs Thatcher the talk of political Europe was a distraction. As she told the Commons: 'I am constantly saying that I wish that they [her fellow European leaders] would talk less about European and political union. The terms are not understood in this country. In so far as they are understood over there, they mean a good deal less than some people over there think they mean.' She signed declarations and the Single Act which contained ambitious language about increasing integration and the need for closer union. Did she just regard these words as the necessary padding or high-flown rhetoric which continental Europeans liked but which were not meant to be taken too seriously?

It was Helmut Schmidt, the former West German Chancellor, who noted caustically that when politicians are tempted to talk about their 'vision' they should take two aspirins and go and lie in a dark room until the temptation has passed. British politics is famous for its pragmatism and empiricism. Yet all politics, British, French, American, wherever, requires some passion, a vision, an idea of what your country is or what your continent could be. De Gaulle famously opened his memoirs with the immortal line: '*Toute ma vie, je me suis fait une certaine idée de la France*' (All my life I have had a certain idea of France). Churchill offered a vision of Britain alone against a Europe enslaved by Hitler and Stalin. With one phrase – the United States of Europe – Churchill's vision inspired a movement towards European unity which needs today more than ever those with a vision of what Europe might be rather than a list of moans about what Europe is.

In Britain, politicians do not do vision. Or if they do it is kept secret. In Britain, vision is politics' *vice anglaise*, available only for private viewings and for adepts. Visit a bookshop in France or Germany and one can usually find a book on Europe written by a politician, journalist or intellectual.

If the British reading public bothers to check Amazon and look for books on Europe, most that are offered for sale are university-level guides to how the EU works or its history. The books taking a strong position on Europe are from anti-European writers or those that find plenty to moan about and which demand major reforms to correspond to the London view of what the EU should be. British bookshelves contain scores of books on Europe but none that has passion, muscular vision, enthusiasm or excitement for Europe.

The first European Book of the Year prize presented in the European Parliament in December each year was won by the late Tony Judt, an academic who had lived in New York for 20 years. His book *Postwar* is perhaps the best history of Europe since 1945. But it is history written in the Anglo-Saxon style of chronological narrative and empirical analysis. Judt had made his name as a writer on the mid-twentieth-century French left and the wartime French Resistance. He was sensitive to the cause of Europe. His 900-page book was a magnificent history, but did not contribute to making the British more European. Each year the jury looks for a book of passion in favour of Europe written by a Brit. So far they have found none until Anthony Gidden won the prize in December 2014.

The most common phrase heard in any discussion on Europe in Britain from those who are not declared Europhobes is: 'I am in favour of Europe but …'. Then follows a litany of all the things that the speaker dislikes about the EU. In the end the sound of Britain on Europe is a long, querulous moan. The teachers of Europe in British universities manage to neutralize their subject and make it just another area of study like mathematics or chemistry or sociology. British universities are not to blame for the lack of enthusiasm about Europe in Britain, but they contribute nothing to overcome this sense of Europe as a problem, or worse, a bore.

So where can the enthusiasts for Europe be found? Here is one.

I saw the European Union as a huge historical achievement compared to anything Europe has seen. By historical standards it was still young – imperfect and often irritating because we had not yet learned the art of working effectively together. Rhetoric had run ahead of achievement, but that was an argument for moderating the rhetoric, not for abandoning the achievement.

Saying 'No' to the EU is foolishness which would have helped to bring about the nightmare which had always alarmed our predecessors: a continental union influencing British lives at almost every turn over which we had no control. We would have reduced ourselves to a weak, though no doubt pretentious nation wedged between the United States and Europe. Each would pay us courteous attention for old times' sake, but the important dealings would be amongst themselves.

This passionate language can be found in the memoirs of Douglas Hurd, one of the leading Conservatives in the late twentieth century, who held high office under Margaret Thatcher and John Major. As in France, the British political memoir is a reflection on yesterday not an appeal to tomorrow.

Hurd's fervent defence of Europe was the last to be heard from a senior Conservative. He was born in 1930. His son, Nicholas, was born in 1962 and followed his father into the House of Commons in 2005. Nick Hurd's view on Europe was very different. In his first speech as an MP the son repudiated everything the father had written two years before. Hurd the son told the Commons that if the EU was to count on his support as a representative of the next generation of Conservative MPs, 'It must first explicitly ditch the principle of ever-closer political union and focus instead on re-establishing the EU's credentials as a force for prosperity, growth and jobs. That means winning the argument for the Anglo-Saxon model of economic liberalism.' Hurd junior was named as a minister by David Cameron because his vision of Europe *à l'anglaise* is precisely that of the British prime minister, without any serious challenge from leaders of other political formations.

In Britain, most of the dominant voices on Europe blame the existence of the Union, its currency, its institutions for the problems the British people face. With no alternative vision, why should the British not consider leaving the Union to be a serious option? A particular obsession of the British right is to portray the EU as a new totalitarian threat. The most important tabloid newspaper for the British middle classes is the *Daily Mail*, with more than 6 million readers. Every few months the *Daily Mail* runs a headline about the 'Fourth Reich' as a description of what Europe has become or will become. One of the intellectual architects of British Euroscepticism is John Laughland, who has taught at the Sorbonne and works for the Paris-based and Russian-funded Institute of Democracy and Cooperation, described by the Russian state propaganda television channel Russia Today as pro-Kremlin. In his book *The Tainted Source*, Mr Laughland has written of what he describes as the 'direct links between Nazi, Vichyite and fascist thought, and the ideology of European integration in our own day'. This theme is echoed by Boris Johnson. He has written that a 'Nazi European Union' was proposed in 1942 with 'single currency, a central bank, a common agricultural policy and other familiar ideas'. The idea of Hitler shaping a common agricultural policy to transfer German money to farmers in France or Italy is wondrous to contemplate. But these are not the vapourings of an eccentric. The Mayor of London is a major British politician.

To be sure, throughout decades, if not centuries of European history endless quotations or references can be found written or spoken by dictators or authoritarian leaders that associate the idea of Europe with some overarching hegemonic search for power over people and their nations. Napoleon complained that 'Europe never stops making war on France, on its values, on me'. In *Tainted Source*, Mr Laughland offers this splutter of rage from 1160 by the English-born John of Salisbury, who was a clerical diplomat and secretary to the Archbishop of Canterbury before his installation as Bishop of Chartres: 'Who made the Germans the judges of nations? Who gave this brutish and impetuous people the authority to determine at their discretion who is to be the prince over the heads of the sons of men?'

One might laugh at invoking a twelfth-century savant in order to make the case against Europe, but the bulk of the British intelligentsia remain suspicious of anything from across the Channel. Here is the prominent British economist Wynne Godley, writing in 1992, predicting doom for Britain if a single currency is established. 'The establishment of a single currency in the EC would indeed bring to an end the sovereignty of its component nations', which would acquire 'the status of a local authority or colony'. On the contrary, he argued, 'so long as it is a sovereign state [...] it can devalue its currency. It can then trade successfully at full employment.' Britain devalued its currency by 25 per cent after 2007/8, as it did repeatedly in previous decades. But while the printing of money by the Bank of England, much higher debt and deficits than in the Eurozone, a housing bubble and the continuing strength of London have made Britain a better-performing state than others in Europe, there is no sense in which Godley's view that devolution was a magic cure-all for economic weakness is true. Paradoxically, the long run of good economic performance 1997–2007 and the return of the British economy to some growth in 2013 coincided with a rise in the value of the pound. Few economists believe now that a country can devalue its way to growth. But the vast majority of economists with public platforms in Britain present Europe and economic and monetary integration as a cause of problems rather than a way of increasing cooperation and common policies to achieve growth and social justice.

Economists dominate much of the available space for public discourse in London on Europe. There are no counter-arguments from other disciplines that offer a positive vision. Europe is presented in such negative terms week by week, year by year, it is almost a surprise that Britain is still an EU member. But this anti-European vision or ideology does not come from nowhere. Someone has to pay for it. Under Mrs Thatcher, the British government was spending £25 million a year promoting the European Community and its single market. A television and radio advertising campaign titled 'Are

EU Ready?' explained to people the new developments in Europe following the Single Act and why they were to Britain's advantage.

When I became the Europe minister in 2002, my budget to explain the EU to Britain was cut by Gordon Brown and Jack Straw to £150,000, the lowest public information budget of any ministry in the British government. Against that the anti-European campaigns had not only the resources of the EU-hostile press that daily printed propaganda against Europe, but also some of the richest businessmen in Britain and the speculators of the hedge funds, derivative trading and spread-betting industries who saw Europe as a threat to their view of how a market economy should be organized.

11

HOW THE CITY FINANCES EUROPHOBIA

If Britain does leave the EU, the City and business will have to accept their share of responsibility. The mood in favour of Europe reached its high-water mark with the formation of Britain in Europe at the end of the last century. From 2000 onwards, businesses began to echo Eurosceptic themes about too much control being exercised by Brussels, too much red-tape regulation and, of great concern to the City's financial services sector, too many proposals that appeared to hinder rather than help the City in its new role as a global financial hub no longer moored in a national, let alone a European framework of rules and obligations.

Many in the City supported David Cameron's view that the EU needed major reform and that a referendum was the mechanism to achieve this. So far no one in the City or no representative business federation has criticized the in–out plebiscite Mr Cameron proposes in 2017. For some, full not semi-detached membership of the EU is vital. Richard Gnodde and Michael Sherwood are the joint CEOs of Goldman Sachs in London. They argue that 'Large international and European companies see a Britain divorced from the EU as a much les attractive place. Threats to British involvement in the EU', they wrote in the *Evening Standard*, 'are threats to British business'. This kind of argument is beginning to surface as the masters of finance in the City wake up to the seriousness of Brexit.

As David Cameron's political rhetoric against Jean-Claude Juncker mounted after the European Parliament elections in May 2014 and Conservative MPs fulminated against EU citizens being allowed uncontrolled access into Britain, the CBI's director-general, John Cridland, warned that 'The EU is our biggest export market and remains fundamental to our economic future. Our membership supports jobs, drives growth and boosts our international competitiveness.'

He was rebuked by the Conservative MEP David Campbell Bannerman, who said the CBI 'isn't doing any serious thinking. It's just maintaining a position where EU membership at all costs is benign for the UK.' The anti-EU senior Conservative John Redwood went further. Speaking at the Conservative Party conference in Birmingham in September 2014, the former cabinet minister said business leaders who spoke against Brexit would pay a 'very dear economic and financial price'. He told companies and CEOs to 'keep out' of the in–out debate, arguing that they should not 'meddle in politics'. In an extraordinary threat, Mr Redwood said anti-Europeans would 'make life difficult for them' and that it could be 'destabilising' for their business. He added that executives could be 'forced out of their jobs'. Mr Redwood is not an anti-European loud-mouth. He spends a great deal of time at meetings and seminars in the City. He represents the axis of money power and political power and was issuing a very clear threat that money power should stay on the Eurosceptic Brexit side of the argument, where it had been for some years.

Some have challenged chairs or CEOs of big companies with a clear stake in maintaining the UK inside the EU over their pusillanimity in opposing political Euroscepticism and supporters of a Brexit referendum. The excuse usually given is that boards are divided and to speak out against the Conservative Party line on Europe would cause difficulties. Now Mr Redwood is seeking to shut down any business opposition to the Brexit referendum with the threat of sanctions by politicians in government against pro-EU firms.

One of the people in his sights might be Dame Helen Alexander. Writing for the *Evening Standard* in mid-2013, Dame Helen, former president of the CBI and now chairman of a City-based events and marketing firm, UBM, asserted as a matter of indisputable fact: 'It is not hard to see why membership of the EU is overwhelmingly in our economic and political interests.' She argued that 'A car, van, bus or truck rolls off a production line in Britain every 20 seconds. Eighty per cent of those are exported and half of those go to Europe, with no tariffs, no export licences – under rules that we have helped to write.' The next day the City-financed Institute for Economic Affairs offered a prize of £100,000 for the best essay describing how Britain would survive and flourish outside the EU.

Dame Helen and the Goldman Sachs chiefs are sincere in their views that for banking, insurance and other City firms that draw profit from the EU and not just the Gulf, Asian or Russian oligarchs, keeping the UK in Europe is important. But for the last two decades such firms have allowed the opposite view to take hold without much challenge.

To be sure, the City and British business do not speak with one voice. British capitalism is split between its international and national components, its industrial and service sectors and many new money-making sectors ranging from universities offering degrees and diplomas to Formula One racing or video production. Britain is also home to movements who portray the EU as a giant capitalist conspiracy to impose a post-national, neo-liberal world order to increase profit accumulation at the expense of workers and citizens. In *Corporate Europe: How Big Business Sets Policies on Food, Climate and War*, the energetic journalist David Cronin depicts Brussels and the European Commission as slaves of modern capitalism, doing whatever big industrial firms or banks desire. This thesis has plenty of followers. Kalypso Nicolaidis, Professor of International Relations at Oxford, writing in the report, *Roadmap to a Social Europe* (*Social Europe Journal* July 2013), declared: 'Jürgen Habermas cogently names the main culprit [for the EU's economic woes]: unfettered capitalism. Absolutely.' British banks in the forefront of lobbying against EU proposals for a financial transaction tax or limitations on bankers' bonuses might disagree with Mr Cronin or Professor Nicolaidis that the European Commission is a servant of modern capitalism. Moreover, when the

European Commission punishes Microsoft, puts Google under pressure to change its operations or prevents the merger between two giant global mining companies, Rio Tinto and BHP Billiton, both star performers on the London Stock Exchange, the view that the European Commission does whatever big business wants has less impact.

The argument that Brussels is the valet of private enterprise also contradicts the view of many in the City and business that the EU seeks to prevent the 'animal spirits', to use Keynes's term, or the 'creative destruction', in Schumpeter's words, of capitalism from operating fully. The association of Chambers of Commerce in Britain produced a report in 2008 saying that EU regulations cost British companies, big and small, €60 billion. A closer examination showed these regulations included not using asbestos or not requiring employees to work 80-hour weeks. They were EU regulations which would apply to Portugal and Poland, Latvia to Malta, to ensure that the single market operated under a single set of rules.

Some British company chairmen and CEOs appear to want common rules for everyone else in Europe, but a régime of exceptions for the City and other British firms. London invented and is home to many gentlemen's clubs. There is a constant demand for the EU to complete the single market in services. But the abolition of national rules controlling the professions, insurance, the price of books or even how taxis are ordered would require an unprecedented transfer of power to Brussels to abolish national rules and regulations on the provision of paid-for services. Completing the single market in services would require more Europe, not less, more directives adopted under qualified majority votes and certainly more rules (called red tape by their opponents) emanating from the European Commission. No one has explained to the gentlemen of the City that in a club everyone has to abide by the same rules, and if the club is called the EU the same obligation applies. Rules once agreed and voted upon cannot be changed to suit just one member of a club.

The CBI and other querulous moaners about the negative impact of EU regulations on British firms or competitiveness never explain how many firms or economic actors in other EU member states seem to do very well indeed while operating within the framework of single-market EU regulations that the leaders of British business have been so negative about. The same business leaders helped create the atmosphere of now deeply rooted hostility to the EU that can be heard all the time in social gatherings of British business.

The City, after all, owes its renaissance in the 1980s not to Mrs Thatcher alone, but to European competition policy which broke open the cartels and protectionisms of fixed commissions which were barriers to open competition. Instead of being grateful to Brussels for ushering in the most glorious era of money-making in the City's history, with Midas-like payments to its top managers, the gentlemen of the City are the source of much of the ideological hostility to and financing of campaigns against Europe. The star of British Europhobia, Nigel Farage, the leader of Ukip, is a former City trader and a regular guest at City lunches and dinners and seminars which form a permanent fiesta of anti-European prejudice at the heart of British business.

If for the left Brussels is too business-friendly and for the right it is hostile to modern capitalism, the functionaries of Europe may pat themselves on the back and think they are equidistant and therefore have found *le juste milieu*. In the British debate, however, the arguments about Europe's relationship with firms are not clinical, legal examinations about which EU directive helps and which hinders. Instead there is a permanent, rumbling hostility, magnified by the press offices of the different employer organizations. This contributes to the negative view of Europe promoted by business. In July 2012, the British Chambers of Commerce organization published the findings of a poll which deserve closer examination.

The British Chambers of Commerce (BCC) today released the results of a poll of nearly 2,000 businesses, which suggest that most businesses (85%) do not want further EU integration. [...]

Commenting on the findings, John Longworth, Director General of the British Chambers of Commerce (BCC), said:

These results clearly show that British businesses do not want further integration with the EU.

Although only a small proportion of firms hold extreme views on whether to leave or stay, nearly half of companies say they want a renegotiated, 'looser' membership within the European Union.

Look carefully at the statement of this leader of British business as he defines as 'extreme' the view that Britain should stay in the EU. His press officer presumably meant to write 'strong' or 'firm' but the use of the adjective 'extreme' is nonetheless revealing. In fact, what British business leaders are doing is faithfully reflecting the anti-European views of the party they support, the Conservative Party, and the newspapers they read – the *Telegraph, Daily Mail* or *Sunday Times*. Nine out of ten of these businesses want Britain to have a different relationship with the EU. The way forward according to this poll is a plebiscite.

Of those businesses that want to see a different relationship with Europe, over half (55 per cent) see a referendum on EU membership as a medium-term issue, to be dealt with in the next one to five years. Another 40 per cent of those firms would like to see a referendum within the next 12 months. A report produced by the London Chamber of Commerce and Industry in May 2013 said that half of London businesses (52 per cent) believe that remaining in the EU under the current terms would be harmful to their economic prospects.

Thus the view of business chimes completely with that of the EU-hostile political and media class, who have been pressing for a referendum either as a means of blackmailing the rest of Europe to concede Britain a special status – full access to the single market but no responsibility to abide by EU rules if Britain does not like them or, if that is not available, to leave Europe and seek a new future outside the EU. What is never heard from business is coherent, consistent, convinced support for Europe.

Support for Europe is not entirely absent in the City. Business for New Europe is a network set up by pro-European publicists. It organizes conferences and publishes pamphlets and has a score of business leaders ready to publish statements supporting British membership of the EU. The main voices in the City and those ready to use their private wealth or the money of their companies are those who dream of a Britain liberated from what they consider the prison of EU membership. One example is Stuart Wheeler, who once gave £5 million to the Conservative Party in 2001 to encourage its Eurosceptic position. When David Cameron did not immediately start a process of withdrawing from the EU, Mr Wheeler transferred his financial support to Ukip, where he is now the treasurer. Mr Wheeler, like Mr Cameron educated at Eton and Oxford, made his fortune by setting up a firm in 1974 which allowed people to bet on the price of gold at a time when physical ownership of the precious metal was not permitted. His company moved into spread betting, which today is a business worth £120 billion in London. Spread betting is the purest form of modern casino capitalism. It took off after the Bretton Woods system, which stabilized world currency relationships, collapsed in the 1970s. In legal terms spread betting is gambling and therefore investors do not pay tax on their gains any more than they pay tax if they win £10,000 on the National Lottery or betting on horses.

Another denizen of the City is Michael Spencer, whose company ICAP is involved in heavy derivative trading and money broking – that is, betting on movements in interest rates. His firm has been investigated for its involvement in the Libor interest-rate-fixing scandal. He has boasted that he has given £2 million to the Conservative Party and was even treasurer of the Conservatives under David Cameron until he resigned following other scandals involving selling shares in his firm shortly before their value dropped by 20 per cent. Spencer is deeply hostile to Europe and has said he would move his company out of Britain and the EU if a financial transaction tax was introduced. For the City, any call, any suggestion, that the activities of banks, traders, hedge funds, lawyers and accountants who advise on tax avoidance, commodity traders, Libor rate manipulators, derivative brokers or spread betting firms should be subject to any regulation or supervision at a European level is heresy, anti-City treason.

Unlike the chemical, food, transport, automobile, energy or telecommunications sectors, which have accepted that the single market cannot exist without supranational regulation so that every consumer knows that the purchase of a good or service is – at least in theory – governed by common rules, the City believes it has no duty or responsibility to accept supervision and regulation other than that which it approves of and does not challenge its interests. Money from the City has flowed and still flows to set up and support anti-European networks. On one occasion I penetrated one of their gatherings.

Thursday, 14 May 1998

In the evening I went to a dinner organized by Carla Powell, the woman whose salon, thanks to her marriage to Charles Powell, Margaret Thatcher's great assistant, has been the most famous in Conservative circles for years. The event is to launch a book on Europe by a man called Rodney Leach who works at the same bank as Charles Powell. We turn up at a posh hotel in Knightsbridge and bit by bit a coven of Europhobes assembles. There is Paul Johnson with his watery eyes and his once flame-red hair now turning white. Then there is William Rees-Mogg looking more gaunt and white-haired than ever but still passionate in his hatred of all things European. Michael Howard appears with his model wife and then Bill Cash. There was one of the Saatchi brothers who was close to the Conservative Party. Then the divine apparition came in. It was Margaret Thatcher coming through a side entrance in a fluorescent light blue dress walking very slowly and sedately like an ageing goddess amongst her fawning serviteurs.

Then an introductory speech from Charles Powell and up stands the author, Rodney Leach, who is introduced as some kind of polymath because he is a great bridge player as well as being a banker and has written his book. He makes a rather tedious speech attacking Europe for its social policies, its federal inclinations and all the usual rant of the Europhobes. I mutter under my breath getting noisier all the time and I see blacker and blacker looks at me. The publisher of the book says I am behaving disgracefully and Mrs Leach is very angry.

At the time I thought I was describing the end of City and business Euroscepticism. I was wrong. It was only just getting under way. Rodney Leach paid for and was first chairman of Open Europe, the most successful and professional of the anti-European think-tanks in London. Its daily online criticisms of Europe, avoiding crude language and usually based on facts (if carefully selected), is effective. Its many staff, including those in an office in Berlin, tirelessly fan out into a world of seminars and conferences and appearances on television and radio to promote the anti-European cause that I encountered in 1998.

Rodney Leach has been rewarded by David Cameron with a peerage and thus made a legislator. From this platform he can continue to preach against Europe. It is a message to other bankers in the City who crave honours, above all that of becoming a Lord. The rewards for financing and encouraging Euroscepticism are to enter Britain's second legislative chamber. Lord Pearson, also prominent in the insurance sector in the City, moved from the Conservative Party to Ukip and was briefly party leader. The think-tank Global Britain, which he founded with two other peers opposed to Europe, is one of the myriad anti-European foundations, think-tanks, even political parties that have been financed from within the City to crusade against the EU.

Over the years they have changed names, leaders and sponsors. Business for Sterling, New Europe, the Referendum Party, No, Open Europe, Global Britain, United Kingdom Independence Party and the latest, Business for Britain. All are dedicated to the simple proposition that the EU is inimical to British interests. Some seek electoral success; others work through the Conservative Party.

The City is not a single-interest bloc. Nine out of ten banks in the British Bankers' Association are foreign-owned. All the major EU banks have important operations in the City. An estimated 300,000 French citizens live in London, most working for French banks and other financial concerns. British capitalism has always been the most open of any European economy to foreign ownership. Foreign-owned firms like Japanese automobile companies set up in Britain in order to have access to the single market. In private they complain about British Euroscepticism. In public they say nothing and lend no financial or political support to any effort to counter the daily disinformation about Europe produced by leading newspapers or the anti-EU campaigns and think-tanks.

Many of the City firms that finance the anti-European campaign are privately owned and thus not accountable to shareholders. The publicly owned firms usually like to steer away from controversial politics. In Britain there are no debates about whether to stay in NATO, or the World Trade Organization, or the UN or to resile from the many treaty organizations that set rules nations have to accept. Membership of these supranational bodies is assumed as normal within the political life of the nation. But the EU has been transformed into a permanent political battleground, where armies fight and no quarter may be given. A great success of the Europhobes in the City has been to make pro-Europeanism appear as a foreign ideology designed to damage the City by those ready to sell out Britain to foreigners. The cultivated men of money in the City with their Covent Garden and Glyndebourne opera seats, Hermès ties, BMWs, Mediterranean holidays, chalets in Verbier and Gstaad and knowledge of fine wines look down their nose at the crude xenophobic language of the populist politicians who take the struggle against the EU on to the airwaves and into the streets. But they have ensured that pro-European voices are placed in the same category, not as the normal expression of the national interest but as partisan, unbalanced, unBritish.

Thus it is completely logical for foreign firms and foreign executives based in London to keep their heads down and avoid taking sides in what is presented as a bitterly divisive domestic dispute over Europe internal to the peculiarities of British politics. In other European countries, the debates over Europe involve Eurosceptic parties or individual politicians seen, fairly or not, as not being part of mainstream conventional politics of government – Le Pen or Mélanchon in France, Bossi or Grillo in Italy, Wilders in the Netherlands, Jobbik in Hungary, Golden Dawn in Greece, the Swedish Democrats or True Finns in Finland. In Britain, anti-EU politics is part of mainstream political debate within the Conservative Party (and in the past the Labour Party) with many legislators in the two houses of the British Parliament supporting Eurosceptic positions. For the most part, the business leader who may have pro-EU views keeps them private if he or she wants to win esteem and make a profit.

Outside the City and outside London, the dominant businesses in the domestic British economy are in public works, construction, housing, public sector contracts, retail, leisure, telecommunications, with a disproportionate number of very small firms and self-employed workers. The indigenous white working class has seen the arrival of workers from new EU member states ready to work for the minimum wage and work long hours for employers. The City may employ French, German, American and Arab professionals of global finance but they are lost within the post-national megalopolis that London has become. By contrast, when the supermarkets of Hull or Liverpool, or smaller towns, suddenly fill with the voices of Poles, Lithuanians or Bulgarians looking for their national food on the shelves of local supermarkets, the presence of Europe in the domestic labour market can be seen as strange and unsettling.

Thus outside London it is harder and harder to find a local business leader who speaks well of Europe. They take their lead from their preferred politicians on the right and from the right-wing press. When I became an MP in South Yorkshire in 1994 there was still an acceptance by many in the local business community that, on balance, being in the EU made economic sense for Britain and was in the interests of their business. A decade later in 2005 I made a BBC programme on the EU constitution and interviewed friends in business in the small town where I was an MP. I could not find one who was in favour of Europe. The scorn about Europe had become deeply engrained. Local businesses who exported nothing and whose businesses were not covered by EU directives spoke of Europe as a foreign power inimical to Britain. They did not know that Britain did more trade with Ireland than with all the BRIC (Brazil, Russia, India, China) nations combined or that half of Britain's trade and millions of jobs depended on exports to Europe. They seemed unaware that the many foreign firms that had invested in Britain – including the Indian company Tata or the Japanese car components firm Toyoda Gosei – had bought or opened local factories because they could export freely to the EU. Europe to those I interviewed was a joke, something to scorn, a source of problems. They did not want to leave. They were not enthusiastic about staying.

They reflected in 2005, the lack of support for the EU in the middle ranks of the British business community. None of the arguments about the economic advantages to Britain of being in the EU appear to have penetrated. In 1975, only three out of more than 400 business leaders said they would vote No in the referendum on the European Community. Forty years later the mood was very different. One of the favourite right-wing economists in the City is Roger Bootle, founder and managing director of Capital Economics. He compared the Treaty of Rome to Hitler's *Mein Kampf* early in 2014 and told a City audience Britain would 'do rather well' if it left the EU. None of the City audience protested at the lurid comparison of the EU to the Third Reich. Far from standing up against Brexit, opposing the plebiscite that can lead to Britain quitting the EU, the City and British capitalism remained silent in the face of the clamour against the EU and no one has dared challenge the 2017 Brexit referendum.

12

THE BRITISH LIKE THEIR PARLIAMENT, BUT NO OTHER

The question of power within the EU, who has it, how are power-holders held to account and what is done with EU power is not just an academic topic. A pervading sense in Britain that somehow the EU is undemocratic contributes to the drift towards Brexit. In particular, the British feel that their parliament has lost some control of the nation's destiny to unknown legislators and officials outside the UK. The call for a return to the unfettered supremacy of the House of Commons has been made throughout the years since Britain ratified the Treaty of Rome in 1972.

It was John Major, when prime minister, who summed up the barely hidden contempt that many British politicians have for democracy in Europe. Challenged in the Commons in 1994 about why he was, once again, at odds with all of his fellow leaders in Europe on a now-forgotten issue the British premier snapped at MPs: 'Most European heads of government couldn't find their way to their parliaments with a white stick.' The then prime minister's condescension hid a real truth. In the UK citizens share the unspoken or rather rarely spoken but deeply felt view that only the British (and perhaps the Swiss) are properly democratic, while other Europeans have yet properly to learn how to be good democrats. The EU is seen as full of young nations where democratic and rule-of-law traditions have still fully to take root.

Professor Ulrich Beck of Munich University, a German writer on European politics, wrote in March 2013 that: 'The crisis of Europe has been analysed from the perspective of political institutions, the economy, elites, governments and the law, but not from the perspective of the individual. What does Europe mean for individuals and what principles can be developed on this basis for a social contract for a new Europe from below.' This demand from a sociologist reads well but would make little sense to British citizens, who consider, rightly or wrongly, that each individual subject of Her Majesty has an individual relation with democratic power mediated by the choice of an individual representative in the British House of Commons. British citizens do not vote for a party list, or for a single dominant leader like a president. Most British Members of Parliament are known locally, have a local home and are obliged every week or two to hold open meetings for their constituents who arrive with many different complaints about how the state is run and how government decisions impact on individuals.

The arrival of first a coalition government in 2010 and then the constitutional issues opened up after the Scottish referendum and Mr Cameron's view that the Commons should have two categories of MPs – Scots and English – are symptoms of a parliamentary and governance system in the UK which is not working as once it did. The House of Commons no longer has the authority and respect of old. The House of Lords, the largest unelected legislature in the world outside China and North Korea and containing men who have bought their right to be lawmakers, is even further removed from any democratic process commanding respect.

Nonetheless, most British adults – citizens and subjects at one and the same time – see their Parliament as the only acceptable source for laws and rules over their lives. This is not to idealize British democracy or its system of representative parliamentary elections on a single-seat, majority basis. The leaders of British politics are found seats which remain safely Conservative or Labour but they are still obliged to buy a local house and turn up to hear complaints and protests from individual citizens. Under France's Fifth Republic there has been endless tinkering with the electoral system. British election systems have not altered much since the nineteenth century. President Sarkozy introduced special constituencies for French citizens living abroad who could elect their own deputies to sit in the national assembly. So now France has deputies for North America, for Asia or for Africa. For a British citizen it would be illogical to the point of being absurd to have an MP representing all of Britain, let alone all of the British citizens living in Spain or the United States. How can one have a politics, would ask the British citizen, where representatives are not to be seen and met most weekends and who really know what is happening in the locality?

This passion for a parliament of fellow citizens controlling the state is in the British DNA. Britain, or more properly England, traces its first attempt to place the King under some control to the Magna Carta of 1215. The first parliament was assembled a few decades later. Conservative, Liberal and Labour historians have traced British politics through the history of the nation's parliament. A leader of Britain's postwar Communist Party was a dull, dour Scot called John Gollan. He and his party opposed Britain joining Europe after 1970. In a pamphlet, *The Common Market: Why Britain Should Not Join*, the general-secretary of Britain's main Marxist political party sounded just like a member of the Le Pen family:

> The supranational apparatus and directing bodies of the Commons Market are in effect a gigantic bureaucracy over and above the national governments with the elected Parliaments exercising no control whatsoever.

The communist Gollan insisted on the sovereignty and supremacy of the British Parliament. As he developed his argument, he sounded more and more like a reactionary old British Conservative, even quoting a writer who was the epitome of the conventional establishment. 'The cornerstone of Britain's political constitution is the sovereignty of Parliament. Sir Ivor Jennings has said "the supremacy of Parliament is the constitution" […] the pro-Marketeers are prepared to sacrifice

British sovereignty to enter the market.' One cannot help hearing Marx and Engels, who used their time in London and Manchester to expose the delusions of bourgeois parliamentarianism, spinning in their graves as the spokesman for British communism used all the arguments of the Conservative right to reject joining other European nations in the EEC. But Gollan knew what he was doing. Any hint that gave the impression of reducing the central authority of the House of Commons is treason in Britain. Like arguing in the Vatican that priests might marry, the argument that British parliamentary sovereignty is not the alpha and omega of British democracy can certainly be advanced but it is likely to fall on deaf ears.

One of the persistent complaints of anti-Europeans is that the public has never been told that becoming part of the European Community did involve a loss of sovereignty. This is simply a lie, but if lies are repeated often enough they are believed. Debates on Britain and Europe since 1945 have been about nothing except the sharing of political authority and sovereignty. The end may indeed have been presented as an economic one, but the means to that end were always spelled out as political and requiring the Commons to share power with other national democratic systems. Over the years, pro-Europeans have gently reminded the public that Britain's sovereignty is not inviolate. In 1965, a group of Conservative MPs published a pamphlet, *One Europe*, advocating the 'full economic, military and political union of Europe'. Much of it was written by Enoch Powell, who became, after 1970, the leading right-wing opponent of Britain joining Europe. As we have seen, one recurring theme in British hostility to Europe is the number of opinion-formers in public life who switch from a rational pro-European position to a fundamental faith that Europe must be opposed as the mortal enemy of British interests. But in 1965, Enoch Powell and another rising Conservative, Nicholas Ridley MP, later one of Margaret Thatcher's favourite ministers, who revealed himself as a crude anti-German Europhobe at the end of his political life, sought to persuade doubters in their own party. In 1965, sovereignty was not a problem. Britain's membership of the IMF, NATO, GATT (today the WTO) and other treaty-based international organizations meant also that 'we have lost much sovereignty', the Conservative pamphlet argued.

When in 1972 the Conservative government sought to persuade Britain of the virtues of European Community membership, their White Paper argued: 'There is no question of any erosion of essential national sovereignty.' But no one ever explained what 'essential' meant. The statement was not a lie, but neither was it the truth. The European Court of Justice as early as 1963 had declared that the Treaty of Rome meant accepting that 'the States have limited their sovereign rights'. Britain's Attorney General at the time noted in 1962 that Europe now had 'supra-national powers which override those of national constitutional bodies and which are incapable of challenge in the national courts of member states'. The same was true of the Strasbourg-based European Court of Human Rights, which would be a meaningless talking shop if the states who signed the treaty setting it up did not accept its rulings.

These were not just lawyers' or politicians' subtle words. They were a truth that was out in the open but not given its due prominence. The reason is the attachment that British culture has to its parliamentary system. The Commons is the constitution, and until the British believe that they have some parliamentary control over what Europe does there will remain a deep, permanent sense that Britain has lost control of its destiny.

The idea of parliament has occupied a central place in the British conception of democracy. In the eighteenth century power quietly slipped from the monarch to Parliament. In the British idea of democracy, the great battles of political control, reform, change, reaction and renewal have all been led by Members of Parliament. The British system of majority voting with each constituency represented by the man or woman who gets the most votes at an election also makes parliament a highly personalized place, with the role of the party or the parliamentary faction being less important than in most continental nations.

Like Saudi Arabia and Israel, Britain is a rare example in the modern world of a nation without a written constitution. Thus there has been little tradition of constitutional debate. British political philosophers like John Locke or Jeremy Bentham have expounded theories of contract. The direct democracy of a Rousseau or the all-powerful Jacobin Republic rarely penetrated British political consciousness. Kant and the German view that law should be supreme never persuaded the British with their preference for contracts between government and governed which could be altered without reference to judges or a written constitution. Parliament itself decides its own reforms. Over years it has both conceded powers and centralized them. Votes for women did not arrive fully until after 1945 but the British Parliament has also agreed to the creation of a National Parliament in Scotland and a National Assembly in Wales with significant degrees of governance in Scotland quite different from arrangements in England.

Initiatives in the Commons – not decisions of ministers – led to the abolition of the death penalty and the right of women to have an abortion a decade before France adopted similar reforms. The British pride themselves on this pragmatic flexibility and willingness to adapt and use Parliament as the means of allowing competing political passions to be channelled into angry verbal debate rather than seeking authoritarian political solutions or being required to mobilize in the street in the name of replacing one regime by another.

Thus when the British enthusiastically helped set up the Council of Europe in 1949 they made sure that its assembly of parliamentarians at which Churchill himself spoke was an assembly of talkers. The real decisions would be taken by the Council of Ministers on an inter-governmental basis. The Council of Europe would not reduce the power of the Commons or impose law on Westminster. The British political class is based on conversation. Few of its leaders aspire to being thinkers or writers. Such parliamentarians who have produced major books tend to write history, in the case of Churchill almost exclusively about himself or his forebears. The rough-and-ready change of governments every decade or so allows each new generation of MPs to think and to hope, with justification, that a little patience will bring the pleasure of office, a ministerial car and a chance to make decisions rather than make speeches.

Very few British MPs go abroad to study, and if they do it is almost certainly to an American university. There is no requirement on the British political elite as there is the graduates of France's École nationale d'administration or for most northern and today many southern Europeans to speak two or more languages. Of course, linguistic ability does not define Europeanism. Helmut Schmidt and Valéry Giscard d'Estaing spoke English, while François Mitterrand and Gerhard Schröder required interpreters. The British political class is monolingual. Most senior politicians on the continent speak more than just their mother tongue. The idea of their British equivalents picking up *Le Monde* or *Die Welt* or *El Pais* would seem just odd in Whitehall or Westminster.

Democratic consent requires a common language. During the Constitutional Convention that sought to draw up the Constitution for Europe that France voted down in 2005, there was much talk about it being a Philadelphia moment, a reference to the Federalist Papers. These great exchanges between James Madison and his fellow Americans as they struggled to work out what kind of a constitution the United States would need in the 1780s were never to be reproduced in Europe. There was simply no common language. Jürgen Habermas would write his essays in a richly textured German that does not always translate so easily. The French politician Pierre Moscovici, now a European Commissioner, could write an impassioned article in *Le Monde* under the title 'Let's Have a President for Europe' and the American-born Oxford professor Larry Siedentop produced a whole book called *Democracy in Europe* that deployed considerable learning acquired over decades of studying European democracy as a political scientist. But none of them ever exchanged ideas with one another. There were no letters written backwards and forwards by Europeans of high intellect. The Constitutional Convention resembled, as does so much in European construction, a peasants' market full of haggling over who should have which powers and what the exact price to be paid for a concession might be.

This idea of a Europe of permanent negotiation and no final settlement actually was closer to the British political tradition than the continental practice of drawing up a legally binding constitution and then living under its provisions. But British political philosophy had become utterly infused with a dull and sturdy pragmatism, and there was no poet to describe or defend the making of European demos. Moreover, most in Britain questioned whether such a thing can, in any case, be achieved without a common language. While it is true that English is becoming a lingua franca, the point about a lingua franca is that it is a lowest common denominator language. It is used for commerce and for essential communication, but not to inspire, move or govern a people whose mother tongue remains the means by which they perceive and define themselves.

Each member state of the EU, each with its own distinct language, has rightly insisted that interpretation and translation should be provided. This necessary cost may have the perverse effect of preventing European mutual comprehension. It is often said that the British and the Americans are 'two peoples divided by a common language' and it is true that the many forms of English in use around the world do not permit the creation of a common political space.

Great hopes have been placed in the European Parliament. However, its staunchest friends and the most devoted admirers of the many highly competent and hard-working members of the European Parliament will find it hard to say that it represents full democratic legitimacy in the way that the House of Commons in Britain or the National Assembly in France, the Bundestag in Germany, the Cortes in Spain or the Sjem in Poland, as well as the other national parliaments of Europe, are considered the accepted sources of law-making, democratic legitimacy and political decision.

In the first direct elections to the European Parliament in 1979 62 per cent of eligible voters turned out to vote. At each succeeding election that figure has shrunk and in 2014 it was down to 43 per cent. If this trend continues we may see that after a few more European Parliament elections there will be more MEPs than voters. For advocates of the Strasbourg Parliament, with its pharaonic buildings in the Alsatian city, as well as the Parliament in Brussels, the trend line is very clear. Despite all the investment that the European Parliament makes in promoting itself it commands less and less support. In 1979, participation in Germany was 66 per cent and 61 per cent in France. Thirty years later, only two out of five voters in Germany and France thought it was worth casting a vote to elect a deputy to the European Parliament.

In elections to choose MEPs held in Croatia on the eve of its joining the EU in July 2013, just 20 per cent of voters took part in the election of Croatia's MEPs. This despite the fact that in 2012 visitors to the European Parliament were paid €23m euros, most of it in cash handouts to visitors. Each of the 751 Members of the European Parliament is entitled to claim payments which cover the cost of travel and accommodation for up to 110 visitors per year. The European Court of Auditors has noted that no receipts are required to be paid. While the trips to Strasbourg and Brussels are certainly agreeable, it is hard to justify the use of taxpayers' money for this purpose, as the more money that is paid to visitors to the European Parliament the more they lose interest and do not even bother to vote.

With 751 members, the European Parliament is much bigger than the French National Assembly, with 577 members, the Bundestag, with 620 members for Europe's most populous democracy, or the House of Commons, with 650 members. It is not as big as the 800-strong House of Lords, the least democratic and most corrupt legislative chamber in the world, and it is no accident that some of the most vehement critics of elected MEPs and/or Europe can be found in the surreal and 100 per cent unelected House of Lords. Most British parliamentarians have never been to Strasbourg or Brussels. They may know an MEP through political party links, but the work of British MEPs is discrete and distinct and isolated from national party political activity.

The election system itself has produced bizarre results in Britain. After 1979, the European Parliament elections were used to protest against first Mrs Thatcher and then her successor as Conservative prime minister, John Major. After the 1994 European Parliament elections British Labour MEPs amounted to more than 10 per cent of all MEPs. This was hailed by some as proof that first, the Labour Party was taking European politics much more seriously and second, that Labour's increasingly pro-European message by 1994 was finding an echo with the public. This was a mirage. The 1994 vote was the high moment of rejection of the Thatcher era of Conservative government. The European Parliament election was used as a protest vote, not as a moment for a mature electoral debate on Britain's place in Europe or the future of the EU.

Fifteen years later, in 2009, exactly the same process of using the European Parliament election as a protest vote against the government of the day could be seen. By then voters were bored with the tired Labour government under Gordon Brown. So just 13 Labour MEPs were sent to Strasbourg from Britain. British voters used the European Parliament to send two members of an extreme racist and antisemitic party – the BNP – to be MEPs at the expense of mainstream Labour, Conservative or Liberal Democrat candidates. Five years later, in 2014, the nationalistic, anti-European and misogynistic Ukip became the biggest party from Britain in the European Parliament. The party had so far been unable to win a single seat in the Commons at a general election, but once again British voters used the European Parliament election to punish the governing parties, especially the Liberal Democrats, who lost all but one of their MEPs.

The European Parliament thus failed to reflect in any way the balance of power in the House of Commons. It was seen as belonging in its own electoral world and although the elections themselves were fully democratic, they did not represent how people were voting in elections that touched directly upon their lives like the choice of Parliament and prime minister, elections to the Parliament and Assembly in Scotland and Wales or the choice of municipal councillors and local political leaders.

In addition, many Labour politicians who sought and won election to the European Parliament in the 1980s and 1990s stayed there for as short a time as possible and spent all their energy trying to win selection as a candidate to enter the House of Commons, as that was seen as where real power lay. The Liberal Democratic leader, Nick Clegg, used the European Parliament as a kind of waiting room until he could enter the House of Commons. Conversely, the European Parliament was seen in many countries as a place where rejected national politicians could find another little space to continue their political lives once their national political career was over.

As a result, the Conservative and Labour parties have never allowed one of their MEPs – despite many being men and women of considerable ability – to have a role on the national political stage. None speaks with an authority that influences political decisions. This is not to disrespect the many MEPs who conscientiously carry out their committee work and seek to form European legislation in the way that conforms to their political values and do so in a sincere, hard-working fashion. But there are also populists like Ukip leader Nigel Farage or Italy's Beppe Grillo, who was a professional comedian before entering populist politics and allying his *Cinque Estrella* (Five Star) anti-immigrant party with Ukip.

At times the European Parliament is more like a students' union convention with stunts in the chamber. Extreme Ulster Protestants like Ian Paisley stood up to scream and shout and hurl abuse at Pope John Paul II when he addressed the European Parliament simply because he was the Pope and thus the arch-enemy of the late Lord Paisley's idea of Protestant supremacy. In a childish publicity stunt, Nigel Farage turned his back on the swearing-in ceremony for new MEPs elected in 2014.

There are approximately 10,000 members of national parliaments in member states. Many of these national parliamentarians feel utterly excluded from the European decision-making process. MEPs reject the creation of a senate of the European Parliament consisting of representatives of national parliaments. The European Parliament claims that the senate consists of the Council of Ministers. To be sure, there are elements in the work of the Council of Ministers which have a legislative component, but ministers take part in these meetings as executive representatives of the governments of their nation-states. It would be much healthier to connect national parliaments to the European Parliament. Another move would be to have far more joint committee work between national parliaments and committees of the European Parliament. But there is a certain arrogance, bolstered by high salaries and the most generous expenses for nearly any elected parliamentarian anywhere in Europe, that impregnates MEPs to the point that they no longer see how unrepresentative they are.

British political leaders pay lip service to the European Parliament but do not really want it around. As we have seen, David Cameron led the Conservative Party out of the pan-European alliance of conservative parties called the European People's Party. He promised this gesture in order to win enough votes to become party leader in 2005. Other than among specialists or party functionaries there is little interest in Britain in the workings of the different political formations like the Party of European Socialists or the European People's Party. We have also seen how British journalists were caught by surprise when each party federation named a candidate to become president of the European Commission following the 2014 elections. As it became clear that the dominant centre-right parties headed by Germany's Angela Merkel were serious about backing their nominee, Jean-Claude Juncker, as Commission president there was outrage in London newspaper circles. How dare elected MEPs presume to think they might have a say in the choice of who should be the Commission president was the line. The press, headed by the normally level-headed *Financial Times*, got up on its high horse and denounced the idea that choosing a Commission president now involved an element of democracy and was no longer based on secret deals and trade behind closed doors.

There were dark hints that this would never happen again. However, both the new Commission president, Jean-Claude Juncker, and the European Parliament president, Martin Schultz, made clear at the Parliament's October 2014 session in Strasbourg that they considered the new mechanism for choosing a Commission president, via a Europe-wide political process as well as the results of the MEP elections, as now being the norm and would be the means to select a new Commission president in 2019. The European Parliament had shown some muscle, if for the first time, but has yet to win the affection of European voters or be seen as legitimate as their national parliaments.

The anti-European press portray MEPs as men and women lining their pockets with expenses and allowances and relish listing the dozens or scores who go off to agreeable conferences in the warmth of the Caribbean to discuss relations between South America and Europe while their voters shiver in the winter cold. Mr Cameron's deputy prime minister, Nick Clegg, criticized the new alliance that the Conservatives had entered into with other nationalistic and populist right-wing politicians in the European Parliament. Mr Cameron was unperturbed. The European Parliament was only useful to him in order to show his contempt for it.

The small number of Labour MEPs – 20 out of 751 – have little impact on British political life. The only MEP well known to a wider public is Ukip's Nigel Farage. In 2009, he admitted at a meeting filmed and shown on television that he had taken £2m in expenses from the European Parliament. He also admitted to employing his wife, paid for by taxpayers – a practice which is illegal in most democracies but commonplace among British MPs and MEPs. As national parliamentarians in England were being crucified over their own expenses, this extraordinary boast produced little concern or condemnation. Mr Farage is a highly popular politician in Britain and appears more often on the BBC or in newspaper interviews than any national politician. He has the rumbustious, straightforward talking style of the golf club know-all, with a cigarette in one hand and a pint of beer in the other as he produces short sentences – often inaccurate, often untruthful – which portray Europe in a uniformly negative light.

Nigel Farage endlessly calls for Britain to withdraw from the EU. Like Senator Joseph McCarthy in the late 1940s and early 1950s in America, obsessed with the Soviet Communist threat to the USA,

Farage believes that Britain is now controlled by outside forces coming from Brussels and hidden Europhile cadres control government and the media to peddle false messages to the British people. He has been awarded the same status as other national identity politicians in Europe – Marine Le Pen in France, Geert Wilders in the Netherlands, Beppe Grillo in Italy and others – who have used Europe and their hostility to the EU as a means to achieve fame and political profile in their own countries. In most cases, anti-European politics shades into anti-immigrant, anti-Muslim, often xenophobic and racist positions. There is a return of anti-Semitic politics, especially in Hungary, where it began with the election of Jobbik candidates to the European Parliament before the anti-Semitic party won seats in Hungary's national parliament. Ukip has now entered into an alliance with an extreme Polish Party, the Congress of the New Right, whose leader says 'Jews are our worst enemies' and dismissed with a sneer what he calls 'the Holocaust Industry'. Mr Farage is unperturbed, as was David Cameron, at being in a political alliance with Poles holding ugly views on Jews.

The European Parliament, with its time-limited speeches, suits the demagogic rhetoric of the quick-fire speaker full of sound-bites and not the deliberative, thought-out speeches of traditional parliamentary oratory. Mr Farage is a master of one-line denunciations and insults. None of the MEPs from the other political parties match him for slippery but effective rhetoric or headline-catching statements and the European Parliament is voiceless in terms of any British politician able to defend its existence with a style or panache that has the same impact as Farage's denunciations.

This matters more in Britain than is realized because the idea of parliament is supremely at the heart of the British political tradition and culture. A parliament that is seen as finding room for defenders of the Waffen SS from Latvia, of anti-Jewish Polish or Hungarian MEPs or unrepresentative, single-issue, protest-vote MEPs who come in for one parliament and then disappear is difficult to take seriously within the British idea of parliamentary democracy. In addition, a parliament which seems to insist only on its own rights and prerogatives and gives the impression of being utterly superior to all national parliaments, rather than a partner with them, is not a parliament that will command respect, affection or support in Britain.

And the British – more specifically the English – will only learn to trust and like the EU when they feel there is some parliamentary control over its decisions and elected representatives who command respect and are known to the voters. The English do not like new sources of government. They turned down the chance to have regional government in northern England in a referendum in 2004 and also used local referendums in 2012 to largely reject having directly elected mayors in big cities. For centuries the English have had two levels of representative democracy – the local council and their national parliament. The English want to know and elect those responsible for cleaning the streets or going to war. The European Parliament confuses and worries them. Is it a rival to the Commons? Is it superior to the British Parliament? Does it make laws? Does it have authority over the Commission or Council of Ministers? Can it supervise EU spending? Can it call to account the many instances of unaccounted EU payments? Experts on EU institutional arrangements can provide answers, but the average British citizen knows little and cares less about the European Parliament and believes simply, if sadly, that a democratic EU is an oxymoron.

13

MYTHS, MURDOCH, LIES: THE PRESS AND EUROPE

Thursday, 11 December 2003

> *'It is just the press with their manic rubbish on Europe. Let's be honest. All these guys living thousands of miles away telling us what to do. We can't do a referendum on the euro with the press so strongly against us.'* [Tony Blair telling me how the press controlled his policy on Europe.]

Tony Blair turned to me with a sad look in his eyes as the Royal Air Force aeroplane taking us back from a meeting in Brussels was getting ready to take off. 'How can I do anything on Europe with the tabloids we've got, Denis?' It was a heartfelt lament. The most widely read British newspapers are full of venom, contempt and propaganda against Europe. They are owned by proprietors who visit but do not live or pay tax in Britain.

Rupert Murdoch had to become an American citizen if he wanted to own a giant media empire covering television and newspapers in the USA. In Britain, Mr Murdoch owns the most important TV news channel after the BBC.

In addition to the *Sun* and the *Sun on Sunday* (which replaced the *News of the World*) Mr Murdoch also owns two more serious papers, *The Times* and *Sunday Times*, but their reporting on EU affairs is biased to the point of parody and most of their regular

commentators are part of the permanent sneer about all matters EU
that disfigures the collective face of British journalism. In the 1930s,
the editor of *The Times*, then owned by the right-wing family group
that now owns the *Daily Mail*, censored reports from his Berlin correspondent that were critical of Hitler. Today no such censorship is
needed as editors mainly want criticism of Europe in their papers.

As the Reuters journalist Paul Taylor told Cristina Marconi and
John Lloyd in their *Reporting the EU: News, Media and the European
Institutions*, published in 2014 by the Reuters Institute for the Study
of Journalism, 'Many news media and many countries don't cover
the EU at all with their own correspondents'. Taylor says that the
aim of the Eurosceptic press is not to present reasoned arguments
against a project, but rather to demolish it through funny, unlikely
stories. 'For some, those who were strongly opposed to what the EU
did, they didn't want the facts to get in the way of a good story.'

To be sure, there is much in EU affairs that needs scrutiny and
exposure. Not all the press criticism of Europe is wrong. There is
corruption, especially as most EU spending is in obscure parts of
European agro-economy and public works contracts where politically motivated spending decisions are often exposed, not least in
Britain. MEPs, unlike British MPs, were not able to speculate in
the London property market using funds provided by taxpayers, but
it has been a long struggle to clean up and make transparent the
pay and expenses of MEPs and there are still opaque areas. One
Ukip MEP, Tom Wise, who boasted about 'repatriating money from
Europe', was jailed for two years after he was found to be using his
MEP allowances to buy fine wines. Other Ukip MEPs have made
extraordinary remarks about women and gays. MEPs from other
countries have been exposed for taking money to act as lobbyists.
A robust press is needed to expose such behaviour.

It should not be forgotten that an entire Commission had to
resign after one of its members was revealed to have been involved
in corrupt practices. A reader of the *Financial Times* may look down
his or her nose at the grotesque distortions in the tabloid press, but
often the self-denominated 'quality' papers miss key stories. And

giving vent to popular or populist passions, even if ugly at times, is an important safety valve in a democracy. The official policy of the German Springer group of papers is to support the EU. But its *Bild Zeitung*, with daily sales of 3.2 million, garish headlines and editorial comment that makes the UK's *Sun* editorials look like something from *The Economist*, can be as crudely and rudely contemptuous of Brussels and EU projects and policy as any British tabloid.

In addition, blaming Eurosceptic editors is too simplistic. A major cause for the persistent anti-European tone of many papers is that they are reporting what senior politicians say. The lurid language about the EU comes from MPs. At any given stage since Britain linked itself by treaty to Europe in 1973 there have always been senior politicians validating the anti-Europe line of the press: Enoch Powell and Tony Benn in the 1970s; any number of senior Labour politicians in the 1980s; John Redwood, Norman Tebbit and Norman Lamont in the 1990s. The Conservative leadership and in government senior ministers from 2000 until today have been ready with anti-EU quotations galore, as have a number of senior Labour figures. There is very little Nigel Farage says that has not been said by a senior Conservative at some stage since 1997. Without the oxygen provided by senior political figures it would have been more difficult for the press to sustain the breadth and depth of anti-EU reporting and comments.

Unlike France, where national newspapers like *Le Monde*, *Libération* or *Le Figaro* have relatively small circulations even if they have high-quality journalism and are papers of considerable political influence, the national newspapers of Britain still are mass-circulation papers, centralized under a tight metropolitan elite of editors and in some cases owned by foreigners and men who pay no taxes in the country where their papers promote anti-EU ideology. The great regional papers of France like *Ouest-France* do not exist in Britain, where the regional press is very weak as other forms of media including free newspapers, radio, social media and the internet have taken so much advertising revenue from printed papers.

Thus the *Daily Mail*, which is owned by Lord Rothermere, who does not pay taxes in Britain, sells 2.5 million copies. It is obsessed with promoting propaganda against Europe. In the 1930s, the *Daily Mail* ran a headline, 'Hoorah for the Black Shirts!' and constantly published articles saying that Jewish refugees should not be allowed into Britain. Fast forward to 2004, when the EU was enlarged to include eight new member states mainly in Eastern and Central Europe. Poles, like the Irish before them, arrived to work in the then-booming UK economy. Britain had given refuge to a quarter of a million Poles after 1945 who did not want to return to live under communism and the British–Polish connection has remained strong ever since. Even before Poland was formally admitted to the EU, low-cost airlines like EasyJet and Ryanair had flights between all major British cities and major cities in Poland. Rather like France and the connections with the Maghreb countries or Portugal, Britain has always sought cheap labour from countries like Ireland in the past or Poland now.

But of course for some politicians any arrival of incomers from a foreign country is unwelcome. Although the Poles on the whole were hard-working, energetic men and women who paid taxes and social security, rented property from many small landlords and added new shelves to every supermarket in Britain as they began to stock delicious Polish hams and pierogi, it was easy to whip up hate against them. The Federation of Poles of Great Britain produced a report in 2009 showing how just one paper – predictably enough the *Daily Mail* – had written 80 ugly headlines and reports full of dishonest caricatures of Polish people in Britain and inciting hate and contempt for them. The federation produced a later report showing the number of violent xenophobic assaults on Poles as a culture of anti-Polish hate was stoked up by the *Daily Mail* and other anti-European tabloids.

After the scandal over phone-hacking that led to the arrest and trial of some of the most senior editors and journalists working for Rupert Murdoch, an inquiry was set up under a senior British judge,

Sir Brian Leveson. He found that 'There is certainly clear evidence of misreporting of European issues.'

Lord Leveson's inquiry heard about the lies in anti-European papers. British papers had published statements that the EU or Brussels was proposing to ban:

- Scottish kilts
- curries
- mushy peas
- newspapers being delivered to houses
- Caerphilly cheese
- charity shops
- bulldogs
- bent sausages and cucumbers
- the British Army
- lollipop ladies
- British loaves
- British-made lavatories
- the royal crest on a passport
- lorry drivers who wear glasses.

Alistair Campbell was Tony Blair's press officer and no special friend of Europe. Indeed as Europe minister, I found it tiresome listening to this intelligent man, who speaks French and German, repeating all the boring prejudices of the British against Europe. But even he confessed his amazement at the litany of lies that poured out about the EU from the media. In his evidence to the Leveson inquiry, Campbell declared:

> If the Eurosceptic press is to be believed, Britain is going to be forced to unite as a single country with France, Church schools are being forced to hire atheist teachers, Scotch whisky is being classified as an inflammable liquid, British soldiers must take orders in French, the price of chips is being raised by Brussels, Europe is insisting on one size fits all condoms, new laws are being proposed on how to climb a ladder, it will be a

criminal offence to criticise Europe, Number 10 must fly the European flag, and finally, Europe is brainwashing our children with pro-European propaganda! Of the UK press and the European institutions – I speak as something of a Eurosceptic by Blairite standards – it is clear who does more brainwashing. Some of the examples may appear trivial, comic even. But there is a serious point: that once some of our newspapers decide to campaign on a certain issue, they do so with scant regard for fact. These stories are written by reporters, rewritten by subs, and edited by editors who frankly must know them to be untrue. This goes beyond the fusion of news and comment, to the area of invention.

Leveson's findings were damning when he stated that newspapers are entitled to be Eurosceptic but they shouldn't make up nonsense about Europe and report it as fact. Lord Levenson went on: 'There can be no objection to agenda journalism (which necessarily involves the fusion of fact and comment) but that cannot trump a requirement to report stories accurately. Clause 1 of the [British] Editors' Code explicitly, and in my view rightly, recognizes the right of a free press to be partial; strong, even very strong opinions can legitimately influence the choice of story, placement of story and angle from which a story is reported. But that must not lead to fabrication, or deliberate or careless misrepresentation of the facts.'

The British love a drink, for example. They buy loads of beer, wine and other alcohol from supermarkets and small shops which are allowed to sell alcohol. What greater threat to British happiness could there be than the lie that the EU was about to close down access to supermarkets except at weekends and force up the price of beer and wine. Here are two stories. Both are lies but printed as fact in two of the most popular, bestselling daily newspapers:

Sun, 21 February 2005

EU health chiefs are drawing up plans to close thousands of British off-licences. [...] The proposal is said to be part of a drive to curb alcohol abuse across Europe. Other measures include a Monday to Friday ban on off-sales and huge booze price hikes through tax rises. A blueprint masterminded by EU health Commissioner Markos Kyprianou also contains moves to control sales through a state-run monopoly.

Daily Star, 21 February 2005

Supermarkets and off-licences will only be allowed to sell booze at weekends under secret plans by barmy Brussels bureaucrats. A leaked document reveals EU chiefs want to ban take-away sales of alcohol from Monday–Friday in an over-the-top clampdown on binge drinking. They also plan to raise the tax on drink sold in pubs.

From beer to bread. In October 1997, the *Daily Mail* told its readers that Brussels was about to abolish the British loaf. The paper wrote: 'Brussels bureaucrats are planning the end of the traditional standard loaf. Under current Weights and Measures laws, standard loaves should weigh either 400 or 800 grams.' Again this was a complete myth, as the briefest visit to the shelves of supermarkets where bread of every size and shape is on sale would show. The editor of the *Daily Mail* would have known that the story was nonsense, but such was and is the obsession of the paper in creating fears about Europe the lie was published anyway.

All the popular British tabloids told readers in September 1994 that Brussels was going to ban curved or small bananas. Again a lie. In response to requests from the banana trade business and the Council of Ministers the Commission proposed some quality standards so that consumers would know what kind of bananas they were buying. But the myth entered British consciousness that Brussels wanted only straight bananas to be sold. It would take a whole book to list all the myths and half-truths in British newspapers about Europe.

It is, however, possible to trace a starting point. The arrival of Boris Johnson as the Brussels correspondent of the *Daily Telegraph* in 1989, a year after Mrs Thatcher's Bruges speech, was the moment when telling lies about Europe became official British newspaper policy. The *Daily Telegraph* was also in foreign ownership and was on the eve of becoming the cheerleader for crude anti-European ideology. Boris Johnson had taken the road to be a journalist in Brussels after being fired from *The Times*, which had hired him as a brilliant young Oxford graduate. Working in the media – newspapers, television, public relations – is a classic start for elite British young men and women who want to go into politics. British politics likes its stars young. Churchill, Blair and Cameron were all noted young future political leaders in their twenties and all worked in the media as they waited to enter the Commons.

Boris Johnson, however, had a small problem. He had been fired from *The Times* for inventing quotations and attributing them to a professor at Oxford who had trusted Johnson. The poor professor was publicly ridiculed after Johnson put words into his mouth that were never said. When Johnson arrived in Brussels his first story sent to the *Daily Telegraph* was that the symbol of European governance, the Berlaymont building in Brussels, was going to be blown up. All that had been announced was that Berlaymont, where asbestos was found, would be evacuated while the asbestos problem was treated. But for Johnson the idea of telling his readers that the symbol of the Brussels system was going to be blown to smithereens was too exciting to be defused by the facts.

Other British reporters who worked in Brussels at the time like Rory Watson, the highly respected Press Association correspondent, say Johnson 'made-up stories', or like David Usborne of the *Independent* say that Johnson 'was fundamentally intellectually dishonest'. Johnson's Old Etonian contemporary, James Landale, now a senior BBC political editor, was a Brussels reporter at the same time as Boris and went into verse about Boris the journalist:

> Boris told such dreadful lies
> It made one gasp and stretch one's eyes.

These accusations against the man who invented Eurosceptic news reporting come from Johnson's fellow Conservatives or Old Etonians, it should be noted, not from the left. Boris Johnson was described by Conrad Black, the owner of the *Spectator*, which Johnson edited as a platform for hyperbolic anti-EU propaganda, as 'ineffably duplicitous'. In even stronger language the right-wing commentator and historian Simon Heffer called Johnson a 'proven liar'. Charles Grant was *The Economist*'s correspondent in Brussels and records how a Johnson story was the front-page 'exclusive' on his paper. Johnson 'reported that Delors wanted to scrap the rotation of the EU presidency and to centralize power in Brussels. The member states would lose their remaining veto rights.' This was simply untrue. The *Sunday Telegraph* front-page headline was 'Delors Plan to Rule Europe'. When a paper indulges in such fantasy the chances of citizens knowing the truth fly out of the window.

Boris Johnson is a charming, witty companion and every exchange I have had with him on Europe has been punctuated by such exaggerations and jokes that it is impossible to dislike the man. If Johnson was simply an entertainer, a comedian, it would not matter. No one, it is argued, believed his fables and myths about the terrible things Brussels was doing or planning to do to Britain. These invented tales were just political comedy and Boris Johnson should be seen as a Eurosceptic music-hall comedian, not as a journalist with some categorical duty to follow the first rule of the profession, which is to tell the truth and to make clear what are facts and what are opinions and beliefs.

Yet this is too glib. The plain fact is that Boris Johnson made up stories and told half- or quarter-truths about Europe, if not downright fibs. He had an elite education, a classical training and has a real understanding of Greek and Roman history and literature. Johnson has foresaken the forensic truth seeking of a Cicero and became a Plautus, a writer of comedies best known for always seeking to titillate and arouse the audience. But he was just the most entertaining liar in a *galère* of journalists that in the last two decades had helped create a climate of scorn and contempt for Europe that serves darker political purposes.

Boris Johnson and the other editors who for more than two decades have published myths, lies and propaganda about Europe could only have acted thus if they had the blessing of their proprietors. In the 1970s, Rupert Murdoch's papers were reasonably honest about Europe and supported the Yes vote in the 1975 referendum. Why and when did he change? His latest biographer, David McKnight, is a fellow Australian who published a penetrating biography and political analysis of Murdoch in 2012. According to McKnight:

> The key to Murdoch's line on Europe is not hostility to EU so much as blind pro-Americanism. One of the consistent themes in the political line which he encouraged on the *Times* was that he saw the EU as a rival to the US. He bitterly opposed those Conservatives who wanted Britain to have a degree of independence and some critical distance from the US.

Professor McKnight's analysis rings true. It explains why Conrad Black, the neo-conservative Canadian admirer of Ronald Reagan and George W. Bush, who became owner of the *Daily Telegraph* as well as the *Spectator*, which has the biggest circulation of any political weekly in Britain, was also anti-European. Black appointed Boris Johnson editor of the *Spectator* to ensure that Britain's most virulent but very clever anti-European propagandist was at the centre of the London press hostility against the EU.

For more than two decades the poor EU Commission Office in London has tried to set the record straight with news communiqués or letters to the editor. It is all in vain. Telling lies about Europe has been fully integrated into public and political discourse. If it is in a newspaper, it is fact. The professional organizations meant to have some oversight of editors' and journalists' ethics in Britain have never bothered to rebuke the lies about Europe or insist on some relationship to truth in reports.

Each country organizes its school teaching and examinations differently. France has its *baccalauréat*, Germany its *Abitur* school-leaving examination and in Britain the end-of-school examinations before

going to university are called A-levels (Advanced Level examinations). Of course a reasonable ambition is to create diplomas or
qualifications that are recognized in different countries. But a discussion paper produced in 2000 was turned by the Europhobe *Sunday
Express* newspaper into this headline. 'Britain's A-levels and university degrees could be axed in an EU plan to harmonise schools and
teaching. They would be replaced by European-style diplomas.' This
was untrue but would worry any British teacher or school adminis-
trator who believed the lie and became concerned that the whole system and structure of examination was to be abolished on the orders
of Brussels.

Occasionally, a British journalist will tell the truth. Charles
Bremner is the long-serving correspondent of *The Times* in Paris and
now the paper's Europe editor. In a remarkably honest column for
his paper in March 2013 he lifted the curtain on how the British
media covers Europe.

> Playing fast and loose with the reality of the EU is a tradition
> across broader sections of media that do not so happily bend
> facts with the domestic scene.

Take a couple of fresh examples.

(1) The Commission suggested earlier this month that all EU
states align their polling days for the European Parliament
elections so that voters do not already have the results from
some countries when they cast their ballots. It was an old idea
and just a proposal to national governments. For part of the
UK media, though, the story ran along the lines of 'Brussels'
dictating voting rules in member states.

(2) This one is typical of the fact-twisting that is so easily committed with the EU's complicated decision-making. The
Commission asked for an 11.2 billion euro top-up to this
year's EU budget. The move, signalled in advance, is part of
manoeuvring over the EU's new long-term budget between

the Parliament and the member states. There is no chance that the states will agree to cough up the Commission's suggested figure. Britain and its northern allies told it that they were opposed, though some smaller increase will undoubtedly emerge from a compromise with the Parliament. Yet much of the British public heard that the 'EU' was 'defying David Cameron' and telling Britain to pay billions more.

The *Express* version was amusing. 'The European Commission's snub to the Prime Minister means that UK taxpayers will now have to pay another £1.2 billion – more than £340 a household.' The *Mail* stated that the Commission threatened to veto the EU's long-term budget if Britain did not go along with its demand. That is nonsense. The Brussels executive body does not even have a vote on the matter, which is in the hands of the member states and the Parliament. But who cares about the detail (neither of those papers, by the way, has a Brussels correspondent). One more serious newspaper reported that 'The European Union has defied Britain's attempts to control its spending'. That is not true because the Commission is not the European Union. It is a service that proposes and administers policies decided by the governments and Parliament.

There are plenty of reasons for all this. The media of all nations play to their public's view of the world. Good mileage is guaranteed by indulging in caricature. Simplifying it, 'Brussels' is a foreign, power-hungry machine that schemes against an honest but gullible and defenceless Britain.

With a few exceptions such as the early Blair era, British governments have been on the defensive on Europe. With media waiting to pounce, they have preferred the us-against-them game to explaining an unpopular cause.

The failings of Europe and antipathy towards the 'European project' are no excuse for its misrepresentation. It's our job in the media to focus on what does not work but we should act straight with a system that has created not just the world's biggest open market but has in recent years anchored former Soviet bloc and poorer southeastern states into the democratic continent.

It is worth quoting Charles Bremner at length because rarely does a senior journalist reveal the truth about how London editors twist the news about Europe. Just as Bremner was writing his admonition, the front page of the *Daily Express* headlined in giant type: 'EU BRAINWASH FOR OUR CHILDREN'. This was about a modest, unimportant guide to Europe that was available to schools if teachers wanted to use it. Before 1939, the *Daily Express* famously told its readers that there would be no war with Germany. Today the paper is permanently at war with the EU and misleads its readers as much as the prewar editors. A British member of the European Parliament, Catherine Bearder, recalls newspaper stories that said the EU would force Britain to have busts of Jacques Delors on motorway bridges, or display the EU badge on England football shirts. She, like many pro-Europeans in Britain, is hardened to the non-stop propaganda against Europe. She notes that she is contacted by Eurosceptic voters who 'point out it is insulting to suggest they are taken in by tabloid tales about the EU. On this we agree: We need honest reporting of the EU. That means journalists going to the European Commission for clarification and comment, which is frequently omitted at the moment despite calls to Brussels press offices being within the budgets of most national or indeed local newspapers.'

When he gave evidence to the Leveson inquiry into the operations of British newspapers, Tony Blair defended the right of newspapers to take a line:

> Those papers who are Eurosceptic are perfectly entitled to be Eurosceptic. They're perfectly entitled to highlight things in Europe that are wrong. What they shouldn't do is, frankly, make up a whole lot of nonsense about Europe and dish that up to the readers, because that's – I mean, how does the reader know that's not correct?

The Leveson inquiry's main focus was not on how the press covered Europe, but so blatant was the abuse of press power by proprietors and by editors who could only keep their jobs if they lied about Europe that Sir Brian Leveson was obliged to issue this rebuke: 'The press have a responsibility to ensure that the public are accurately informed so that they can engage in the democratic process. The evidence of inaccurate and misleading reporting on political issues is therefore of concern.' In Britain there are very few mechanisms to ensure correction of inaccurate reporting is published.

The only mechanism for correcting untruths in the British press is a committee set up and controlled by editors themselves. The biggest-circulation serious papers and tabloids – the *Daily Mail*, the *Sun*, the *Daily Telegraph*, the *Daily Express*, *The Times* and the *Daily Star*, whose combined readership is over 15 million – have been engaged in a 20-year propaganda campaign against Europe. The left-wing *Guardian* is more nuanced, and the *Guardian's* current European editor in Brussels, Ian Traynor, is painstaking and honest as he seeks to be accurate even in reports that criticize the EU. But the *Guardian's* coverage of the euro has been consistently hostile, with the paper's economics editor, who controls how the *Guardian* covers the single currency, even sitting on a committee set up to oppose Britain joining the euro. His journalistic impartiality sits uneasily with political participation in a movement opposed to the euro and he has never missed an opportunity to tell *Guardian* readers that the single currency cannot and will not work.

Britain has the *Financial Times*, the gazette of global business. The *FT* cannot afford to be anything other than scrupulously accurate about the EU. Its comment pages are open to pro-Europeans and anti-Europeans alike. Sadly, however, the *Financial Times*, by far Britain's best paper, is a minority sport. At £2.50 it is too expensive for ordinary citizens to buy and in many places where newspapers are sold outside of London there is no *Financial Times* on sale. The *Independent* has always been a pro-European paper but it has no correspondent in Brussels as its circulation and income has got smaller and smaller. It now depends on the generosity of its

Russian oligarch owner to stay alive. Britain has no tradition of mass circulation weekly journals like *Nouvel Observateur* (now renamed *L'Obs*), *Der Spiegel* or *Time*. Their equivalents would be the separately edited Sunday newspapers but these mirror the same prejudice as their daily brothers and offer the reader little respite from the anti-European propaganda demanded by offshore proprietors.

The BBC, of course, is required to be more impartial and in its news bulletin reports it avoids propaganda. But its journalists work in the same culture of cynicism and scorn for the EU. The BBC political editor, Nick Robinson, has never managed to disguise his contempt for the EU, while the flagship BBC Radio 4 *Today* programme seems to take its editorial line on Europe directly from the *Daily Mail* and the *Spectator*. Another key BBC politics presenter, Andrew Neil, is resolutely Eurosceptic. The BBC has never seen itself having any duty to expose the lies of the Europhobes. It will allow a pro-European some space, but the BBC's phone-in news programmes or programmes where audiences ask politicians questions always seem to be filled with anti-European fanatics with no balance to ensure that the neutral viewer or listener gets a fair account of a European issue. BBC grandees and those who opine on BBC news reporting tend to live in London and reflect what they see or hear on flagship television and radio news and current affairs. But BBC local radio is important and widely listened to. Its phone-ins, which are the cheapest form of programming, are overwhelmed by anti-EU comments inspired by what participants read in the tabloids. Few if any of the BBC phone-in presenters have the knowledge on how the EU actually operates to check or challenge this prejudice.

The BBC has turned the anti-European Nigel Farage into a national hero by giving him weekly appearances on the most-viewed television programmes to denounce and denigrate everything in Europe and call incessantly for a referendum to vote Britain out of Europe. Mr Farage's and his party's appeal is principally on the single issue of quitting Europe, though Ukip MEPs make unpleasant, often sexist and sometimes xenophobic and anti-Muslim (despite having one Muslim MEP) remarks about foreigners living and working in Britain. Certainly at the European Parliament elections, which more and more are the occasion for protest votes about Britain's EU membership, Mr Farage scores well. He is a direct speaker who insults everyone and livens up programmes, to the delight of editors, But nowhere else in Europe would someone who had never been elected to a national post, whose party has no programme of government or little policy to offer the people beyond the single issue of quitting Europe be given the kind of respectful treatment and enormous coverage that the BBC gives Mr Farage.

As Charles Bremner, *The Times* Paris and Europe correspondent, sadly notes:

> It's impossible to write a news story about the EU that's not negative anywhere these days. Things were already pretty much that way when I was *The Times* Brussels correspondent in the late-90s. What always strikes me is how the standard pitch casts the UK as a frail virgin who is always being ravished by dastardly continentals. If only the Brussels crowd were half as clever as the pantomime version makes out.

Lord Beaverbrook, the great newspaper proprietor of the first half of the twentieth century, candidly admitted, 'I run the paper [the *Daily Express*] for the purpose of making propaganda and with no other motive.' For more than two decades his successors have run a non-stop propaganda war against the EU via the papers they own. If Britain does quit Europe, Mr Murdoch and the other anti-EU proprietors will have won their biggest victory.

Occasionally an alarmed reader tries to protest about the biased coverage of Europe. *Daily Mail* reader Jon Danzig protested early in 2014 about what he said was 'the *Daily Mail*'s entirely inaccurate story with the headline, "Sold out! Flights and buses full as Romanians and Bulgarians head for the UK"'. Mr Danzig complained to the Press Complaints Commission (PCC), the discredited body paid for by newspaper proprietors that was meant to defend the public against inaccurate and mendacious newspaper reporting. In this case the PCC upheld Mr Danzig's complaint that the *Daily Mail* had breached the PCC Editors' Code on Accuracy. But the PCC has not compelled the newspaper to make a proper correction and to admit in public that they broke the Editors' Code. The PCC will not publish their ruling, and according to Mr Danzig, 'The *Daily Mail's* so-called "corrections" on this issue have been small and obscurely tucked away; they make no reference to my complaint; do not explain the context of the corrections and the reasons for them; do not state that the paper broke the Editors' Code, and do not even have to refer to the PCC ruling. If this is the only consequence for sloppy, incorrect, alarmist and often xenophobic journalism, nothing is ever going to change, is it?'

Mr Danzig speaks for everyone in Britain who dreams about journalists reporting any aspect of EU affairs with the same care for facts as they do about, say, Britain's membership of NATO.

14

HOW THE EUROZONE HAS MARGINALIZED BRITAIN

Friday, 19 January 2001: UK–France Colloque, Versailles

The star turn was Gordon Brown. He had come down in a train from Brussels to Paris with Laurent Fabius. There had been an Ecofin meeting and clearly during the train journey Fabius had worked as much charm as possible. He spoke first before the dinner. His speech was full of praise at what Brown had accomplished in turning round the UK economy and offering leadership in Europe. He flicked into English at the end and with a charming French accent said, 'Dear Gordon, we want Britain and we want you to be at the heart of Europe. Please, that means that Britain will have to join the Euro.'

But the surprise of the evening was Gordon's warm response to Fabius. Unfortunately he couldn't pronounce his name. He kept referring to 'Lorrenne' as if the former French Prime Minister, now Finance Minister, had the same first name as the American film star Lauren Bacall. But he was warm in his enthusiasm for the single currency. 'We want to see the single currency succeed. We think it makes sense. We see no constitutional or political reasons not to join. The economic tests remain but we expect it to succeed and we want to be in it.'

The problem of monetary stability in Europe has been at the heart of so many European tragedies and dilemmas in the past century. The creation of the single currency has been seen by many in Britain, including many pro-Europeans, as a step too far. The Eurozone's difficulties and lack of growth have confirmed those concerns. It is not that the existence of the euro is the main cause for the drift to Brexit, but the recurring crises linked to the single currency, especially since the crash of 2008, has done nothing to encourage pro-EU commitment in Britain.

Ninety years ago France's prime minister, Raymond Poincaré, denounced the frivolity of monetary policy across the Rhine in Weimar Germany. 'Germany', he thundered in 1923, 'has realised no reforms. Germany has made no effort to stop the worsening of its financial, economic and monetary situation. [...] The indefinite depreciation of the mark, the incessant increase in the cost of living, the economic and financial disorder are such that this can lead Germany, from one day to the next into catastrophes of the most lamentable kind.'

Today it is the turn of Germans to lecture wayward European countries, especially France, on their inappropriate budgets and lax fiscal policy based on borrowing and not controlling public expenditure. Thus the wheel of history turns. Yet the search for monetary stability in Europe culminating in the creation of the euro has been at the heart of European construction. And it is a process, of course, that Britain has always shunned. The love affair of the British with their currency is hardly sustained by economic history. Twice postwar Labour governments were forced to devalue the pound against the dollar. In 1949 and 1967, these devaluations were seen as national humiliations highlighting Britain's slow decline into a second-rate power. The end of the Bretton Woods system and the lifting of all capital controls at the beginning of the era of globalization removed the need for countries to indulge in formal devaluations that had done damage to the reputation for economic competence of the two Labour prime ministers, Clement Attlee and Harold Wilson.

Since 2007, the British pound has been seen as weak and at times has come to start trading dangerously close to parity with the euro. It revived in 2014, but when the UK stops printing money, increasing deficit spending or stoking a housing bubble, what will happen to the national currency? Of course the pound's rate against the euro, the dollar or other world currencies will alter, and the pound remains an important currency for speculators who can no longer speculate against all the different European currencies that preceded the euro. By the summer of 2014, blue-chip British exporters were complaining that the high value of the pound meant their profits were being seriously reduced. In the 1950s and 1960s, under the Bretton Woods system there was relative stability between currencies whose value in the world market was decided both by the innate economic strength of the country, the sense that its budgets were well managed and ultimately by a formal decision of the government to maintain the exchange rate or move it up or down.

This era of stability came to an end in 1971 when President Nixon decided to abolish the Bretton Woods system and let the dollar float freely. He wanted both guns and butter – to run a hugely costly war in Vietnam while at the same time promoting domestic harmony by putting money into the economy, increasing the minimum wage and looking benignly on American trade union negotiations with industrial employers in the automobile and steel industries.

One of the reasons General de Gaulle refused British entry when the British prime minister, Harold Macmillan, sought to join the Common Market in 1961 was that the weakening of sterling and Britain's lack of budget discipline – compared to de Gaulle's strong franc policy – meant in de Gaulle's eyes that Britain was not strong enough in terms of its currency and finances to join the six founding members of the EEC. De Gaulle told the French cabinet that Macmillan was 'this poor man, to whom I had nothing to give'. De Gaulle toyed with the fantasy of returning the world to a gold standard in the 1960s, but his death and the looming disintegration under Nixon's dollar egoism launched Europe on its hunt for monetary stability.

In 1970, Luxembourg's prime minister, Pierre Werner, produced the first serious examination of economic and monetary union. By then, France's President Pompidou and the social democratic team of Willy Brandt and Helmut Schmidt in power in Germany were looking to expand the original six EEC members to include Britain. The Anglophile Helmut Schmidt never made any secret of his wish to include the more liberal and trade-focused British economy. The Werner report produced various recommendations, which put into play the process that within a quarter of a century was to lead to the creation of the euro.

These first stirrings of economic and monetary union coincided with the arrival of the pro-European Edward Heath as prime minister in 1970. His finance minister, Tony Barber, spent the war years in captivity after being shot down as an RAF fighter pilot. He was thus of the generation in Britain determined that new arrangements were necessary to ensure Europe never again reverted to the nationalisms that led to war. He told France's then finance minister, Valéry Giscard d'Estaing, that Britain was ready to 'join in any arrangements for linking the currencies of the community more closely together [and] would be willing to move as far and fast as the rest of the community'. There was more British support for monetary union from Roy Jenkins, who became president of the European Commission in 1976. A former chancellor and leader of the pro-European wing of the Labour Party, Jenkins initiated work by the Commission to draw up plans for what became the European Monetary System. He was aided by two former finance ministers by then running France and Germany. Valéry Giscard d'Estaing and Helmut Schmidt spoke together in English as they worked in parallel with the British president of the Commission, to lay the first foundations for monetary integration.

Across the Channel, however, London was less than enthusiastic. Officials at the Treasury had always opposed monetary union. It was alien to their belief that having the pound sterling as an independent currency with the supposed virtues of flexibility and the power to set interest rates held firmly in the hands of national governments was a *sine qua non* for sound financial administration.

There was absolutely no self-awareness at the Treasury that their system of running the British economy since 1950 had coincided with a serious decline in Britain's economic standing. Treasury officials routinely moved across to work for banks, although there was no direct corruption in the sense of bribes paid to obtain government decisions in monetary, investment or currency policy. Instead there was a cosy little self-referring world of central bankers, finance ministry senior officials and the City which rejected the idea of working collaboratively and accepting some pooling of authority by setting up a European monetary union.

Denis Healey, Labour's Chancellor of the Exchequer between 1974 and 1979, was suspicious of European integration. He said that combining the pound sterling with continental currencies did not correspond to Britain's outlook on the world. Healey argued:

> Europe did not come first in our international league table. America came first economically, politically and defence-wise – it was infinitely more important than our relationship with Europe, that was the fundamental reason why Britain did not join the EMS; it was still a more important argument than the issue of the rigidities of the EMS and whether we would be locking ourselves into the wrong exchange rate.

James Callaghan, the British prime minister, also spoke to US president Jimmy Carter and asked him to try and discourage his colleagues in the newly created G7 group from going ahead with the European Monetary Exchange Rate System.

As in 1950, France and Germany ignored the vapourings of the British politicians and moved ahead to create what within a few years was a coherent and working system of linking European currencies so there were no sudden movements thus reducing the possibilities of speculative attacks against them. President Mitterrand's decision in 1983 to turn away from the cause of his left-wing protectionist ministers and instead move in the direction of European integration marked by the Single European Act two years later created the terrain of monetary stability that allowed the euro in due course to be born. The French franc and German mark seemed already by the middle of the 1980s to be the same currency. They never varied by a centime or a pfennig.

By contrast, the British pound was like one of the stalls at a fun-fair with balls on jets of water bouncing up and down as people try and shoot them off. One day the pound was strong and buying 13 francs and a few months later it was weak and buying only eight. For some this yo-yo performance of the pound sterling under Mrs Thatcher seemed bizarre economic management. However, many British people enjoyed the yo-yo pound's ups and downs. If the pound was strong they would buy holiday apartments in Majorca or Florida or a gîte in the Dordogne. If the pound was weak, well one just went on holiday inside Britain and used the weak pound to boost exports.

Under Mrs Thatcher, who removed all capital controls, the pound became just another commodity whose value should be decided by the decisions of speculators sitting in front of their screens. The so-called Big Bang in the City which turned London into the world centre of casino capitalism meant huge fortunes could be made on trading – or betting on – currencies, including the pound. The attempts on the continent to bring in monetary stability were seen as old-fashioned and not particularly relevant. Not all policy makers shared this light, almost flippant view of the value of constantly moving exchange rates. Inflation remained a persistent problem in the UK, and at the end of the 1980s Mrs Thatcher's two key lieutenants, her chancellor, Nigel Lawson, and her foreign minister, Sir Geoffrey Howe, both orthodox liberals in economic terms, decided that one way of bringing inflation under some control was indeed to seek more stability for the pound. They had realized that any weakening of sterling as a world currency immediately increased prices for all the raw materials, goods and food that Britain had to import.

The two men argued Britain should enter the Exchange Rate Mechanism (ERM) and insisted to Prime Minister Thatcher that this should become government policy. Thus the UK entered the ERM in October 1990. But far from this process moving Britain towards a more sympathetic position on European monetary integration, the reverse took place. A political crisis broke out that in a matter of months ended Mrs Thatcher's premiership and destroyed the reputation of her successor. Monetary union and the move towards the euro – seen as the logical next steps of European integration and a necessary corollary of the single market – became defining political issues in Britain in a fashion that happened nowhere else. The turbulent two years in the ERM turned many in Britain permanently against the single currency in a way that hasn't changed in the intervening two decades.

Britain's entry into the ERM turned out to be a major mistake. In 1950 and 1957, Britain had not been present to help write the first two chapters of European construction. Britain had turned its back on the early efforts at stabilizing Europe's currencies. Now, late in the day, Britain embraced ERM but entered in the wrong way, at the wrong time, at the wrong exchange rate. This quickly became clear after Mrs Thatcher fell from office and was replaced by her Conservative successor John Major. He was suddenly propelled into Number 10 as the candidate who had made the fewest enemies when the time came to choose a successor to Mrs Thatcher. He went along helplessly with the advice of British state functionaries, who as so often confused their technical expertise with the real-time politics of operating in Europe. Mr Major narrowly won a fourth consecutive Conservative victory in 1992 but found that the rising tone of hostility to Europe emanating from the deposed but still vocal Mrs Thatcher was infecting his entire party.

Sensing the arrival of the euro, global speculators sought to make as much money as possible by trading different currencies. George Soros bet heavily against the British pound. In a forerunner of crises affecting Greece and Cyprus and southern European states the British government begged for help from Germany. But Chancellor

Kohl and his finance minister, who were looking with horror at the mounting cost of the unification of Germany, were in no mood to help the increasingly Eurosceptic British. Interest rates in London in the autumn of 1992 had to be raised to 15 per cent to try and defend the pound.

The result was that the pound was forced to leave the ERM in what was a complete humiliation for the new government, which was also trying to persuade its increasing cohort of anti-European MPs loyally to endorse the Maastricht Treaty in the House of Commons. The day Britain was forced to leave the ERM became known as Black Wednesday. Norman Lamont was forced to resign as Chancellor of the Exchequer and never again held office. The abrupt termination of his political career because of Europe has turned him into a prominent Eurosceptic. After a decade of aggressive, self-confident economic policy from Mrs Thatcher here was a British government utterly unable to control its economic destiny and humiliated in the eyes of its own citizens and the world because of its participation in a European project.

The debacle of the ERM expulsion changed British politics. The Conservatives became even more suspicious about any form of monetary union or any attempt to fix exchange rates. The Labour Party, in the form of its hitherto Europhile finance spokesman, Gordon Brown, who at the time was seen as the pro-European leader of the next generation of Labour leaders, decided that merging the pound sterling with other European currencies was a risk too far. So Britain stayed out of any plans that Paris, Berlin and Brussels had to create a single currency. The pound sterling was also fluctuating from its immediate market-driven devaluation after leaving ERM, when it sank very low, followed by a gradual and then rapid strengthening as the British economy picked up in the mid-1990s.

When Tony Blair entered power in May 1997 the pound was again extremely strong. The over-valued pound was one barrier to euro entry, but, as we have seen, far more important was Blair's promise of a referendum on euro entry. The currency was successfully introduced first as the accounting unit for member states in

1999, with all national bank notes and coins being replaced by euros at the beginning of 2002. However, few in political life in Germany or France believe that had a condition for abolishing the German mark or the French franc been approval in a referendum there would have been a Yes vote. This is especially true in Germany, where no one believed then or believes now that a referendum to replace the German mark by the euro could ever have been won.

Thus the poison pill of the plebiscite stayed Blair's hand. The idea of organizing a referendum to say Yes to the euro never seemed remotely possible politics. Predictably Gordon Brown, who had become less and less enchanted with Europe and more and more anxious to keep Rupert Murdoch and the other offshore newspaper owners on his side as he began manoeuvring to replace Blair as prime minister, produced a report that said the time wasn't right for Britain to join the euro. The divisions over the Iraq conflict and later the French and Dutch No to the European Constitution reduced still further any hope that Britain would join the euro, and the question of the UK's entry into the euro faded away as possible politics. In 2005, the new Conservative leader, David Cameron, said that Britain would never join the euro. Labour politicians were careful to avoid using the word 'never' and would say that Labour was ruling out the euro in the lifetime of the next Parliament. By the time Labour went into opposition, the party's opposition to the euro had grown.

Sunday, 6 June 2012

> *I look at the papers and there is a disgusting piece by Ed Balls about immigrants. Real ugly populist rubbish with a boast about keeping Britain out of the euro thrown in for good measure.*

Ed Miliband, the current Labour leader, has had to make concessions to the growing hostility to Europe in Britain. He criticized the decision to allow citizens from new EU member states to work in Britain. In January 2013 he told the BBC, 'Britain is not going to be joining the euro and it won't be joining the euro if I am prime minister'.

In April 2013, Britain produced a new design for its £5 note. It bore the picture of Winston Churchill and all saw the symbolism of attaching Britain's greatest prime minister to the national currency. Most of the public and all MPs accept that the pound is not going to be replaced by the euro.

The crisis that exploded with the collapse of banks in 2008 made matters worse. Gordon Brown had had a bust of Alan Greenspan, champion of neoliberal deregulation of banks and chairman of the American Federal Reserve, installed in the Treasury, where it can still be seen. Greenspan had presided over the anti-regulation ideology which helped create the 2008 crash. The British financial world, including its nominal political chiefs in government as well as the functionaries at the Treasury, gradually gave up believing that banks should be required to show any responsibility or have adequate capital reserves. The years of deregulated speculation turned global banking into an activity which would not even have been permitted in the casinos of Las Vegas.

The fools' gold of banking bonuses and high incomes for employees in the City of London were allowed to develop to the point of destruction by Labour ministers. Both Gordon Brown and his chancellor, Alistair Darling, were from Edinburgh and returned to the Scottish capital for constituency duties and to be back among family and friends. They seemed unaware that the Edinburgh bank, the Royal Bank of Scotland (RBS), Britain's biggest, was technically insolvent by the end of 2007 on account of its exposure to the pyramid schemes of sub-prime mortgage lending which the bank gambled on heavily in the United States. They claim to have been surprised by the collapse of the bank in autumn 2008 and the consequent transfer of billions of pounds of public money. About 10 per cent of national wealth had to be transferred to RBS and other UK banks to keep them afloat. A few senior bank executives took early retirement, but there has been no real sanction on the sometimes criminal activity which did so much damage to Britain. The after-effects are still a dead weight around the British economy.

The defence of politicians is that no one told them what was going on. But a general has to know what is happening on all his fronts and in all corners of his battlefield and it is never an excuse when defeated to say, 'Oh I wish I had had better intelligence and information'. However, for British Eurosceptics, the main consequence of the banking crisis was to prove to their own eyes that keeping out of the euro was a good idea. They looked with glee at the troubles first of Ireland, then Greece and Portugal or Cyprus, or the difficulties the Spanish and Italian governments faced in borrowing money. Almost without exception the commentators on the economy in the British press as well as most Conservative and not a few Labour MPs blamed all these difficulties on the existence of the euro. The press started using the term 'Grexit' to argue that Greece should exit from the euro as if that was a miracle cure for Greek financial problems.

The refusal of Berlin to offer help to beleaguered southern nations, culminating in the proposed raid on the savings of depositors in banks in Cyprus, also proved to the satisfaction of British Eurosceptics that being in the euro was bad for an economy.

A study by Commerzbank in London in 2013 showed that the devaluation of the pound that began when Gordon Brown became prime minister in 2007 had not led to any increase in British exports. On the contrary, prices of essential services like gas and electricity and mobile phone tariffs were going up because of imported inflation. Foreign direct investment was not coming to Britain despite the low pound, and British investments overseas – for two centuries an important source of income into the country – were also declining because of the weak pound. Nonetheless, the new prime minister, David Cameron, and his Eurosceptic foreign secretary, William Hague, insisted again and again that Britain would never join the euro. What had been a project of possibility 20 years ago when Mrs Thatcher's ministers forced her to enter the ERM had become a politics of rejection of the euro as another, younger Conservative prime minister took power.

The point is not to debate the merits of the single currency, the policy of the European Central Bank and what needs to be done in order to get growth going. It is that the British believe their hostility to the single currency has been confirmed by its recent troubles. Opinion polls in Germany and France still show up to two-thirds of citizens saying they want to keep the euro. In a debate in Athens in February 2012 between me and Professor Nouriel Roubini, the New York professor argued that Greece should leave the euro if the Greeks wanted to recover economic well-being. Twelve hundred people were present to hear a debate broadcast on BBC World Television. Before the debate, 78 per cent of those present said they wanted to keep the euro and did not want to return to the drachma. After the debate and despite Professor Roubini's eloquence the vote in favour of Greece staying in the euro had gone up to 80 per cent. In other words, even in the most troubled of countries no one thought that quitting the euro was an answer.

In contrast, in Britain, public opinion, all the anti-European press and the governing party made clear that they thought the euro was a disaster. The euro remains a contested project, as David Marsh, the currency's historian, has shown. His latest book, *Europe's Deadlock: How the Euro Crisis Could be Solved – and Why It Won't* (2013), marshals the arguments against the euro. But despite the urgings of the London commentators there are few takers in France, Austria, Spain, Italy, Belgium or The Netherlands for a return to francs, schillings, lire, guilders and so on. The euro is here to stay.

Britain's Eurosceptics and the press made much of the launch in Germany of a new political movement, Alternative für Deutschland, which called for a return to the Deutschmark. British commentators enjoyed explaining why France under President Hollande was in a lamentable state. *The Economist*, the organ of the global gospel of economic liberalism, argued that France's economic weakness could bring down the euro. No one in London seemed to have a mirror to look in their own faces as they lectured the rest of the EU on why the euro was a bad project and why a return to francs and D-marks to rejoin the pound in a paradise for money traders and speculators was better for Europe. But the simple fact was that since the euro's launch in 1999, Britain had had no stake in the future of the single currency. Quitting the EU would not mean the upheaval of leaving the euro. Far from the euro acting as a cement to hold Europe together, Britain's politics of sticking to the pound made the possibility of leaving the EU less of an upheaval than would be the case for countries using the euro.

The British press reported with glee the attack by the French Socialist Party on Mrs Merkel and her politics of austerity. Nothing gives British politicians of all colours more pleasure than to see Paris and Berlin at each other's throats. That both France and Germany shared the same currency but were at war over fiscal and economic policy proved to British Eurosceptics that the single currency brought with it no peace, happiness or economic cooperation and coordination. For those wanting to use a referendum to take Britain out of the EU, the single currency and its problems appeared to have become an ally.

15

CAN BRITAIN EVER LEARN TO LOVE EUROPE?

For the British, Europe is about interest, not identity. It is about a balance sheet of advantages and disadvantages. When the new prime minister of Italy, Matteo Renzi, talks about Europe as Italy's destiny and the need for a United States of Europe, the British sip their Scotch and think such language proves that Italian politics after the years of Craxi and Berlusconi has indeed been taken over by talkers, not doers. The most ideological of David Cameron's ministers, Michael Gove, a clever Conservative politician with close links to the Republican right in Washington, told the BBC he would vote to leave the EU if there was a referendum tomorrow. So would Jamie Oliver, the best-known chef in Britain, whose television programmes and books about cooking have made him more famous in Britain than Albert Bocuse in France. They reflect the view that in the balance sheet of future British interests, Europe adds more negatives than positives. This absence of a permanent positive culture in favour of Europe is a major contributor to the growth of Brexit tendencies.

The word 'Europe' for the British covers everything from the European Commission to the European Court of Human Rights, whose judgements delaying British authorities from deporting terrorists have outraged Conservative and Labour politicians alike. Europe is the presence of men and women earning money doing jobs in Britain which do not go to British workers. Europe, for employers who do not like dealing with trade unions, is a list of social rules or, if they have employees on the continent, the obligation to create a European Works Council. Europe, for many on the left, is a liberal capitalist arrangement with a European Court of Justice always upholding the rights of trans-frontier companies to get around existing national arrangements between unions and employers.

Europe is what the people are told it is by their press and many of their leading politicians, both Conservative and Labour, over the four decades of British membership. That vision has been mainly negative, increasingly so in this century. Persuading the British to have warm feelings for Europe is hard. As I have argued in this book, the political and media hostility to 'Brussels' over the past quarter of a century has brought British public opinion to the point where a vote to leave the EU in a referendum is more than possible. But wait a second. The hostility to Europe is not exclusively a British disease. In 2010, Jean-Claude Piris, the wise chief legal adviser to the Council of Ministers, argued in his book, *The Lisbon Treaty: A Legal and Political Analysis*, that:

> The Lisbon Treaty has not corrected the major asymmetries which still characterize the EU's architecture, which might be a factor of instability in the future, in case of stormy weather. The absolute priority should now be to try and improve the EU's democratic legitimacy and its visibility for the citizens, especially through better control by each national parliament over the participation of their government in decisions taken by the EU.

A few years later the crisis of the 'EU's democratic legitimacy' has worsened. The euro crisis and the failure of European leaders, whether national or at EU level, to find a solution has significantly reduced public confidence in Britain in Europe. I sensed this happening as Greece started to become Europe's problem child.

Monday, 22 March 2011

The Greeks are in a dreadful state. Having lived for years without reforming the way they spend public money or even having reasonably open and accurate accounts the international markets have now caught up with them and want huge, savage deficit reduction cuts to take place as quickly as possible. I read a very stupid article in the Guardian *by a Greek professor at London University saying it is all a plot by the northern European capitalist powers against the periphery of Greece, Spain and Portugal. What utter drivel. The Greeks have lied to and cheated themselves as much as to Europe over who gets the money the state raises. Each ministry has its own pay and pension scheme. Some pay a bonus of a 13th month's pay each December but in other ministries 14 months are paid instead of 12 and in the Ministry of Foreign Affairs it is 16½ months. Different ministries have got different arrangements for free travel or cheap mortgages.*

The new PASOK government under George Papandreou doesn't know what to do. It is appealing for European solidarity because Greece is a member of the Euro zone but Greece doesn't play the foreign policy game on Kosovo, or Cyprus, or Macedonia and there is not much sympathy for Greece in northern Europe. Mrs Merkel has become very hard line as she faces a German public opinion that simply isn't prepared to keep on being the banker of Europe especially when the Germans themselves are having to tighten their belts and accept longer working life and lower social expenditure to try and keep the German economy strong.

It is not widely understood beyond the Rhine that while Germany is rich, Germans are not. The extra taxes imposed to pay for reunification or the standstill of wages imposed by Gerhard Schröder to recapitalize German industry mean that average pay in Germany is lower now than in 2000. Indeed, if the share of the national economy going in salaries in 1980 was the same today, German workers would have an extra €180 billion a year in spending power. So when southern Europeans ask German workers to either increase taxes or reduce social spending to provide more money to Greek, Portuguese, Spanish or Italian banks and spendthrift ministers there is a natural resistance from politicians seeking re-election in Germany. Both the German reluctance to pay for others' mistakes and the unwillingness of political elites to undertake deep social democratic reforms that could relaunch the European economy have brought about Europe's lost decade. The euro crisis, as Hugo Dixon and Wolfgang Münchau point out, is sleeping, not over.

The British press have enjoyed portraying Europe plunged into austerity with the massive rejection of traditional political parties who seem unable to respond to the crisis. To be sure, Britain is no exception and has seen an increase in poverty – expressed by the explosion of food banks to help feed the hungry poor and rising inequality – as the government has imposed on Britain many of the measures – public service cuts, wage standstills, reductions in citizen benefits – that the IMF-ECB-Commission troika have imposed on Eurozone members in southern Europe. Britain has dodged some of the pain by printing money and allowing a housing bubble to reflate, as well as leaving debts and deficits higher than required under Eurozone discipline. Britain is also no exception to the rise of populist anti-Brussels demagogy. Other EU member states have seen a sharp rise in opposition to the EU since the Eurozone crisis developed. In Britain the hostility to the EU was already high and now it has got worse. Using Eurobarometer opinion polls, the European Council on Foreign Relations (ECFR) published dramatic figures which show the collapse of faith in EU institutions across Europe both in the richer north and the Eurozone countries that have required bailouts in the south.

As José Ignacio Torreblanco of the ECRF rightly noted: 'The damage is so deep that it does not matter whether you come from a creditor, debtor country, euro would-be member or the UK: everybody is worse off. Citizens now think that their national democracy is being subverted by the way the euro crisis is conducted.' In Britain, half the population distrusted the EU already in 2007, ten

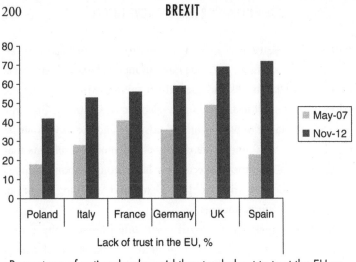

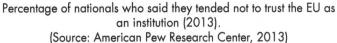

Percentage of nationals who said they tended not to trust the EU as
an institution (2013).
(Source: American Pew Research Center, 2013)

years after the pro-European Tony Blair became prime minister. A poll
published in 2013 by the American Pew Research Center, which does
respected and reliable cross-border estimations of political opinion,
showed that in Britain only 41 per cent had a favourable view of the EU.
In France, the collapse of support for the EU was dramatic. Forty-one
per cent of French people polled were in favour of the EU, compared
to 60 per cent in 2012. So the British case is not an exception. France
may now be where Britain has been for some years. The difference is
that British politics is now organized to turn this loss of confidence in
Europe into an existential question of staying in or leaving the EU.

Just before these dramatic opinion polls were published, José
Manuel Barroso, European Commission president, 2004–14, said
that the European 'dream' was under threat from a 'resurgence of
populism and nationalism' across the EU. 'At a time when so many
Europeans are faced with unemployment, uncertainty and growing
inequality, a sort of "European fatigue" has set in, coupled with a
lack of understanding. Who does what, who decides what, who
controls whom and what? And where are we heading to?'

Obrigado, Sr Barroso, but surely it is the duty of EU leaders to,
well, lead? Is it wise to keep using the word 'dream' as if evoking

the subconscious were to bring people closer to embracing Europe? In 1772, Jean-Jacques Rousseau wrote: 'Today there are no longer the French, the Germans, the Spanish or the English. Despite what is said there are only Europeans.' Rousseau's dream of doing away with the national peoples of Europe and fusing them all into a single European entity is perhaps the worst of the many wrong turnings down false pistes that the makers of Europe have undertaken. Like Francis Fukuyama, they thought there would be no more history or that national stories in the French sense of *histoire* (meaning both story and history) would be over and only Europe had a future. The Europe of conflict and confrontation had been transformed into a Europe of consensus and compromise. But the curse and course of history is that it never ends. The European finality that Joschka Fischer, one of postwar Europe's greatest foreign ministers, pleaded for is an impossible dream.

Europe is a journey, not an end. It is landscape that nature always changes, not finished architecture. Luuk van Middelaar's book *Le passage à l'Europe. Histoire d'un commencement* is both the most lyrical and, given he is Dutch, the most down-to-earth description of the making of Europe since 1945. The English title of van Middelaar's book, published a year later, is slightly different: *The Passage to Europe: How a Continent Became a Union*. Van Middelaar agrees that neither a European finality nor a return to a past and an imagined *Europe des patries* is on offer.

> The current financial crisis represents a new test for the beginnings of certainty enshrined in the treaty. When a storm becomes too fierce and wind blows your ship towards the open sea, it is better to have a good compass than an anchor, better to rely on your sense of direction than on rules. So the euro crisis, like others before it, is forcing the circle of member states to politicise itself, to increase its capacity to act and take responsibility.

He concludes with Hegel's wisdom: 'Amid the pressure of great events, a general principle gives no help. The pallid shades of memory struggle in vain with the life and freedom of the Present.'

In Britain, there is another maxim of Hegel's relevant to our tortured relationship with the rest of Europe's nations, north, south, west and east of the island of Great Britain as well as to the EU. The German philosopher insisted that 'To be independent of public opinion is the first formal condition of achieving anything great'. In Britain, politicians are slaves to public opinion on Europe. Few are willing to challenge the constant negativity in the press or even to question whether men who pay no taxes in Britain should have such power to dictate public opinion. The last big leader on Europe was Margaret Thatcher. She defied opinion polls and the Labour Party in the early 1980s to lead Britain deeper into Europe with the Single European Act. Despite obtaining the British rebate in 1984 she supported a major increase in funding for the European Community budget.

Contrary to the conventional wisdom in Paris that Britain only wants to see Europe enlarging itself with new members, it was Paris, not London which insisted on the early entry of Greece into Europe in 1981 without any control on the clientalist and corrupt nature of Greek politics and state administration. Again it was Mitterrand and not Mrs Thatcher who championed the entry of Spain and Portugal under their socialist leaders, Felipe Gonzalez and Mario Soares, both close to Mitterrand and unknown to Mrs Thatcher.

Germany was the main advocate of Poland and the states with common borders with Germany joining the EU. Both Jacques Chirac and Tony Blair promoted themselves as architects of the opening to France's old friend and Britain's wartime ally, Poland, but in truth it was necessary for Germany's economic future and security needs to surround itself with countries linked in peaceful cooperation under the obligations of the EU treaties.

It may seem strange to say Margaret Thatcher was the last British prime minister who was ready to defy public opinion and support more Europe given how she later became the champion of Euroscepticism, opposed all further integration after she left power and wrote about Britain leaving the European Union in her last book before the shadow of memory loss and decline fell across her. Tony Blair was utterly convinced in his European beliefs. His pro-European sincerity should not be called into question. But he was never willing to challenge public opinion, hiding behind referendums that were never held on the euro or the constitution. His vision of Europe was that of deregulated business, especially in the City of London, even though the more he appeased financiers and the press, the more they attacked the EU.

Euroscepticism, as has been noted, has an appetite that grows with feeding. All citizens should be sceptical about what those in power do. It is the first condition of democracy. However, Euroscepticism is about ideology, not questioning. As John Lloyd and Crista Marconi write in their Reuters Institute report: 'Euroscepticism takes the position that the euro currency, and often the Union itself, are burdens on the nation-state and on national economies, and must be sloughed off.' Complaints about and rejections of EU proposals by Tony Blair and Gordon Brown did not align British public opinion positively with being in the EU. People heard only the criticism and rejection, and politicians found no time to make a positive case. Today, hostility to Europe is far worse and not limited to Britain. As Laurent Joffrin, until recently the editor of France's biggest-selling weekly, the left-wing and Europhile *Nouvel Observateur*, has rightly argued: 'The European Union has got progressively cut off from the people. It is made of anonymous committees run by like-minded technocrats locked away in their ivory towers of certainty and speaking their own private language no one else understands. In most member-states a referendum on Europe would result in an overwhelming No vote.'

The Spanish political philosopher José Ortega y Gasset insisted on the importance of generation in shaping a nation's destiny. As he wrote in *The Modern Theme*:

The changes in vital sensibility which are decisive in history appear under the form of a generation. A generation is not a handful of outstanding men, nor simply a mass of men: it resembles a new integration of the social body, with its select minority and its gross multitude launched upon the orbit of existence with a pre-established vital trajectory. The generation is a dynamic compromise between mass and individual. It is, so to speak, the pivot responsible for the movement of historical evolution.

Britain has never had a European generation. At any given moment since 1945 there have been leaders, sometimes a significant group of opinion-formers and a large number of citizens, either as economic actors, as intellectuals, even as tourists culturally aware of Europe, for whom getting closer to Europe was a worthwhile project. But this never coalesced into a generation that accepted Europe and saw membership of the EU as a source of hope, ambition and desire.

So today Britain is poised to say bye-bye to Europe. Scotland came close to saying bye-bye to England. The England–Scotland union was 307 years old and for most of those years not under serious challenge until Scottish nationalist-separatists turned what might be called Angloscepticism into serious politics. The idea that a union between Britain and Europe that is just four decades old and has been under constant pressure, with many calling for divorce, can easily withstand the populist passions of anti-EU politicians and the press is not persuasive. Mr Cameron is not going drop his call for a referendum and start to make the argument that the European Union of nation-states is worth some investment and support.

Politicians are told never to say never. Yet it is hard to imagine Mr Cameron or any of his generation of Conservatives giving up their Eurosceptic beliefs. In addition, as millions of votes go to anti-European parties, the iron law of politics – 'First get yourself elected' – trumps any wish to find a *modus vivendi* with Europe. In Britain, the politics of the plebiscite have become the politics of

Europe. The British will have to wait for a leader ready to defy public opinion if the nation is to remain fully and wholeheartedly in the EU. Such leaders are rare. None is available today.

Pro-Europeans think that if they get better platforms for their arguments they can turn the tide of Eurosceptic public opinion. European political leaders come to London and say that Brexit would be a disaster for their own country. But the pro-European community and Britain's friends in other European capitals cannot undo the plebiscite promise made by Britain's political leadership. Perhaps a non-Conservative government can avoid a referendum, but at the price of turning the Conservatives in opposition, Ukip voters and the anti-EU media into a braying force-field demanding a referendum over the next years. Europe will dominate the next period of British politics whoever is the next prime minister.

How then can Britain begin to like Europe? A cynical historian told me it was easy. 'Just ensure that Britain had been invaded and occupied in 1940.' That first great impulse to European unity that continued right on to the moment when the world saw a tall German and a short Frenchman holding hands at Verdun in 1984 has always been foreign to Britain. Instead we might look at the time when Europe seemed to make sense to the British. It was above all the time when economic growth was what Europe was good at and which seemed to escape Britain's economic managers. Let there be ten or even five years growth at 3 or more per cent a year in the big Western economies – France, Germany, Italy, and Benelux – and Britain will become more Europe-friendly.

As Jean-Claude Piris argued, restoring or rather finding a role for national parliaments in the definition of European democracy and legislation is worth an effort. The British will never be in love with the European Parliament and will never accept that 700 years of their parliamentary history is on the way out. The answer is not to reject the European Parliament or to pretend that a national parliament alone can debate and decide the economic, social, environmental and international policy of a nation as if neighbours and alternative policies did not exist. As Europe minister I tried without success to argue that national parliaments could stop EU legislation if a number of them held up a red card of opposition. The idea failed to find the support to be included in either the Constitutional or Lisbon Treaty. So why not bring together the Strasbourg assembly and the national assemblies of Europe by creating a Senate consisting of national parliamentarians?

In addition, members of the European parliament could be elected by thirds every two years at the same time as other national elections so that they fully represented the political will of the nations rather than being brought in on a protest vote against the party in national power. A rigorous rule forbidding dual mandates and saying that no national politician can become an MEP within two years of losing an election nationally would stop Strasbourg becoming the place where displaced national politicians are given an income and expenses while they await a return to national politics.

The same should apply to the European Commission, which is now used by former prime ministers and senior national politicians who are out of play in national politics but can get one final period of high pay, chauffeur-driven cars, red-carpet receptions and someone else to write their speeches and articles.

Of course the Commission must be reduced to a size that corresponds more to the cabinets of ministers in most EU member states. If Switzerland, the seventh biggest economy in Europe, can be run by a Federal Council of just seven men and women, why are a further 21 needed to run an EU whose budget is only 1 per cent of Europe's income? David Cameron might have made a stand and a start by refusing to nominate a British Commissioner and challenge other EU governments to do the same. Alas, the prime minister chose a man, a party loyalist with no known interest in Europe.

The new Commission president, Jean-Claude Juncker, has tried to reorganize the Commission into seven clusters of Commissioners, each headed by a vice president, mainly from smaller EU member states. It will be interesting to see if all the Commissioners from big countries like Britain, France and Germany accept supervision or surveillance from other

Commissioners who in theory, and under the treaties, have no right to dictate what they do.

Juncker's reorganization of the Commission was barely noticed in British politics, and he has been given little credit for seeking to meet one of the demands of EU reformers – namely, a more stream-lined Commission.

Free movement of people is a core European freedom. More than 2 million British citizens live and work in other EU member states and would be the first to suffer if free movement of European citizens was reversed. We all enjoy getting on an aeroplane in Britain and going where we like in Europe. If that is our right, it must also be a right for others. But many citizens do feel that the EU equals a loss of control over national borders. Britain is at fault with its refusal to have a system of identity cards and its peculiar national health and social security systems that allow free medical treatment and welfare benefits without any reciprocal responsibil-ity to make some payment. In one of the richest areas of London, Belgravia, two out of five houses or apartments are not lived in. They have been bought for investment purposes by oil-rich sheikhs, Russian oligarchs or Greek ship-owners. As homelessness grows, Europe needs a policy of housing which stops homes being bought as a chip in the casino of modern frontier-free markets but never lived in. Britain could create a proper apprenticeship system and encourage technical education so that firms hired first of all their young trainees before turning to foreigners. The Agency Workers Directive, slowing the supply of cheap, unregulated workers by outside agencies, should be enforced. But stopping a British ski teacher from working in Chamonix is as stupid as sending home all the French citizens working in the City of London. A Europe of national protectionisms would be a disaster.

Europe needs to have a defence profile worthy of its history and desire to influence world affairs. France and Britain are shrinking military nations. They are slowly becoming members of the Euro Defence Club of Germany, Spain, Italy, Denmark or Sweden, where defence spending as a share of GDP is below 2 per cent, sometimes

much lower, just a shade above 1 per cent. According to the
London-based security think-tank IISS, European NATO members'
defence spending in 2012 was, in real terms, around 11 per cent
lower than in 2006.

Both Britain and France will hang on to their nuclear-power status, which gives the entry ticket as permanent members of the UN
Security Council, but the rest of their military spend will allow them
to provide bands and parades for visiting dignitaries or state funerals
but putting an army into the field is now beyond Europe's capability.
The intervention in Libya was only possible because of US reconnais-
sance and intelligence capabilities. President Hollande made much of
his reception in Mali after French soldiers chased out Islamist jihadis
early in 2013, but they have simply gone to the hills or crossed into
Libya to try and capture it as an Islamist state under jihadi control.
When Britain joined the US/French-led attacks on Islamic State in
Iraq the headlines screamed 'Britain at War'. The war consisted of
two ageing fighter-bombers, which were sent over the enemy terrain
but returned to base without dropping any bombs as they could not
find targets. The attacks seemed as pointless as the warship in Joseph
Conrad's *Heart of Darkness*, sporadically firing shells pointlessly into
the jungle. Without greater European integration of defence, especially in terms of arms production, it is hard to see individual EU
nations as major military powers.

The obvious answer would be to Europeanize Europe's defence
and military spending and profile. Europe's combined military
spend is still pretty big, but each nation insists on maintaining its
own fragmented defence industries producing different armoured
vehicles, fighter-planes, rifles, helicopters and naval vessels. Each
country is producing its own drones when a common Eurodrone,
based on the Airbus model of inter-state cooperation, makes
more sense. There was a move in 2012 to merge BAE, Britain's
main defence contractor, and EADS, the European aerospace and
defence giant. But it was torpedoed by German Chancellor Angela

Merkel under pressure from German defence firms who feared competition.

There is no defence lobby of weight left in Europe other than parochial local industries. No one dares question the sacrosanct development budgets even though the military probably contribute more to stability and the possibility of peaceful open market growth than all the armies of development workers. Another suggestion is that defence spending should be excluded from the limit of 3 per cent of GDP for government borrowing – in other words, a form of defence Keynesianism that would be welcome by skilled workers, who see jobs evaporating as politicians raid defence budgets.

At a Franco–British summit in 2003 I observed President Chirac as he turned to the British prime minister and said, 'You know, Tony, there is only one group more conservative than the military and that is the defence industry.' Sadly there is no political leadership around to knock sense into European soldiers and defence firms before it is too late.

Mr Cameron believes that if he wins another term as prime minister in 2015 he can successfully renegotiate new terms for Britain's membership of the EU. One possibility is that there will be a new treaty that Britain will veto unless London obtains major derogations. The rest of Europe does not want to open the Pandora's box of negotiating a new EU treaty, which in more and more member states would require a referendum for ratification. They want to focus on restoring growth and jobs in Europe and have little patience with British Conservatives' obsessive hostility to Europe. Perhaps there will be some kind of fudged statement promising a review or new working parties in line with British desires. Or there will be vague expression of future opt-outs in conformity with Mr Cameron's right-wing economic ideology. But British Conservatives, in their speeches, writings, television interviews and election manifestos, demand more.

They want an end to common European policies on security, policing, justice, fisheries, agriculture, external policy, common positions at the UK and its agencies. They demand a veto for the House of Commons over EU policies judged unacceptable. They fail to notice that what is sauce for the British goose is sauce for the French or Italian or Polish gander, in the sense that many national parliaments in Europe would love to veto EU norms or directives, including on market access, that Britain considers in its own national interests. An EU that does just what Britain wants is the dream of most Conservative MPs elected to the Commons this century. And now, as noted, many Conservatives say Britain should also leave the European Court of Human Rights and the Council of Europe and resign from the European Convention on Human Rights because it stops British ministers doing as they wish.

It is genuinely hard to see how all these demands can be satisfied in the short time between the election in 2015 and Mr Cameron's proposed in–out referendum in 2017. Nor is there any certainty that Rupert Murdoch and other newspaper proprietors will be ready to support anything short of Britain becoming semi-detached from the EU, with the rest of EU member states having to capitulate to British demands. If Labour wins, the demands for a referendum will intensify and the Conservatives under a new and even more virulently anti-European leader, such as, for example, Boris Johnson, will move further to the right and demand complete withdrawal, not renegotiation or repatriation of powers.

It is not difficult to imagine Rupert Murdoch wishing for revenge on the Labour leader, Ed Miliband, who defied Murdoch by supporting an investigation into the criminal activity of journalists hired by Murdoch newspapers to smear people and hack into phones. The British are full of good sense but they are also people of deep passions who love to oppose as much as they like to cooperate. The dislike and distrust of the EU is now so strong in Britain that perhaps it would be better if Britain did say bye-bye. Perhaps not 'adieu' but a 'bye-bye' for a period of separation for the next stage of British and European history. In 1945, Britain could, with some reason, be proud it had saved Europe and allowed millions of Europeans – including my father, wounded as a newly commissioned infantry officer in the 1939 campaign in Poland – to continue the fight or if they lived enslaved on the continent to know that Britain would not let Europe perish. After 2015, the grandchildren of that generation may begin digging Europe's grave.

AFTERWORD: WHAT HAPPENS NOW?

Monday, 2 May 2011

> *I am in Brussels and go out to meet Ian Traynor. He is in a mixture of despair and contempt about the EU as a whole. 'It's just going nowhere. They are paralysed. Nobody knows what to do. Cathy Ashton is in a difficult spot. She won't talk to people. There is no sense of anything strong and clear happening here at all. I think back twenty years to when my old* copain, *John Palmer, held the same job as Ian – the* Guardian's *Europe editor. John was full of enthusiasm about Europe and it infected everyone who ever met him. And there was a giant political project to be done around sustaining the creating of a Europe without all the nationalisms and friction of the past. Labour had to be part of it, he argued. Even if, of course, John came to it with his own at times overheated ideology and exaggerated hopes and primitive anti-Americanism nonetheless he had vision and ideological purpose and commitment. I like Ian as much as any foreign correspondent I have worked with. Above all he knows the Balkans, which I care about. Today he can do no more than reflect the utter draining away of any confidence or vision or purpose or sense of travel that now pervades all of Brussels. My poor Europe. What's happened to you?*

The reaction from the British right to David Cameron's promise of a referendum to allow a vote to quit the EU was to welcome its

High Noon tone of a final show-down with Brussels. At the Ukip end of the xenophobic right there was a sense their fox might have been shot. For ten years the cry of the Eurosceptic right has been 'What do we want? – A referendum! When do we want it? Now!' The prime minister has bowed to their wishes. As Matthew D'Ancona, the chronicler of Cameron's government, records in his book *In It Together*, Cameron's policy guru, Steve Hilton, 'had been arguing since before the 2010 election that the Conservative Party should be systematically preparing Britain for exit'. Whether in the intimate moments of policy-wonking inside Downing Street or on the floor of the House of Commons there was no one offering the prime minister an alternative line on the EU. Cameron's referendum pledge was the minimum the prime minister could get away with to keep his party in line.

A red-faced, angry Nigel Farage said Cameron was lying, and like previous Conservative calls and semi-pledges on referendums this, too, was a promise made to be broken. But Cameron's in-the-camera statement 'There will be an in–out referendum' was unambiguous. He did not say a 'yes–no' vote but an 'in–out' choice, and then said he hoped Brussels would make unspecified concessions to allow Britain its own personalized space within an EU open to British goods and services but with the UK exempted from other common obligations written into all the treaties since 1957.

The second reaction was from the continental EU establishment, which gave vent to its scarcely disguised dislike of Britain. There was a Pavlovian 'How dare he?!' element to this, as the punditocracy thundered about *l'Albion perfide* in French, Spanish, Italian and even Swiss papers. Thomas Kielinger, *Die Welt*'s thoughtful London correspondent, criticized the crude attack on Cameron from the then German foreign minister, Guido Westerwelle, in an op-ed Westerwelle wrote in *Die Welt*. Kielinger argued that Cameron's declaration that there were serious reforms needed in the EU posed a question that could not be wished away. This is common, platitudinous ground, and Dutch and Finnish politicians said Cameron was making a fair point.

In a slightly different register Jean Pisani-Ferry (then director of the Bruegel think-tank and now a senior French government adviser) said the creation of a Eurozone EU with its own rules, interventions and source of authority was creating a new Europe. The bi-EU (BIEU) was not two-speed, nor a question of inner and outer zones but it was leading to something new, with a Eurozone EU operating differently from a non-euro EU. Cameron speaking for a UK that would 'never' join the euro was entitled to point out that some new settlement was needed. The Brussels–Strasbourg left and federalist liberals also enjoyed attacking Cameron, with predictable denunciations from Daniel Cohn-Bendit or Guy Verhofstadt. But they might ask why so few people vote in European Parliament elections and why so many racists, xenophobes and populists sit in the assembly. The European Parliament is part of the democratic deficit problem faced by the EU, and Cameron is not wrong to ask how national parliaments can be better involved in European affairs.

Surely even the most Europhile of political leaders or the devoted militants of the European movement have to ask why the EU is mired in a decade of slow or no growth, rising unemployment, catastrophic levels of youth unemployment and huge protest movements captured by nationalist identity parties that encourage and validate atavistic and xenophobic politics. The OECD says that Germany will be condemned to possibly decades of growth of little over 1 per cent. That is the recipe for social chaos, especially as an ageing population demands more and more public support paid for by a smaller number of taxpayers. An obvious answer is to open Europe's borders to the near Europe in Ukraine, Turkey and the Maghreb. But this is rejected by anti-immigrant and anti-foreigner politicians of right and left. Another move would be to lessen protectionist barriers, especially in the field of agriculture. In 1994, King Hassan of Morocco told Jacques Delors in Rabat that Morocco had 5 million peasant farmers who wanted to export their tomatoes to Europe. Delors explained that the Spanish, French and Italian agro-lobby would not permit this to happen. 'OK. I understand your difficulties', replied the king. 'But if Morocco cannot export tomatoes, in ten years' time we will be exporting terrorists.' Ten years later, in March 2004, Islamist terrorists from Morocco exploded bombs at Madrid's Atocha railway station killing nearly 200 and wounding more than a thousand.

So perhaps a huge shake-up, a volcanic shift of Europe's frozen tectonic plates is needed to move all Europe's leaders in national capitals as well as in Brussels and Strasbourg to slough off their inertia and provincial reflexes of defending national or Brussels *acquis*.

The third response was to ask what happens between now and 2017, the putative date of an in–out UK referendum. As Conservative Party leader, David Cameron has indulged his party's venomous dislike of Europe, which is seen, like the Catholic Church in the nineteenth century or communism in the twentieth, as a foe of Britain's culture, traditions and needs. As he struggles to win votes from Ukip and maintain control over his fractious party, no one should be surprised to see a reversion to the genuine, EU-hostile Cameron.

He has never explained how he can obtain the renegotiation he demands. In fact he has never spelled out exactly what he wants from the EU in order to avoid a Brexit vote in his 2017 referendum. The European Commission and Council have no legal authority to start negotiations with Britain or any other EU member state that wants a unilateral set of derogations from the treaty. Cameron appears to be placing his hopes on a completely new treaty that some believe is required to give full legal authority to the new Eurozone arrangements. But France and other Eurozone countries like Ireland or de facto Eurozone countries like Denmark have made clear their opposition to a new treaty that would require ratification by referendum and plunge Europe into years of fraught treaty negotiation followed by uncertain plebiscites. It would be a rerun of the disaster of the first decade's constitutional treaty negotiations followed by its rejection in France and The Netherlands and then the hastily cobbled Lisbon Treaty with its new offices of president of the Council and foreign affairs supremo, which have not worked as hoped.

The idea of reliving that decade *horribilis* just to appease Mr Cameron is not very enticing to other EU leaders. There may be room for a narrow treaty to place a new Banking Union on a clear legal basis, and in Berlin, where EU policy-makers have to look over their shoulders at the German Constitutional Court in Karlsruhe, calls for a modest treaty have been made. Yet at the same time German officials at the highest level explain to any Brit they meet that Berlin cannot make major treaty derogation concessions to the UK unilaterally. Social Europe, which Conservatives loathe, is not a problem in Nordic nations, where Mr Cameron claims support. Germany is governed by a coalition in which the pro-union German Social Democratic Party holds key posts. Denmark and Sweden have social democratic prime ministers. So the hopes of a rewrite of the treaty to allow an investment and trading special advantage to the UK by a return to sweatshop pay and hours are unlikely to be accepted by German, French, Italian or Nordic governments where pro-Social Europe parties are in power.

David Cameron is caught in the dilemma of serving his party, which rejects Europe, and leading a state whose high officials and business leaders do not want to risk a rupture. There has been an endless tango between the prime minister and his followers. Initiatives like quitting the European People's Party, passing a Referendum Act which promises a plebiscite on any future sharing of powers with European partners (except on Turkey joining the EU) or finally offering an in–out referendum are all measures initiated by Cameron to show he is listening to and acting upon his party's hostility to Europe.

The prime minister also proposed a 'review of competences' that was meant to examine whether the balance was right between the powers Britain exercised and the powers it accepted Brussels should have. Acting on Mr Cameron's instructions, the Foreign and Commonwealth Office asked other EU partners to join in this review of competences, but other than Bulgaria and Italy, which submitted a banal, obvious statement, other European countries simply ignored the invitation. Why should Berlin or Stockholm or even Dublin get involved in an exercise which was about internal party politics in Britain? As it happened, the first report of the review of competences, published just after Parliament rose for its summer recess in 2013 so as to ensure no querulous protests from Eurosceptic MPs, turned out to be unremarkable to the point of banality. The report drawn up by FCO officials decided that the balance of powers between the UK and EU was broadly right and did not need major change. This is a clear message from the British state's official machine that plunging ahead with a referendum that could risk an exit from Europe was not in Britain's interests.

Some (but not many) business leaders and even the Japanese government in a remarkable intervention have urged the prime minister to stay in Europe. How does he satisfy his MPs, party activists, Ukip voters and the anti-EU press while at the same time appeasing the power-holders in the deep state and business who see the referendum process as too risky? It is Mr Cameron's dilemma and no one knows, not even the man himself, how to resolve it.

Where is the British left in all this debate? Its absence has been marked. Can the British left and Labour as an alternative government define a coherent European policy? Labour MPs have lost the ability to make the case for Europe or, for the most part, even to understand what is happening in other EU capitals. The mono-lingualism of Britain's political class has not helped. There were no efforts to create a knowledgeable cadre of Labour politicians with experience of Europe.

Labour remains without a coherent EU policy also because the left as a whole does not have one. The left cannot make up its mind if the EU is 'a capitalist club', as *Tribune* put it, a component element of a neo-liberal Davos world order or what? Not since Tom Nairn's scornful eloquence in his 1971 essay *The Left against Europe* has there been a single book which offers a left perspective on Europe. The *Guardian* is culturally pro-European, but also hostile to the euro and economic integration. Politicians or intellectuals who try and place a broadly pro-European comment in the *Guardian* are rejected in favour of the Marxist musings of a Slavoj Žižek or the inpenetrabilities of a Jürgen Habermas. Many Labour MPs have run with the current of public opinion of prejudice against workers from EU member states. There is a belated recognition that calling for fair wages and the full implementation of EU social directives would better protect both indigenous and incomer workers. But Labour is now calling for 'fair', not free movement without defining what is 'fair'. Has Labour forgotten that the EU is based on four core freedoms of movement – of capital, goods, services and people? Trying to decide what is 'fair' movement of people also raises the question what might be 'fair' movement of capital, goods or services. Open that Pandora's box and the single market begins to unravel. There are 10,000 British citizens receiving unemployment benefit in Germany. When Labour, in a bid to chase the Ukip working-class vote, says that no EU citizen in Britain should be eligible for benefits until they have spent two years working in the country, have their spokespersons worked out what that might mean if reciprocally applied to British people living and working in other EU countries?

However, those pro-Europeans on the left, including the present writer, have spent too much time defending the institutions and personnel of Brussels and Strasbourg. There are serious discussions organized by thoughtful outfits like Policy Network and London is home to two excellent EU think-tanks – the Centre for European Reform and the European Council on Foreign Relations. But these are ring-holding discussant bodies, not campaigning, politically focused institutes. Trade unions have lost their early 1990s enthusiasm for Europe, or at least the Social Europe John Major refused to sign up for. Labour did embrace Social Europe, but trade union organization in the EU remains wholly national and all the social rules in the world cannot alter economic laws of market competition and the desire of workers to have access to the cheapest possible goods. The left has no Nigel Farage or Boris Johnson – cheeky populist communicators – to mock the lies and dishonesties of the Europhobes. The BBC follows the *Daily Mail* or *Spectator* line on most EU questions and has given Nigel Farage more space and status than any politician from the pro-EU Labour or Liberal Democratic parties who actually win parliamentary elections.

The anti-EU think-tanks know what they want and say it. The liberal-left's policy groups give the impression of apologizing for the EU and finding a dozen things that are wrong with European constructions before grudgingly admitting that perhaps the EU has some positive aspects. Other pro-EU outfits like Business for New Europe or the new organization, British Influence, support chiefly the liberal single market aspects of the EU and cannot endorse Social or Foreign Policy Europe or an EU developing as a world-political region distinct from the United States or the BRIC countries. They aim to convert the Conservatives and take Labour's pro-EU position for granted. This may be a serous mistake, as a populist left hostility to Europe in the style of a Jean-Luc Mélenchon in France or Syriza in Greece can easily emerge.

In this sense, David Cameron is exposing the extent to which most of the British political class has no real vision of Europe. Like him, politicians of all parties lurch opportunistically from one EU moment to the next, deciding on policy responses not out of ideological belief or principle or the result of mature political debate (no one recalls the last time a Labour conference had a serious discussion on Europe) but tactical advantage and headline-grabbing.

So will Brexit happen? In his book *Au Revoir, Europe: What If Britain Left the EU?*, David Charter, a journalist who works for Rupert Murdoch at *The Times*, where he has been a political editor and Brussels correspondent and is now Berlin correspondent, concludes with a chapter outlining a new relationship Britain would have with Europe after a referendum effects the rupture sometime before 2020. His book is a long requisitory against the EU. As a responsible journalist, Charter lists some counter-arguments advanced by pro-Europeans like Peter Mandelson for Labour and Shirley Williams for the Liberal Democrats. The problem is that Baron Mandelson is 61 and Baroness Williams 23 years older. Both are energetic and clever. Sadly, however, it is indicative of the Europe debate in Britain that so many of the pro-Europeans have reached retirement age.

To stay in Europe, British politics needs those who believe in Europe. But the faith has gone. President Lyndon Johnson, who, whatever his failings over the war in Vietnam, was one of the most successful politicians in American history, always emphasized the importance of belief in a cause to succeed in politics. 'What convinces is conviction. You simply have to believe in the argument you are advancing: if you don't you're as good as dead. The other person will sense that something isn't there', Johnson declared.

In Britain, the conviction politicians all want Brexit. Labour does not, but Labour politicians begin their argument on Europe by listing the problems and the parts of Europe they do not like before concluding that, on balance, staying in the EU makes sense for Britain. By contrast, the Eurosceptics are people of passion and profound belief. Their faith may be based on a worship of false gods and infected by populism and sometimes xenophobia, but they have conviction and they believe in their own arguments.

David Charter sympathizes with the critics of Europe. Drawing from his experience as a Brussels correspondent he lists the many failings of the European institutions from the Commission to the Parliament. When he was a correspondent working in the British Parliament in Westminster he could have multiplied a hundredfold stories on the failures of British ministries, big and small, projects that do not work, transfer payments to the agriculture or defence industries or to welfare payment recipients that cannot be accounted for. The NHS, the police and other taxpayer-funded agencies as well as local councils also are accused of maladministration, corruption and being run for the benefit of state functionaries, as well as elected officials who abuse pay and expenses. Yet no one says that such failings are the existential fault of the British state, its police and doctors or of local councils. The UN and many of its agencies are poorly run, with well-founded accusations of financial incompetence and sometimes corruption. No one, however, suggests quitting the UN with the vehemence that British Eurosceptics promote a departure from the EU as the answer to the problems British citizens confront.

Mr Charter imagines a Britain outside the EU by the beginning of the next decade:

> By deciding to leave the EU, the UK had forfeited its place in the room where any future decisions were made about trading rules in the European Union. But public opinion seemed reconciled to this, given that British officials did not sit in the US Congress or China's State Council to influence their internal trade rules either. The situation that Britain ended up in was curiously like that created for the Channel Islands in 1972 ahead of UK accession.

Is being reduced to a larger version of the Channel Islands quite the future for Britain outside the EU that Margaret Thatcher had envisioned? It's true that for the City speculators who fund anti-Europe campaigns the prospect of Britain being a giant fiscal paradise where the rich pay few taxes and the poor get poorer may have some attractions.

David Cameron has unleashed a political process that began with his promotion of anti-European hostility from the moment he became leader of the Conservative Party in 2005. A decade later that process can all too easily end in Britain quitting the EU. An in–out plebiscite means what it says. Labour and the British liberal-left's failure to provide an explanatory narrative and political support for the EU ever since the party turned from outright Euroscepticism 25 years ago may now cost Labour dear if the impression grows that Cameron at least has a policy and a determination to go through with it come what may.

Politics does not happen by accident. Francis Fukuyama famously wrote that history had come to an end in 1990. He was celebrating the long Euro-Atlantic era of peace and prosperity after 1945 that by 1990 had also seen an end to dictatorship in Europe, an end to authoritarian military rule in Latin America and South Korea and a wider victory for freedom – economic, social, for women, for gays, for people of different races – than ever before in human history.

But Fukuyama was recording the high moment in just another cycle of history. Today there is evidence that Europe is at the end of its latest 60- to 80-year cycle of peace and stability. For the past four centuries, the European continent has endured periodic outbreaks of violent conflict, which are usually ended by treaties and new political arrangements, which usually last around six or seven decades before conflicts break out again.

War today in Europe should be unthinkable, though it wasn't in the Balkans 20 years ago, in Georgia five years back or eastern Ukraine after Putin's Russia annexed Crimea as casually as Germany annexed the Sudetenland in 1938. The sending of NATO troops and armour and fighter-planes to eastern Europe in response to Russian aggression and annexation in Ukraine showed how political differences could take on a military hue, as does the commitment of armed forces to subdue Islamist extremists in Iraq and Syria. The passage from peace to conflict can take many forms, and Europe is simply conforming to its history as forces arise seeking to persuade nations to turn their back on the arrangements put in place after 1945.

The course of European history appears, then, to be two or three decades of conflict followed by 60 or 70 years of peace, as exsanguinated Europeans agree, in Churchill's words, that jaw-jaw is better than war-war. In the seventeenth century, the Thirty Years War destroyed Europe. The British contribution took the form of a civil war and decapitation of a king. In 1648 peace broke out, as the Treaty of Westphalia imposed a 60-year truce on conflicts based on whether Catholic or Protestant Europe would be dominant.

Sixty years later, at the beginning of the eighteenth century, Europe was again locked in conflict. The war of Spanish succession lasted a decade. It dragged the newly unified nation of England and Scotland into continental conflict. Britain's first great army commander, the Duke of Marlborough, campaigned a thousand miles away from his island home. Britain had to drop Shakespeare's romanticism about 'this sceptred isle' protected by the sea from European entanglements. The Treaty of Utrecht imposed another long peace on Europe until the convulsion of the 1780s launched a 15-year conflict that in turn required the Congress of Vienna to write rules for a long period of peace and prosperity for participating nations.

Europe again enjoyed its 60 years of peace until a united Germany decided it wanted to be a world power like Britain and France, with their empires and colonies. Germany was too late for imperial conquest in Asia or Africa and instead went to war with France to prove its might.

The conflict was short and sharp but stored up endless trouble, as Germany rejected the Rhine as a natural frontier and occupied part of eastern France. Today Russia believes it can ignore international law and redraw the frontiers of Europe as Moscow annexes or occupies territory of other sovereign states – Ukraine and Georgia. In 1878, the Congress of Berlin settled things down for a while, until Europe returned to war between 1914 and 1945. The Versailles Treaty bought a little breathing space, but with communism and fascism becoming locked in mortal twentieth-century combat, much as Catholicism and Protestantism had been in the seventeenth century, Europe was ravaged by civil war and military conflict until 1945.

Again, Europe sought to make treaties to guarantee peace and prosperity. The treaty setting up NATO kept American soldiers in Europe and the successive treaties of European integration from 1950 to the Lisbon Treaty of 2007 sought to build prosperity based on open borders, open markets and a supranational authority to tame the national economic and power-play passions that had done so much damage previously.

Today, Europe is at the end of its latest 60-year cycle of peace. Of course, no war in the sense of full-scale military conflict appears to be on the horizon. But who can be sure? Keynes warned in 1937 that 'The idea of the future being different from the past is so repugnant to our conventional modes of thought that we, most of us, offer a great resistance to acting on it in practice.' But suppose the unity of the EU is not the future? The era of conflict that is now opening is political rather than military. The peace treaties and post-conflict agreements of Westphalia, Utrecht, Vienna, Berlin, Versailles and the various European integration treaties since 1950 ran out of steam as new political generations rose who wanted to construct a different world – usually one in which a single nation, religion or ideological perspective would prevail. Across today's Europe we can see powerful centrifugal forces appealing with success to national passions for a new settlement.

As military budgets leave Europe increasingly defenceless and as the United States pulls its forces and matériel out of Europe, there may be new military threats not on mainland Europe but in peripheral areas like the Near East, North Africa or even small residues of European puissance like the Falklands. Today, Europe's shrinking and fragmented national arms industries and national military doctrines will be unable to rise to any serious military challenge.

But the real problem is political. Britain is not the exception in its deep unhappiness with the way Europe is run. Every opinion poll shows growing discontent in most European nations. Nigel Farage is the most European of British politicians – every EU member state now has its Nigel Farages denouncing Europe and finding an audience and votes.

We can all hope that Europe will not relapse into war as in past times when a 60-year peace runs out of steam. Nevertheless, the omens are not good in terms of cooperation or compromise to achieve growth while maintaining the social cohesion, cultural and religious tolerance and supranational rule of law that have been the hallmarks of Europe's long era of tolerance and communal living since 1950. National passions and rigid beliefs are again on the march as Europe heads for troubled times.

Thus the European question is set to dominate British politics for the next few years. As Matthew D'Ancona rightly observes, if David Cameron wins a second term in office and fulfils his in–out plebiscite promise, 'the Conservative Party's energies would be utterly absorbed by Europe, as never before, for up to eighteen months'. Mr D'Ancona, a former prize fellow of All Souls College, Oxford, should know better. Britain's EU question will not be over in a matter of months. Until leadership returns to British politics the Europe issue will rumble for years. Like the question of free trade or the question of Irish religious and national rights and identity, the Europe conundrum will continue to determine the course of British politics for some time yet. As Jean Pisani-Ferry mordantly notes: 'In Europe, the experts have lost their legitimacy. Nowadays, angry citizens are in charge, and politics is driving financial policy. But politics in Europe is national, and what one national parliament regards as the only solution another parliament regards as unacceptable.'

So as Greeks paint Hitler's moustache on to Mrs Merkel's face and the once tranquil social democratic haven of Sweden sees its capital burn as angry, alienated citizens protest they are excluded from the world of white IKEA Sweden, a new Europe of anger and rejection emerges. In that sense, Britain leaving the EU may be the signal for a new period of European conflict after almost seven decades of stability and prosperity that began with the first treaty of European integration in 1950. For many inside Britain, and for some elsewhere in Europe, the debate on what form Europe should take if we are to avoid a new period of conflict is better conducted if Britain is outside the EU. The assumption that Brexit will not or cannot happen is wrong. The rest of Europe and the rest of the world had better get used to the idea that while a team from Manchester and Chelsea will still play in the European Champions League and British singers will still come last in the Eurovision Song Contest, the moment is fast approaching for the British to say bye-bye, Europe. And then the decisions that both Britain and its fellow European nations will have to take in order to survive in a new world order will become acute. A Brexit may force Europeans into taking decisions on real integration that Europe has been afraid of since 1950. Or it may confirm a new period of nationalisms and the slow Balkanization of our common Europe. Mr Cameron's plebiscite will be the beginning of a new Europe.

EPILOGUE

Books are not predictions. I set out in two editions of this book why I thought Brexit was likely to happen. There is no satisfaction in being proved right. 'I told you so' doesn't figure in my vocabulary and the fate of Cassandras who try and warn their fellow citizens of ills that may befall them is not encouraging. I concluded the end of the book with my view, 'Mr Cameron's plebiscite marks the beginning of a new Europe'. I have no reason to change that conclusion even though we now know Britain voted to leave the EU on 23 June 2016.

Yet in politics, as in life, nothing is pre-ordained. David Cameron did not have to lose his bet on Brexit and thus lose his position as prime minister. But from the moment he returned in triumph to Number 10 in May 2015, having seen off the challenge of Labour's Ed Miliband and no longer needing the all-but-disappeared Lib Dems as coalition props, he seemed to make every wrong strategic and tactical choice in his campaign to win his referendum.

Half the Conservative MPs now sitting in the Commons owe their political careers to David Cameron. In 2015 he was in a strong position. To be sure, the promise to hold a referendum on Europe had been in the manifesto. But Cameron had also pledged to hold a referendum on the 2007 EU Lisbon Treaty at the time of 2010 election and had wriggled out of it.

Ukip had made no impression in the general election and the only parliamentary seat they held was that of a well-entrenched

Conservative MP, Douglas Carswell, who had joined Ukip in 2014. Professor Matthew Goodwin, who rose to prominence as an academic pundit on Ukip, had predicted Ukip would win six House of Common seats in March 2015. Ukip made headway in the sense of winning seats when the issue was Europe. They increased votes in European Parliament elections in 2004, 2009 and 2014 when they won 4.3 million votes and the largest number of seats in the European Parliament.

If Europe was on the ballot paper, Ukip were a formidable force. The first-past-the-post electoral system stopped Ukip from making a parliamentary breakthrough. When voters had to choose MPs to take decisions across the board on how Britain is governed they were not interested in Ukip. There were a few Ukip councillors, often inheriting council seats from the extreme right-wing, anti-immigrant British National Party. But Ukip councillors were erratic and came and went without ever consolidating into a national force in local government to challenge other parties.

In short, Ukip were a nuisance to David Cameron and more than that to the Labour Party, which had lost the support of many white working-class voters in recent years, much as Labour had in the 1980s when Labour votes in the 1983 and 1987 elections were 27 and 30 per cent respectively. But Cameron had seen the Liberal Democrats eliminated as a force in the Commons and saw Labour writhing in misery at the loss of its Scottish seats and soon the election of a leader, Jeremy Corbyn, who was a divisive figure. Like other leftist disarmers who headed Labour in the 1930s and 1980s he was not seen as a future prime minister.

So was Cameron's first unforced error the decision to hold the referendum at all? Had there been no one in Number 10 wise enough in 2013 to point out to David Cameron the potential outcome of calling a plebiscite on such an emotional issue as Europe? George Osborne, a shrewd political strategist, was against the move, but what of Ed Llewellyn, Cameron's Eton classmate and chief of staff to the prime minister from 2010 to 2015? Llewellyn had worked closely with Chris Patten, a Europhile Tory grandee, and was far from being a Eurosceptic. Did he not urge his friend and boss to avoid granting Ukip their main demand – a referendum on Europe?

And even in May 2015, it would have been possible for Cameron to delay or defer his plebiscite as he had done with the promise to hold one after 2010 on the Lisbon Treaty. But no one in the higher reaches of the state apparatus was willing to say 'No, Prime Minister' to David Cameron any more than they were willing to say 'No, Prime Minister' to Tony Blair on Iraq or indeed 'No, Prime Minister' to Cameron when he repeated many of the mistakes of the Iraq intervention in Libya after 2011.

Officials who worked in Number 10 now admit privately that the referendum bill was rushed through parliament in too much of a hurry. 'I am still kicking myself that we did not extend the vote to 16- and 17-year-olds as we did in the Scottish referendum', one senior Number 10 insider told me. In the 1979 referendum on devolving power to Scotland and Wales there was a stipulation that at least 40 per cent of the total electorate had to vote Yes and that figure was not reached. In June 2016 only 37 per cent of the registered electorate voted Leave, so had the same rules been applied as in 1979 Brexit would have been defeated. But Number 10 ignored all precedent or examples from other countries where a major constitutional upheaval demands a 60 per cent or two-thirds majority.

In addition Cameron had been deliberately making it harder for younger voters to be on the electoral register. He ordered a new system to be put in place so that instead of a household or a university recording who lived in a family home, rented flat or student accommodation, and thus could vote, each voter now had to be registered individually. This meant that there was a 9 per cent drop – around 1.9 million – between 10 June 2014 and 1 December 2015 of 18- and 19-year-olds who were eligible to vote. This gerrymandering was aimed at helping the Conservatives in the 2015 election and then the 2016 London mayoral and municipal elections, as on the whole young voters don't vote for right-wing candidates. Cameron insisted on forcing through changes in October 2015 designed to help his party and had a Commons majority to do so. But in consequence a large number of young pro-EU votes were not available for his referendum.

Having placed his own obstacles in the path of victory Cameron and the Number 10 apparatus went to sleep for nine months. The prime minister continued to denigrate the EU, describing Brussels as 'bossy and bureaucratic', hardly language designed to generate pro-EU votes. The whole tone of senior Conservative Party discourse in the summer and autumn of 2015 remained as it had been since William Hague changed the Conservative Party into one that was ideologically hostile to the EU, even if stopping short of Ukip demands to quit. At the Conservative Party conference in October 2015, the then home secretary Theresa May won cheers as she cried: 'The numbers coming from Europe are unsustainable!' – the language of Ukip for the previous ten years.

There was no political preparation by Cameron to win the plebiscite he had now legislated for. None of the long arms of the Conservative Party were reaching out to try and get businesses to talk to employees or even to square the press. Ministers were not despatched to find arguments in favour of Europe. Indeed many of Cameron's key ministerial team like Iain Duncan Smith, Michael Gove, Chris Grayling and Theresa May continued stoking anti-EU fires as they blamed the EU for too many foreigners working in Britain, or pointed the finger at low economic growth across the Channel. They never asked why productivity was 30 per cent lower in the UK than in France, or why the UK runs huge balance of trade deficits with most other countries, or why, if EU regulations were such a burden on business, it was perfectly possible for German or Dutch or Danish or Austrian firms to win export orders and be profitable in their home markets?

Commonwealth countries had a far greater share of foreign-born residents in their population than the UK. Canada has 20.7 per cent; New Zealand 25.1 per cent; and Australia 27.7 per cent compared to 11.3 per cent for Britain. Twenty-seven per cent of the Swiss population is foreign born and have helped make Switzerland Europe's richest country as well as proving that being outside the EU is no bar to high levels of immigration. But no Tory minister or MP was willing to make these self-evident points.

Instead of throwing every resource of the state into helping the prime minister win the referendum he decreed after May 2015, clearing all Whitehall decks from the summer of 2015 to secure the stated aim and policy of the government, the Number 10 operation appeared to have gone to sleep.

Instead government officials poured all their efforts into securing some kind of pledge card from the European Union that Cameron thought would be sufficient to defeat the Leave campaign. Cameron went on a grand tour of Europe to see the German chancellor, Angela Merkel, the French president, François Hollande, and other leaders to ask for some special concessions for the UK that he could present to voters as showing Britain had a new status in the EU and could be excluded from its legal treaty obligations. The problem was that no one in Number 10 appreciated that all 27 other heads of government in the EU had their own internal political difficulties.

To meet Ukip-Tory anti-EU demands on stopping Europeans working in Britain required a fundamental re-writing of the existing EU treaties as non-discrimination against workers from different European countries had been a fundamental principle since the days of the first Coal and Steel Community in 1950.

Cameron did not like the term 'ever-closer union', which referred to peoples, not states, and which was in the preamble to the EU Treaty since the Treaty of Rome. For the rest of Europe this expression was 'apple pie' wordage, rather like the reference to 'life, liberty and the pursuit of happiness' in America's Declaration of Independence. The phrase 'ever-closer union' had indeed been removed from the formal Treaty language of the EU in the 2004 Constitutional Treaty when I was Minister of Europe. After the French and Dutch voted down the Treaty in their referendums in 2005, and I ceased to be Europe minister, the phrase was re-inserted in the Lisbon Treaty. No Tory MP at the time showed any interest in its removal nor any concern about its return. But by 2015 the term 'ever-closer union' was held up as proof by Eurosceptics that the EU was about to dissolve all its component nation-states into a single entity. This was complete nonsense but on Europe any nonsense could be said and was often believed.

In February 2016, there was a declaration from the European Council and Commission stating in guarded, hedged words carefully written by lawyers that the UK was told that it could have an opt-out from the reference to 'ever-closer union' at some future stage when the next EU Treaty was drafted. Cameron was told that the UK could make future EU workers wait a bit longer before claiming benefits. These moves to prevent what was dubbed 'benefit tourism' were already broadly accepted in Germany and other countries which had experienced similar waves of arrivals in the labour market from poorer EU member states. In the UK every study showed that European employees made a significant net contribution to the economy and the government budget, paying far more in direct and indirect taxes than they received in the form of benefits or NHS treatment.

Finally, Cameron did win an important concession as it was agreed that being in the EU's Single Market meant that the UK could raise objections if it was proposed to create new Eurozone rules which might discriminate against the City. In fact, the European Court of Justice was poised to issue an important ruling in favour of London as it decided that a proposal from the European Central Bank that all trades in euros, including derivatives and clearing contracts made in euros, should take place within the Eurozone. This was extremely lucrative business for the City with a volume of euro trades and clearing worth $120 trillion and most foreign banks and finance houses were based in London on the assumption they would be able to trade across the entire EU market of half a billion consumers. As long as the UK was fully in the EU the City would be protected was the message.

Cameron sought to return home saying he had now brought about 'a reformed European Union' and finally in March 2016 went on the offensive saying it was in Britain's interests to stay in a 'reformed EU'. No one believed that the February deal, which was predicated on some future treaty or confirmed what was happening anyway, amounted to a major reform and before long Cameron dropped the claim he had brought about 'a reformed European Union'. Instead, nine months after returning to Downing Street in May 2015, he finally began to campaign in March 2016. Again it is still inexplicable that the state machine did not start organizing in June 2015 a coordinated, coherent, comprehensive campaign to secure the prime minister's wish of winning the referendum.

At a London party in January 2016 I saw an old friend – a senior civil servant who was permanent secretary of a department of state whose minister was a staunch Europhobe – I said: 'I am very worried about Brexit.'

'Oh, don't worry, Denis, Jeremy has got it all organized!'

The Jeremy in question was not the hapless leader of the Labour Party but Sir Jeremy Heywood, the Cabinet Secretary and Head of the Civil Service. I don't doubt the sincerity of my friend who, like other Whitehall chiefs, would have gone to Whitehall meetings to be told that all was well in the campaign to win the referendum. But to anyone on the ground up and down the country talking at events about Brexit it was clear Jeremy had not got it organized and from the first days of the campaign it was clear that the different Brexit groups were much better placed.

After the referendum, the former Canadian High Commissioner in London, Jeremy Kinsman, lacerated David Cameron in an open letter he published in Canada. It is worth looking at an abbreviated version of what he wrote.

Dear David Cameron,

- Referenda are the nuclear weapons of democracy. In parliamentary systems they are redundant. Seeking a simplistic binary yes/no answer to complex questions, they succumb to emotion and run amok. Their destructive aftermath lasts for generations.
- Never call a referendum without being sure of the outcome. You called this one primarily for reasons of tactical political positioning.
- You should have been sure you had a high-performance team before you leapt. Ambitious defectors from your cabinet and untrustworthy political rivals undermined you.

- In any referendum over separation, the 'independence' side appeals to the patriotic heart. The thinking of the Leave side is magical. It plucks at a dimly remembered but glorified past (that was never as good as nostalgia makes it), and offers a future that is imaginary.

- Your appeals to the nation's head didn't get through. In a post-factual political age, reasoning doesn't reach the heart. To win, you needed to mobilize convincing passion behind the case that the status quo is both preferable and improvable.

- You let the Leave side get away with claiming that the EU would negotiate as an equal partner with equal stakes as the UK because the volume of trade was roughly equal. The reality is that respective stakes are starkly unequal. On trade, the UK is dependent on the EU market for 45 percent of its exports. The EU is dependent on the UK for only 8 percent of EU exports.

- Why didn't the Remain campaign say more about non-industrial benefits from the EU? Is it because of a visceral inability to praise its merit after years of denouncing it? The contribution to the EU budget by the UK has been exaggerated beyond belief. It only accounts for 1.3 percent of the UK's budget. On the other hand, British farmers love the 55 percent of their income coming from the Common Agricultural Policy. The cultural and arts community needed its 230 EU grants. The one third of university students hoping for Erasmus support for study in Europe will be stuck at home.

- Many who voted Leave say it was because they are unhappy over Britain's 'domination' by the EU. Why didn't you demystify this toxic fable?

- Immigration is the issue people say they care about most. Do EU workers actually replace British workers? Sixty percent have jobs lined up before they arrive because UK employers need them. Unemployment across Britain is only 5 percent. Could the NHS do without the 10–20 percent of its professional staff that is from the EU?

- You must accept the principle that the free movement of labour is fundamental to being a member of the EU's single market. It's delusional or deliberately misleading to have gone along with the notion that Britain can deny this essential principle and still have full access.

- Your European colleagues liked you. In their guts, they know that the British lift the EU game in many ways. But they will not reward England's nativists because you and their many British colleagues are pleasant and professional. They were never going to give the UK a break in negotiations to unravel 43 years of gradual integration and institutionalized accommodation. They have identity-driven nativist adversaries baying at them in their own capitals.
- Allow me to observe that partisan politics is all you have ever done. It's a handicap. Professional politicians over-react to tribal voices and noises from their camp. In your case, it's against the continuous drumbeat of jingoistic anti-EU right-wing journalism.
- The referendum shouldn't have been a response to party politics. Its significance is existential. It can't be undone. But people can't be expected just to absorb the pain and stay calm and carry on. There is real disbelief those about to take charge know what they are doing. Public antipathy and division will increase. The elected Parliament is against Brexit. Your friends abroad are aghast.
- I understand why you walked away abruptly. But given that your decisions ultimately enabled this crack-up, you can't leave for good without being clear about the size of the casualty ward to expect.

Jeremy Kinsman is one of Canada's most experienced diplomats and has served as his nation's ambassador in top capitals and is now a leading public-policy thinker and writer in Canada. I quote him not just because I agree his analysis is spot on (and I wish many like him had written like this before the referendum) but it is useful to see ourselves as others see us.

The Electoral Commission decided the question on the ballot paper was whether the voter wished to Remain in the EU or Leave the EU so the two camps became dubbed Remain and Leave. The Leave camp split into two groups – a broader Leave campaign which attracted top Tory MPs like Boris Johnson, by far the most effective populist communicator in British politics since Enoch Powell though with oodles more comic empathy than Powell ever managed. Michael Gove was the closest the Cameron generation of Tory MPs had to an intellectual as he forced arguments through their paces to satisfy himself as to their rigour. From the European Parliament came one of the most fluent of polished anti-European advocates, Daniel Hannan. Jacob Rees-Mogg MP, who had become a favourite of the back benches with his exaggerated eccentricities, was an effective speaker to whom audiences brought up on the *Daily Telegraph* and *Daily Mail* responded fervently.

The Leave campaign was led by a veteran right-wing but very effective campaigner, Matthew Elliott. He had turned an obscure campaign outfit called the TaxPayers' Alliance into a much quoted source for attacks on Gordon Brown as chancellor (1997–2007) and then prime minister. Elliott's speciality was to package statistics into media cluster bombs so that one figure emerged and all the normal qualifications and setting-in-context a responsible economist or statistician or tax-expert would feel honour-bound to include just fell away. There was endless money in the City or Mayfair hedge funds for anti-European propaganda and organization. Elliott had already set up a Brexit front organization called 'Business for Britain' and his network was ready to roll out as soon as the campaign started.

Some Tories hedged their bets and stayed close to David Cameron just in case he won. Sajid Javid, the Business Secretary, said he would have never entered the EU, would have voted No in 1975 and would vote No in any referendum on a future treaty. Oliver Letwin also said that 2016 was not the time to leave Europe but when the next treaty revision came around then the opportunity would arise. These were the advocates of *Brexit Interruptus* – withdrawal, but not just yet.

After her tirade against the EU at the autumn 2015 Conservative Party conference Theresa May was seen as a natural to lead the Brexit campaign. But she is a cautious, hesitant politician and stayed nominally loyal to her prime minister though she made little effort in the campaign to help the Remain camp. On the contrary, in late

April 2016 she made a speech saying Britain should withdraw from the European Convention on Human Rights (ECHR) and leave the Council of Europe. This was not on the referendum ballot paper but after the EU itself, the ECHR was the most hated institution amongst anti-Europeans and the Europhobe press. So Theresa May was sending a clear message of reassurance to Tory Eurosceptics that she remained with them and even if they did not win EU withdrawal she would urge withdrawing from the ECHR.

Ukip set up its own Leave campaign as the Tory MPs refused to ally themselves formally with their political opponents even if the message – Get out of Europe – was identical. Nigel Farage toured the country making the same speech that he had been making for 15 years. An insurance salesman who had made billions very publicly bankrolled the Ukip operation. Farage is a speaker of conviction and passion. He has the demagogue's gift of distilling a complicated set of interlocking relationships into simple slogans. All UK laws are made by the EU. Not true. Britain pays £350 million a week to the EU. Not true. There is no growth in Europe. Not true. The Europeans had caused the unemployment in Greece or Spain. Not true.

But the demagogue is not interested in truth. He wants to rouse up emotions and present a dragon that, if the people only fall in behind, can be slain. In fact, there was little to choose between the Tory Leave campaign and the Ukip Leave campaign. Both were the culmination of more than 20 years of attacking the EU across the board.

It was surreal to hear a senior Tory, Andrea Leadsom, say on the *Today* programme shortly before the Queen's Speech that 60 per cent of all UK laws were decided in Europe as if Her Majesty the Queen was in Brussels taking dictation from Commission officials on what she could or could not put in her speech announcing future legislation. No one on the programme challenged this palpable untruth.

Another Brexit minister, Penny Mordaunt, was challenged when she kept insisting that 75 million Turks were about to join the EU and Britain could not stop this happening. When the BBC interviewer, who knew a little about the EU, pointed out that the UK had a veto (along with 27 other member states) she snapped, 'No, we don't' and continued to maintain what was a complete untruth or, in plain English, a lie.

The Leave battle-bus was emblazoned with the slogan that if the UK left Europe there would be £350 million a week to spend on the NHS. Again a fabrication as the UK gets back from the EU its mammoth agricultural subsidy budget, £700 million annually for university research, regional subsidies of hundreds of millions of pounds for South Yorkshire, Wales or Cornwall as well as Erasmus scholarships and funding for environmental and cultural projects.

Boris Johnson blustered and blustered when tackled on this point but the damage was done as millions of TV news viewers saw Johnson and other Leave Tories standing in front of the bus with the untrue slogan beamed into their homes.

A Leave leaflet pushed through letter boxes said that 'Britain's new frontier was with Syria and Iraq' and another one showed a map which stated that Turkey was 'set to join the EU' and in a slightly different tint next to Turkey were its neighbours, Syria and Iraq. At the beginning of the campaign Johnson said that the EU was following in the path of Hitler in seeking to create a super-state. Even by Johnsonian standards the statement was grotesque and over the top. Johnson, of course as he always does, said his remark had been misinterpreted but he knew exactly what he was doing in planting in voters' minds the insinuation that being in the EU was something Hitler might have wished for. In the 1930s a famous demagogue said 'If you tell a big enough lie and tell it frequently enough it will be believed'. There is no need to mention his name though Johnson does rather like to in speeches and books when denouncing Europe. Nigel Farage's Ukip Leave campaign and the Tory Brexit Leave campaign were indistinguishable. Both focused on immigration to the exclusion of most other themes. Those who hoped there might be a rational debate on the nature of modern sovereignty and a real balance sheet discussion of the pros and cons of the Single Market or the City of London enjoying trillions of euro-related trades or being the centre for clearing the common currency were disappointed.

The ghost of Enoch Powell smiled approvingly on the Leave campaign as they brought to a climax his warnings from the 1960s that allowing foreign immigrants into Britain meant the end of our way of life. Farage was pictured in front of poster with the slogan 'Breaking Point' showing a long snaking queue of shabbily dressed Levantine-looking men and women and the clear implication that thanks to lax frontier controls they would arrive in Britain. In fact, the picture was from a border crossing in the Balkans of desperate refugees fleeing wars and with Britain outside the Schengen zone there was no obligation on Britain to accept any of them.

But the bigger the lie and the more frequently it was repeated the more it was believed.

It should be stressed that there were many on the mainstream Leave side who were uneasy about references to Hitler and the sheer populist xenophobia against fellow Europeans. Others had long-standing and genuine concerns about sovereignty and parliamentary supremacy. But their arguments were like a gentle flute drowned by the great brass bands marching with a simple tune of anti-immigrant fear and dislike. Against the daily demagogic stirring of hate there was little that the Remain side could do.

The official campaign was called Stronger In. It was chaired by a former Marks & Spencer boss, Lord Rose. He made one speech at the launch and was rarely seen again. The three directors were a Conservative pollster whose polls for the campaign and for 10 Downing Street were consistently wrong, a Liberal Democrat who has been strategic director of the Lib Dems when they were eliminated from the political map at the general election in 2015 and a nice Labour man, Will Straw, who had chosen an unwinnable seat to stand in and duly lost in the 2015 general election. The campaign issued forecasts about the ills that would befall the economy if voters voted to Leave. These were not demonstrable lies in the sense of the Leave lies but they were projections and it was quickly pointed out that the problem with many an economic projection is that it can turn out not to happen. The campaign was master-minded from Downing Street and George Osborne's Treasury and was dubbed 'Project Fear' and was based loosely on similar tactics that had worked in the 2014 Scottish referendum.

Indeed many of the tenors of that campaign, like Gordon Brown and Alistair Darling, were sent back into action but they sounded like yesterday's men. All the old-timers like Michael Heseltine and Neil Kinnock and John Major made valiant efforts to speak for the UK staying in the Europe, but the Remain campaign failed to find new, next generation voices that commanded respect and compelled attention.

Above all, the prime minister, David Cameron, put himself in the front line and turned the entire referendum into a personal vote of confidence in himself. It was spooky to hear such passionate pro-European words from a man who had found nothing positive to say about the EU or Brussels in his previous life in politics since the 1990s.

President Obama and Japan's prime minister Shinzō Abe and the head of the IMF and OECD and bosses of Goldman Sachs, and Hitachi, and other denizens of Davos spoke or wrote warnings about the dangers of Brexit.

But how was this playing in Bradford or Bootle or Bolsover? The Stronger In–Remain campaign was too late in the day. It sounded and looked like the elite establishment of globalization's chattering class.

It might have helped if the opposition parties had leaders who could make an impact. After Paddy Ashdown, Charles Kennedy and Nick Clegg, the Lib Dems were led by an affable but little-known MP, Tim Farron. But Labour was in a far worse position. It had elected as leader Jeremy Corbyn, a leftist from the 1970s who had learnt nothing and forgotten nothing since that era. He was not pro-Brexit but he had never shown any enthusiasm for the EU. He wanted a more socialist Europe in which trade unions were strong, open market trading arrangements were suspicious and the EU, today dominated by centre-right and nationalist populist parties, should move sharply to the left.

Perhaps if he was a commanding speaker, able to dominate TV studios, find words that convince and convey hope, Corbyn might have enthused core Labour voters including the millions who felt they had lost out as globalization and its EU variant dissolved borders, allowed cheap products made by slave-labour wages in Asia to fill high streets, without any compensating social investment by government.

Corbyn refused to speak alongside Cameron and why indeed should Labour give the Tory prime minister who had called this plebiscite out of cynical internal party opportunism any slack? But in consequence Labour was absent from parade during the vital weeks leading up to the vote. Labour veterans like Alan Johnson and Hilary Benn made Remain speeches and the bulk of Labour MPs and MEPs did their best with local canvassing and street stalls. But their voters had been reading the *Sun*, the *Daily Mail*, the *Daily Express* and the *Daily Star* for years and had absorbed all the propaganda against the EU over the decades. Even those who took the *Guardian* read Sir Simon Jenkins calling for Brexit as often as he could and other star *Guardian* columnists fulminating against Europe and the EU, which they blamed for the continent's many economic and social problems.

In the normal story-telling of an election campaign there are key moments, important events, a brilliant speech, a ghastly error, a turning point which allows a narrative to emerge to explain the result. In the case of the Brexit plebiscite nothing like this occurred. The Leave establishment had the better tunes and by far the better demagogues.

They spoke to all those who were unhappy with their income, the lack of jobs or affordable housing for their children, the sense that their supermarkets and town centres were being crowded out by men and women speaking unintelligible tongues, that infant school classrooms had too many children who could not speak English, that every visit to a GP or a hospital meant sitting in waiting rooms with people who were foreign and clearly could have contributed much to the financing of that very British invention, the NHS.

In other countries insurance and health schemes were based on contributions so you had to pay to get something. In the workplace there were much stronger social rules and works councils to stop undue exploitation. Britain, under all its prime ministers since 1990, had focused on creating as many low-paid jobs as possible and importing trained workers to do jobs that the lack of compulsory training in the UK meant few British workers were equipped to fill. A total of 57,000 EU citizens worked in the NHS because the Royal Colleges which impose the closed shops of the medical and nursing professions had never allowed sufficient British men and women to qualify to fill the demand for medical professionals.

The referendum vote was the chance to express the protest that had been simmering for decades against the existence of two-nation Britain. One statistic sums up the fault-line. Fifty-two per cent of British households are net recipients one way or another of state handouts – pensions, child benefits, disability allowances, working tax credits, social service care and so on. Forty-eight per cent are net contributors to the UK national budget – they pay more in taxes than then they receive in benefits.

That was precisely the divide in the referendum: 52–48. Of course many well-off people voted Leave and many state-dependent people voted Remain. But when a nation has so many unable to earn enough money to stand on their own feet without having to be helped by a state handout of one sort or another then a sense of unfairness can set in. And when life is seen as unfair the natural reaction is to find someone or something to blame. The rich are too rich and they are all those who are saying vote Remain! Let's give them a kicking! For years we have been saying our children need jobs but the politicians ignored us! Let's give them a kicking! We are proud of our nation, its history, its language, its culture. But we are told we must accept new beliefs, cultural practices, shocking treatment of girls and women, and tolerate those who preach support for radical religious ideology which at its far extremes plants bombs on the London Underground. Let's send the elites who have been patronising us a message! The Scots and the Welsh have been given parliaments and can vote for their own arrangement but London keeps all power in London and ignores the needs of the North and the Midlands so let's let England arise and speak! Our sons and daughters cannot find houses to live in while rich Europeans and other bankers flock to London and make living costs unaffordable so let's vote against them!

This was not a general election where voters look at the palette of choices on offer from different parties and leaders. This was a one-off chance to vent anger, to give two glorious English fingers to the boss class, and the elites who seem to do so well out of Europe and out of cheap imported labour but have forgotten how the other half lives, especially far from metropolitan cities and university towns.

This was an English nationalist vote and the majorities in most of England outside of London are striking. To be sure, if David Cameron had not fiddled the electoral register or if a threshold of 40 per cent of all eligible votes had been required Brexit would not have occurred.

The Remain camp could not or did not know how to overcome those handicaps. The other two big losers of the campaign were the pollsters and the media. The polling companies had a terrible campaign. In a world in which vote-winning machinery depends enormously on knowing precise details of how policies and personalities are playing, where votes can be won and where it is a waste of time trying to find them, the absence of any reliable polling was a disaster for the Remain camp. The Leave camp were less bothered by polls. They were fixated on amplifying the same message about Europe that Boris Johnson and Iain Duncan Smith had been pumping out since the early 1990s and Nigel Farage all this century. There was no variation – it was immigration, immigration, immigration and control of frontiers with a little room left over for the UK's budget contribution and a smidgeon on parliamentary sovereignty.

Remain had the trickier uphill task. From the early days some online opinion polls were showing a narrow Leave lead usually a little over 50 per cent – a figure which was reflected in the final vote in the ballot box. What was unusual was that telephone polls – traditionally thought to be more reliable – were showing a much stronger Remain majority and did so up to the last moment. There were no polling shocks as just before the Scottish referendum in September 2014 when a lead for an independent Scotland suddenly materialized. This galvanized the London establishment into offering more fiscal support and autonomy to Scotland within the UK as well as more power for the Scottish government and parliament. The latter was headlined as the 'VOW' and suggested a new Scotland with new powers and rights while staying part of the UK.

Neither Jean-Claude Juncker nor any of the heads of EU governments had it in their power to come up with last-minute bribes or offers of a new status outside the legal obligations of the EU treaties. So there could be no surprise for the fading Remain campaign. The pollsters have been wringing their hands since the campaign at their failure to provide accurate polls. Their explanation – put simply – is that in polling everything works on a previous sample which is adjusted and brought up to date for new circumstances. The plebiscite was a one-off, as the one in 1975 was too far away and it was difficult in the science of polling to be absolutely confident that the sample polled was fully representative. All the polling firms made clear their unease and worked hard as polling professionals to be accurate so their failure was probably beyond their control. But it meant for the Remain camp that there were no reliable pointers to where they were short of votes which might have led to work to focus on those categories instead of pumping out a general message about economic doom and gloom if Brexit won.

The Remain campaign made no attempt to paint a broad picture of Britain as a leading nation with a key role to play in shaping a post-national grouping of countries pledged to peace and democracy and working collectively, instead of behind national frontiers, to promote commerce, culture and modern citizenship with its respect for gender, gay and green rights.

The newspapers, BBC and other broadcasters helped Leave to win. By focusing on phoney balance or false equivalence the BBC allowed Leave's unqualified lies to go unchallenged because later in the bulletin or programme they would run a statement from the Remain side challenging what had been said. It is as if Leave would say that thanks to EU membership Britain would start driving on the right. Instead of the *Today* or 6 p.m. news editor saying: 'Wait a minute, that's rubbish' they said 'Get a quote from Remain saying they are sure we will keep driving on the left'. So again and again, prominent Leave campaigners would say 60 or 70 per cent of our laws are made in Brussels, or 80 million Turks were about to arrive in Britain as Turkey was 'set' to join the EU, or that an EU Army was about to be set up – all part of the 'Bigger the Lie, the More it is Believed' tactics of the clever propagandists behind Leave. These would go unchallenged by the BBC prominenti who dominated the coverage on air and would only be corrected later, if at all, when a Remainer would say 'That's not true'. By then it was too late and instead of putting forward a positive case for being in Europe, the Remain team spent all their time chasing down lies that the BBC should never have allowed to be broadcast unchallenged in news and current affairs programmes.

The newspapers maintained their well-established line on Europe. The off-shore owned press – the mass circulation tabloids like the *Sun* and the *Daily Mail* just sustained their long-standing propaganda line against the EU. They were joined by the *Daily Express* with only the *Daily Mirror* and its much reduced circulation trying to make the case for the EU. The most widely-read broadsheet paper is the *Daily Telegraph* with its star columnist, Boris Johnson. It sustained its traditional hostility and disdain for Europe in its news and comment pages.

Neither Rupert Murdoch nor Lord Rothermere, proprietor of the *Daily Mail* and the *Mail on Sunday*, pay taxes in Britain but they still presume to dictate to the British people what politics they should support. Murdoch and Rothermere split their bets with the Sunday editions of their main papers coming out in favour of Remain.

This however could not offset the relentless year-on-year anti-European tone of both papers since the moment Margaret Thatcher turned against Europe. Nothing could offset the years and years of hard and soft Euroscepticism that the BBC had platformed this century nor the relentless anti-European news reports and comments that much of our press, including left-liberal papers like the *Guardian*, had published. To be pro-European in fashionable gatherings of the political-media-business class in London was to be treated as a benighted idiot who did not understand the course of history. After Brexit, writers like John Lanchester in the *London Review of Books* or Zadie Smith in the *New York Review of Books* wrote powerful essays on how bad Brexit was for their idea of Britain. But they wrote nothing before the vote. The left-liberal intellectual class allowed the rise of anti-Europeanism to sink deep, deep roots without much protest.

I experienced this first-hand as I toured the Waterstones chain of book-stores from Glasgow to Canterbury during the Brexit campaign to debate with pro-Brexit Tory MPs and MEPs and discuss a short book I wrote, *Let's Stay Together: Why Yes to Europe* (also published by I.B. Tauris). At all the meetings, full of decent, thoughtful, bookish people, the vote on a show of hands was to Leave. So while I firmly believe the Leave campaign was meretricious and based on falsehoods I accept fully that those who voted Leave did so on what they believed and what they had been told over many years, not just the weeks of the campaign.

And so before people went to bed at the end of Thursday 23rd, the first results came in from northern, working-class Sunderland showing a clear majority for Leave. The final vote showed the young, London, Scotland and university cities in southern England voting for Remain but a big vote from the Midlands and above all the North for Leave. Overall, no one could dispute that 1,269,501 more people had voted to Leave than to Remain. So the vote was clear enough.

***

Now Britain has embarked on a strange period of its history. Having spent centuries aiming to spread its influence and commerce on the continent it has now been decided by a plebiscite vote to reduce that presence and influence. The prime minister, David

Cameron, who called the referendum, resigned the day after. This was the right thing to do as the whole referendum was a vote of confidence in his decision to break with parliamentary traditions and opt for a continental-style plebiscite.

The Conservatives moved quickly to elect their new leader and prime minister. For some, Boris Johnson, who had led the Brexit campaign against David Cameron, seemed the natural successor. But Johnson's hopes collapsed swiftly as his co-star in the Leave campaign, the cerebral Tory minister Michael Gove, announced that, rather than supporting Johnson, he planned to run himself as leader and hence prime minister.

This scuppered Johnson's chances and did little to help Gove as many reminded him of the saying that 'he who wields the dagger never wears the crown'. So with Johnson the populist demagogue and Gove the intellectual out of the way, who was left? Theresa May had cultivated a Eurosceptic image even if nominally she stayed loyal to David Cameron in the campaign itself. And loyalty is perhaps the most prized virtue in a Conservative Party that has survived nearly three centuries of change but regularly emerged as a governing party because it knew how to stay together rather than commit regular political regi-cum-suicide.

May's main claim to fame after she entered the Commons in 1997 was that she described the Conservative Party as 'the nasty party' in a speech to the party conference in 2002. She held different shadow portfolios under David Cameron without making a special mark in any of them. Chris Grayling was the shadow home secretary in 2010 and would have expected to assume the high office of state. But Grayling made a very offensive homophobic remark saying hotel keepers should be allowed to ban gay couples. Grayling was demoted from cabinet rank and Theresa May was given the home secretary post instead.

Her main theme during her six years as home secretary was controlling immigration and attacking the European Court of Human Rights in Strasbourg and the European Court of Justice in Luxembourg whenever they upheld some appeal against a British court, usually involving deporting someone the British tabloids had got worked up about.

She had no known views on economic or foreign policy but she had proved that through hard work and political skills it could no longer be said that the Home Office was the graveyard ministerial post in British government. And all the time she went to constituency meetings and worked harder than most ministers at being a politician who served the party faithful, came to their events and dinners and shook everyone's hand.

Having seen the two front-runners, Boris Johnson and Michael Gove, cut each other's throat there was an odd interlude when an MP called Andrea Leadsom who had performed well in the Leave campaign by simplifying and then exaggerating all the Leave falsehoods decided she should run to be prime minister. She had little experience but she was for a short while the darling of the more fanatical anti-Europeans like Iain Duncan Smith.

But after making unpleasant remarks about Mrs May's lack of children and seeing the extent of media scrutiny into dubious claims that she had been a major executive in the City as well as into her private finances she withdrew and Theresa May sailed into Downing Street without even facing a serious election.

So in the space of less than a month 17 million had voted Britain out of Europe and no one had voted for Theresa May to be prime minister. The Labour Party had meanwhile sunk to new depths as most frontbench Labour MPs resigned their posts as shadow ministers in protest at Jeremy Corbyn's leadership style. As in the 1930s, the 1950s and the 1980s Labour turned in on itself in opposition and made no impact on key political issues. At a moment in British history when a momentous decision had been made on the basis of lies and with a little over a third of the electorate following Ukip and the *Daily Mail* out of Europe it was little short of a tragedy that Labour was unable to contribute to the political debate that now got under way or hold the new prime minister to account on what decisions she now has to take.

Mrs May gave some indication of her thinking with her appointment of three prominent Brexit campaigners – Boris Johnson, David Davis and Liam Fox – to key cabinet rank ministerial posts charged with negotiating the post-Brexit relationship with Europe and the rest of the world. Johnson, who had never held ministerial rank, was given the senior post of foreign secretary; David Davis, who had briefly been Europe minister in the 1990s under John Major, was made secretary of state for Brexit; and Liam Fox, who had been forced to resign as defence secretary in 2011 over a scandal involving a close personal friend getting improper access to highly secret material in the Ministry of Defence, was made minister for international trade – a key element in the Brexit process.

In short, all three men were better known for their anti-Europeanism than for having held high continuous office and had not proved their ministerial ability. It became clear that no one had the faintest idea in Whitehall what to do next. Britain had no officials with any experience of negotiating trade agreements as all trade deals were an EU competence.

There was talk of the UK following a Norwegian model. Norway is in the European Economic Area (EEA), to which all 28 EU members belong, but not in the EU. This means that Norway has to accept free movement of EU citizens and in per capita terms Norway has three times as many EU citizens living and working within its border as the UK. In addition, Norway has to accept all EU laws and directives and make a financial contribution to Brussels as if it were an EU member state. Norway does keep control of its fishing and agricultural subsidies but many queried if the British taxpayer was really prepared to fork out even more money in subsidies for all the different types of British farmers. On the contrary one cry of the Leave campaign was that outside the EU's Common Agricultural Policy it would be possible to import food cheaply from poor countries at the expense of food produced by British farmers at a higher cost.

It was thus hard to square the EEA Norway option with the claim of the Leavers that Britain should vote to end or limit movement into the UK from elsewhere in Europe and that voting for Brexit meant no more EU regulations or directives and no more money going to Brussels.

Moreover, outside the EU, even in the EEA, it was made clear that the City would lose its lucrative trade in euros and euro derivatives and clearing – a total volume of $120 trillion. Many banks from America, Asia and Europe were based in London precisely because the City had become the Wall Street of the EU operating under EU Single Market law and able to raise money and trade anywhere in the Single Market of 500 million consumers. In the aftermath of the referendum, several banks and multinationals spoke of moving their headquarters to Dublin, Paris or Frankfurt.

Jean-Claude Juncker again repeated as the European Commission shut down for its August summer break that the EU would not grant tariff-free access to the internal market for UK goods and services if Britain did not accept free movement of workers from within the EU. 'There will be no access to the internal market for those who do not accept the rules – without exception or nuance – that make up the very nature of the internal market system', Juncker underlined.

He also noted that the UK would need some time to prepare its position. First Britain had to invoke Article 50 of the EU Treaty, which is the mechanism which allows a government to give two years' notice of its intention to leave the EU. These negotiations covered the status of UK citizens employed by the Commission and the transfer of EU institutions like the European Medicines Agency and European Banking Authority out of London to an EU member state. There are many EU payments that come into the UK for university research, Erasmus scholarships plus all agricultural subsidies. Agreement would be needed on when they would cease and when Britain would stop sending its contribution to Brussels. The Article 50 talks are meant to last two years but can be extended if both Britain and the EU agree that more time is needed. Michel Barnier, a veteran French politician, who had twice been an EU Commissioner as well as holding high ministerial office in France, was named as the EU negotiator for Brexit. Both Boris Johnson and Liam Fox made grandiose statements about the future of Britain outside Europe but it was David Davis who would do the formal negotiating. No one doubted that the final word would lie with Prime Minister May.

What happens in Scotland? The first minister Nicola Sturgeon spoke repeatedly of her desire to see Scotland stay in Europe but that is not compatible with staying in the UK outside the EU. So would a new referendum be needed and what would be the outcome? These questions are not for the Article 50 negotiations and Washington has made clear to the new trade secretary, Liam Fox, that the United States could not begin talking to the UK about a new trade arrangement until Britain was completely out of the EU.

The new chancellor of the exchequer, Philip Hammond, said it would take six years to extricate fully the UK from Europe and other international legal and trade experts think it could be much longer. Spain announced in July 2016 that after eight years of intense negotiations it had concluded a trade deal with China to allow the export of plums from Spain to China. Trade deals alone take years, often a decade, to negotiate as both partners seek to maximize advantage. Anyone can conclude a trade deal if the other nation is given all it wants. Britain runs a balance of trade deficit with most major economies. Indeed one of the sources of the Brexit vote was unhappiness in working-class England at the extent to which free trade meant the arrival of much cheaper goods made in China, Asia and other low-cost producing nations where trade unions and fair wages do not exist. So those who voted Brexit may be in for a shock when they find their champions opening the British market to yet more dumped goods from China and elsewhere which will mark the final death of British-based manufacturing as goods made at much lower prices by low-wage or even slave labour arrive in UK high streets.

So as the summer holiday season got under way after the Brexit vote Britain was still in the EU and no one in government was able to say when or on what terms the final divorce would take place. There was considerable economic turbulence in the weeks following Brexit. The pound slumped to its lowest level against the dollar since the 1980s and various investment funds had to stop withdrawals as there was what the *Financial Times* described as 'a stampede out of the UK' as foreign investors contemplated what might be years of uncertainty before a new economic relationship with the UK and the EU was in place. Some commentators were sanguine or even upbeat, welcoming a lower pound as it meant holiday-makers would have 'staycations' in Britain as going abroad became more costly. But the *Mail on Sunday* reported that British pensioners living on the continent would lose £400 a month because of the pound's loss of value following Brexit. Others pointed to the London stock market going up, not down. However more and more chief financial officers said there was now a hold on investment for 2017 as the uncertainty of Britain's future economic relationships left too many unanswered questions.

The hopes of some anti-Europeans that Brexit would start a chain reaction leading to the disintegration of the EU were not realized, or at least not yet. If anything opinion polls showed there was a surge of support for the EU as the Dutch and the Danes and Italians and others realized what they would lose if the EU disintegrated into nation states behind closed frontiers. In the aftermath of the Brexit vote many papers were produced by think-tanks and commentators but often they projected the author(s)' own wishes and many demanded a massive re-writing of the existing EU treaties, which is not going to happen in the 2014–2019 mandate of the European Parliament and Commission.

Many of the British complaints about the EU were shared on the continent. But at the same time few countries had such an organized level of opposition in mainstream politics, the press and the finance-economic establishment. Countries in Eastern Europe refused to obey instructions to take in refugees from the Middle East and in Greece a left-populist party took power but then after some initial excitement buckled down to work with the EU to reform the Greek economy. No one beyond the far-right fringe across the Channel thought of actually leaving the EU. That was a British speciality.

So Britain is out. While heads of government obeyed the rules of courtesy when Mrs May went to see them, there was little doubt that behind the scenes no favours were going to be given to the Tory and Ukip political forces that had done so much damage to European unity.

What happens next is for another book. But the history of Britain and Europe is far from over. And I believe there are many in Britain who will not accept their country's isolation from Europe. Some will fight, fight and fight again to keep the country we love part of the European Union family of nations. The referendum result must be accepted. But democracy does not end with one casting of votes in the ballot box. Brexit is but one event in the long, complex history of Europe. The next chapters remain to be written. You can read them in my next book on Brexit.

FURTHER READING

In Britain, the Centre for European Reform (www.cer.org.uk) has in nearly two decades of existence published many reports an all aspects of the EU and Britain's role therein. British Influence (www.britishinfluence.org) is a recent website that at last presents daily facts and arguments on Europe that to some extent offset the prevalent Eurosceptic reporting in British papers and their very thin coverage of political developments in EU member states, which help shape EU politics and policy. Open Europe (www.openeurope.org.uk) is a Eurosceptic think-tank but it carries a wide range of news reports, especially from outside the UK, which are helpful for anyone trying to make sense of Europe's direction of travel. The Bruges Group (www.brugesgroup.com) carries a great deal of anti-EU material but set within the bounds of reasonable discourse. For business hostility to Europe, Business for Britain (www.businessforbritain.org) is a good start, while Business for New Europe (www.bne.org) offers facts and arguments for business in favour of EU membership. The Brussels-based Bruegel think-tank (www.bruegel.org) is the most academically rigorous of the general think-tanks on EU affairs. Two daily news and comment sites based in Brussels – www.euractiv.com and www.eureporter.com – have online archives to consult.

It is reasonably easy to navigate EU institutional websites and those of the British Parliament. It would be helpful if someone put together all the debates and speeches in the Commons and Lords on the question of Europe since 1945. It would be a major, but worthwhile, task, as nearly every key fact or argument about Britain's relations with the rest of the Europe is on the record somewhere in Hansard. Publishing these statements, exchanges, debates, speeches and questions would at least give the lie to the oft-repeated myth that every MP and peer merely signed up for an economic, free-trade arrangement. The European Commission and European Parliament have accessible websites with a great deal of core information. The European Council of Ministers (not the same thing as the European Council, the quarterly meeting of EU heads of government) also has a good website.

The books listed below – many with their own extensive bibliographies – have been helpful in the evolution of my thinking on Europe and the preparation of this book.

Anderson, Perry, *The New-Old World* (London, Verso, 2011)
Attali, Jacques, *Europe(s)* (Paris, Fayard, 1994)
Bache, Ian and George, Stephen, *Politics in the European Union* (Oxford, Oxford University Press, 2006)
Beck, Ulrich, *German Europe* (Cambridge, Polity, 2013)

Bergounioux, Alain and Grunberg, Gérard, *L'utopie à l'épreuve. Le socialisme européen au XXe siècle* (Paris, Éditions de Fallois, 1996)

Blair, Tony, *A Journey* (London, Hutchinson, 2010)

Bootle, Roger, *The Trouble with Europe: Why the EU Isn't Working – How It Could be Reformed – What Could Take Its Place* (London, Nicholas Brealey, 2014)

Boris, Pascal and Vaissié, Arnaud, *La France et le Royaume-Uni face à la crise (2008–2014)* (London, Cercle d'outre-manche, 2014)

Brady, Hugh, *Twelve Things Everyone Should Know About the European Court of Justice* (London, Centre for European Reform, 2014)

Bullock, Alan, *Ernest Bevin: Foreign Secretary, 1945–1951* (Oxford, Oxford University Press, 1985)

Butler, Nick, Dodd, Philip, Flanders, Stephanie, Garton Ash, Tim, Grant, Charles and Hughes, Kirsty, *Reshaping Europe: Visions for the Future* (London, Centre for European Reform, 1996)

Campbell, John, *Edward Heath: A Biography* (London, Jonathan Cape, 1993)

Charlton, Michael, *The Price of Victory* (London, BBC, 1983)

Charter, David, *Au Revoir, Europe: What If Britain Left the EU?* (London, Biteback, 2012)

—*Europe: In or Out?* (London, Biteback, 2014)

Clarisse, Yves and Quatremer, Jean, *Les maîtres de l'Europe* (Paris, Grasset, 2005)

Corner, Mark, *The European Union: An Introduction* (London, I.B.Tauris)

Crosland, Susan, *Tony Crosland.* (London, Jonathan Cape, 1982)

Dahrendorf, Ralf, *Why Europe Matters* (London, Centre for European Reform, 1996)

D'Ancona, Matthew, *In It Together: The Inside Story of the Coalition Government* (London, Penguin, 2014)

Dell, Edmund, *The Schuman Plan and the Abdication of Leadership in Europe* (Oxford, Clarendon Press, 1995)

Delors, Jacques, *Mémoires* (Paris, Plon, 2004)

Dixon, Hugo, *The In–Out Question* (London, Amazon Books, 2014)

Ferenczi, Thomas, *Pourquoi l'Europe?* (Paris, André Versaille, 2008)

Firsoff, V.A., *The Unity of Europe* (London, Lindsay Drummond, 1947)

Fredet, Jean-Gabriel, *Fabius, les brûlures d'une ambition* (Paris, Hachette, 2002)

Garton Ash, Timothy, *In Europe's Name: Germany and the Divided Continent* (London, Random House, 1993)

Giddens, Anthony, *Turbulent and Mighty Continent: What Future for Europe?* (Cambridge, Polity, 2014)

Gimson, Andrew, *Boris: The Rise of Boris Johnson* (London, Simon & Schuster 2012)

Giscard d'Estaing, Valéry, *Europa, la dernière chance de l'Europe* (Paris, Éditions XO, 2014)

Godley, Wynne, 'The Hole in the Treaty', in Gowan and Anderson, *The Question of Europe*

Goulard, Sylvie, *Europe: amour ou chambre apart* (Paris, Flammarion, 2013)

Gowan, Peter and Anderson, Perry, eds, *The Question of Europe* (London, Verso, 1997)

Grant, Charles, *Delors: Inside the House that Jacques Built* (London, Nicholas Brealey, 1994). Subsequently translated into French, Japanese and Russian

—*How to Build a Modern European Union* (London, Centre for European Reform, 2013)

Guigou, Jean-Louis, *Le nouveau monde méditerranéen* (Paris, Éditions-Descartes, 2012)

Habermas, Jürgen, *Ach, Europa* (Frankfurt, Suhrkampf, 2008)

—*La constitution de l'Europe* (Paris, Gallimard, 2013)

Haffner, Sebastian, *Churchill* (London, Haus Publishing, 2013)

Hamilton, Daniel S., *Europe 2020: Competitive or Complacent?* (Washington, DC, Center for Transatlantic Relations, 2011)

Hayek, F.A., *The Road to Serfdom* (London, Routledge, 1944)

Heathcoat Amory, David, *Confessions of a Eurosceptic* (Barnsley, Pen and Sword, 2012)

House of Commons, 'How much legislation comes from Europe?', *Research Paper 10/62* (London, House of Commons, 13 October 2010)

Hurd, Douglas, *Memoirs* (London, Little, Brown, 2003)

Johnson, Boris, *The Churchill Factor. How One Man Made History* (London, Hodder and Stoughton, 2014)

Judt, Tony, *Postwar: A History of Europe since 1945* (London, Viking, 2005)

Julliard, Jacques, *Les gauches françaises 1762–2012* (Paris, Flammarion, 2012)

Kielinger, Thomas, *Grossbritannien* (Munich, C.H. Beck, 2000)

Lapavitsas, Costas, *Crisis in the Eurozone* (London, Verso, 2012)

Laughland, John, *The Tainted Source: The Undemocratic Origins of the European Idea* (London, Little, Brown, 1997)

Leach, Graham, *EU Membership: What's the Bottom Line?* (London, Institute of Directors, 2000)

Leonard, Mark, *Why Europe Will Run the 21ˢᵗ Century* (London, Fourth Estate, 2005)

Leparmentier, Arnaud, *Ces Français, fossoyeurs de l'euro* (Paris, Plon, 2013)

Liddle, Roger, *The Europe Dilemma: Britain and the Drama of EU Integration* (London, I.B.Tauris and Policy Network, 2014)

Lloyd, John and Marconi, Cristina, *Reporting the EU: News, Media and the European Institutions* (London, I.B.Tauris, 2014)

Loew, Peter Oliver, ed., *Polen denkt Europa* (Frankfurt, Suhrkamp, 2004)

McCormick, John, *Europeanism* (Oxford, Oxford University Press, 2010)

McKnight, David, *Murdoch's Politics: How One Man's Thirst for Wealth and Power Shapes Our World* (London, Pluto Press, 2013)

MacShane, Denis, *François Mitterrand: A Political Odyssey* (London, Quartet, 1982)

—*International Labour and the Origins of the Cold War* (Oxford, Clarendon Press, 1992)

—*Britain's Voice in Europe: Time for Change* (London, Foreign Policy Centre, 2005)

—*Heath* (London, Haus Publishing, 2006)

Marsh, David, *The Euro: The Politics of the New Global Currency* (London, Yale University Press, 2009)

—*Beim Geld hört der Spaß auf. Warum die Eurokrise nicht mehr lösbar ist* (Berlin, Europaverlag, 2013)

Menon, Anand, *Europe: The State of the Union* (London, Atlantic, 2008)

Mets, Marillis, ed., *Let's Get Europe Moving Again* (Paris, CEPS – Centre d'Étude et de Prospective Stratégique, 2013)

Middelaar, Luuk van, *The Passage to Europe: How a Continent Became a Union* (New Haven and London, Yale University Press, 2013)

Millward, Alan, *The Reconstruction of Western Europe, 1945–1951* (London, Methuen, 1984)

Moisi, Dominique, *La géopolitique de l'émotion* (Paris, Flammarion, 2008)

Monnet, Jean, *Mémoires* (Paris, Livre du poche, 2007)

Morgan, Janet, ed., *The Backbench Diaries of Richard Crossman* (London, Hamish Hamilton and Jonathan Cape, 1981)

Morgan, Kenneth, *Michael Foot: A Life* (London, HarperCollins, 2008)

Nairn, Tom, *The Left against Europe* (London, Penguin, 1973)

Ortega, Andres, *La fuerza de los pocos* (Barcelona, Galaxia Gutenberg, 2007)

Orwell, George, *The Collected Essays, Journalism and Letters of George Orwell*, 4 vols (London, Penguin, 1970)

Peet, John and la Guardia, Anton, *Unhappy Union. How the Euro Crisis – and Europe – Can Be Fixed* (London, Profile Books, 2014)

Peyrefitte, Alain, *C'était de Gaulle* (Paris, Gallimard, 1994)

Pimlott, Ben, *Harold Wilson* (London, HarperCollins, 1992)

Pinder, John and Usherwood, Simon, *The European Union: A Very Short Introduction* (Oxford, Oxford University Press, 3rd edn, 2013)

Piris, Jean-Claude, *The Future of Europe* (Cambridge, Cambridge University Press, 2012)

Priestley, Julian and Ford, Glyn, eds, *Our Europe, Not Theirs* (London, Lawrence and Wishart, 2013)

Pryce, Vicky, *Greekonomics: The Euro Crisis and Why Politicians Don't Get It* (London, Biteback, 2013)

Raffy, Serge, *Le Président* (Paris, Fayard/Pluriel, 2013)

Redwood, John, *Our Currency, Our Country: The Dangers of European Monetary Union* (London, Penguin, 1997)

—*The Death of Britain?* (London, Palgrave Macmillan, 1999)

Retinger, Joseph, *Memoirs of an Eminence Grise*, ed. John Pomian (Brighton, Sussex University Press, 1972)

Rocard, Michel and Gnesotto, Nicole, *Notre Europe* (Paris, Robert Laffont, 2008)

Rosen, Greg, *Old Labour to New* (London, Politico's, 2005)

Sassoon, Donald, *One Hundred Years of Socialism: The West European Left in the Twentieth Century* (London, I.B.Tauris, 2014)

Schaub, Jean-Frédéric, *L'Europe a-t-elle une histoire?* (Paris, Albin Michel, 2008)

Schmidt, Helmut, *Handeln für Deutschland* (Berlin, Rowohlt, 1993)

—*Mein Europa, mit einem Gespräch mit Joschka Fischer* (Hamburg, Hoffmann and Campe, 2013)

Schmidt, Helmut and von Weizsäcker, Richard, eds, *Innenansichten aus Europa* (Munich, C.H. Beck, 2007)

Siedentop, Larry, *Democracy in Europe* (London, Allen Lane, 2000)

Solana, Javier, *Reivindicación de la política: veinte años de relaciones internacionales* (Barcelona, Random House Mondadori, 2010)

Springford, John, Tilford, Simon and Whyte, Philip, *The Economic Consequences of Leaving the EU* (London, Centre for European Reform, 2014)

Steiner, George, *The Idea of Europe* (Tilburg, Nexus Institute, 2004)

Thatcher, Margaret, *Statecraft: Strategies for a Changing World* (London, HarperCollins, 2002)

Torreblanca, José Ignacio, *La fragmenatación del poder europeo* (Barcelona, Icaria, 2011)

Wall, Stephen, *The Official History of Britain and the European Union*, vol. II, *From Rejection to Referendum, 1963–1973* (London, Routledge, 2012)

Walter, Norbert, *Europa. Warum unser Kontinent es wert ist, dass wir um Ihn kämpfen* (Frankfurt, Campus, 2011)

Young, Hugo, *This Blessed Plot: Britain and Europe from Churchill to Blair* (London, Macmillan, 1998)

Youngs, Richard, *The Uncertain Legacy of Crisis: European Foreign Policy Faces the Future* (Washington, DC, Carnegie Endowment for International Peace, 2014)

Zielonka, Jan, *Is Europe Doomed?* (Cambridge, Polity, 2014)

INDEX

Acheson, Dean 59
Acton, Lord 4, 131
Adenauer, Konrad 31, 60
Agency Workers
  Directive 207
Airbus Industrie 97
Alexander, Danny 91
Alexander, Helen 140
Alternative für
  Deutschland 194
Amsterdam Treaty 85, 90
Angloscepticism 204
anti-immigrant
  prejudice 61, 62
arms industry 87
anti-Jewish 116
Arrest Warrant,
  European 18
Ashton, Lady 105, 125
Attlee, Clement 14,
  37, 184: attacks European
  integration 45

Balfour, Arthur 21
Balls, Ed 94
bananas 172
Bank of America 8
Bank of England 137
Barber, Tony 186
Barroso, José Manuel
  98, 200
BBC 66: 1975 strike 66:
  Today, hostile to
  Europe 180: turns Nigel
  Farage into national hero
  180, 219
Bearder, Catherine 178
Beaverbrook, Lord 181
Beck, Ulrich 21, 152
Beffa, Jean-Louis 88
Berlaymont 173
Benn, Tony 49
Berlin, Congress of 223
Berlin Uprising 1953 xxiii
Bevin, Ernest 41, 43–4
Bild Zeiting, die 168

Black, Conrad 174, 175
Blair, Tony 54, 55, 84ff,
  173, 178, 190, 191,
  202, 203: allies with
  George W. Bush 85:
  blocks Guy Verhofstadt as
  Commission president 98:
  EU as *Realpolitik* 99:
  and Europhobe
  tabloids 166: Eurosceptic
  Foreign Secretaries 86:
  A Journey 98: offers
  referendum on Euro
  entry 86: offers
  referendum pledges 5:
  opens UK labour market
  to EU workers 101: and
  Rupert Murdoch 91:
  unpopular over Iraq 105
Blocher, Christophe 12
Boothby, Robert 30
Bootle, Roger 6, 150
Brandt, Willy 113, 185
Brazil 10
Brecht, Bertolt xxiii
Bremner, Charles 176ff,
  181
Bretton Woods 61, 66, 185
Brexit 225: and
  Eurozone 184: first use xi:
  soft 8
British Bankers
  Association 148
'Britain in Europe' 91, 94
British Chambers of
  Commerce (BCC) 3,
  142, 143–4
British influence 219
British National Party
  (BNP) 96, 104, 116
Brown, Gordon xxxiv, 54,
  55, 64, 87, 104, 160,
  160, 183, 190ff
Bruegel think-tank 214
budget, European 25
Bundesbank 69

Bush, George W., 32,
  85, 175
business: hostility to EU 92:
  threatened by John
  Redwood 140
Business for Britain 3
Business for New Europe
  145, 219
Business for Sterling 147
Butler, Nick 26, 96

Callaghan, James 51, 187
Cameron, David 16,
  107, 163, 173, 193,
  205, 216: alliance with
  anti-Jewish politicians,
  Poland 164: campaigns
  against Jean-Claude
  Juncker 120: election as
  Tory leader 114: in–out
  referendum pledge xiii:
  personal charm 21:
  Scottish referendum xxii:
  shower room talk 111
Campbell, Alistair 100, 170
Campbell Bannerman,
  David 140
Camus, Albert 41
Canada xxxi, 60
capital controls 188
Carswell, Douglas 7, 119
Carter, Jimmy 187
Cash, William xviii, 106,
  109, 146
Castle, Barbara 41
Cavendish, Camilla xxi
Centre for European
  Reform 218
Channel Islands 221
Charter, David 64, 219ff
China 8, 102
Chirac, Jacques 37, 85, 96,
  102, 202, 209
Churchill, Winston 28–33,
  40, 173, 192
Citibank 8

City, the 139, 192:
   renaissance in 1980s
   helped by EC 143
Clarke, Kenneth 80, 91,
   123, 128
Clegg, Nick xxiv, 13, 117,
   160, 163
Clinton, Bill 32, 40,
   89, 100
closed shop 69
Cohn-Bendit, Danny 214
Commerzbank 193
Common Agricultural Policy
   8, 25, 36
Commonwealth 51, 59, 83
Communist Party of Great
   Britain 65, 153
Confederation of British
   Industry (CBI) 3,
   140, 142
Confédération générale du
   travail 68
Congress of Europe
   1948 31
Congress of New Right
   (Poland) 164
Conservative Party:
   encourages anti-EU
   views in business 92:
   Government defeated
   1974 65: hostile to EU x:
   patriarchy 62: says no to
   Treaty of Rome 57: turn
   to Euroscepticism 63
Constitutional Convention
   157
Constitutional Court,
   German 216
constitutional treaty 191
Contribution to European
   budget xviii, 5: Mrs
   Thatcher's 400 per cent
   increase 64
Cook, Robin 42, 55, 86, 90
Council of Europe 29, 33,
   39, 44, 156, 210
Council of Ministers
   161, 172
Cridland, John 140
Cronin, David 141
Crossman, Richard 47
crown, Danish 20
Currie, Edwina 81

D'Ancona, Matthew
   213, 225
Daily Express 178, 179
Daily Mail 2, 136, 169, 172

Daily Star 172, 179
Daily Telegraph 119, 172ff
Danzig, Jon 182
Darling, Alistair 192
Davis, David 114
de Gaulle, General 29, 33,
   36, 59, 132, 185: vetoes
   UK entry 48
de La Rochefoucauld 57
de Villepin, Dominique 100
defence spending 208
Delors, Jacques 54, 74,
   77, 174, 214: 1988
   TUC speech 67:
   and Conservative
   euroscepticism 69: and
   Margaret Thatcher 64
Denmark 20
Der Spiegel xxvi, 180
Devaluation (pound
   sterling) 184
Dixon, Hugo 6
Downing Street 103
Dulles, J.F. and Allan 32
Duncan Smith, Iain 81,
   111, 115
Dyson, Sir James xxviii

Economic and Monetary
   Union (EMU) 69, 88, 92
Economist 42, 168, 194
Eden, Anthony 58
Eisenhower, Dwight D. 32
Énarque 17
Estonia 20
Euro 184: economic
   tests 95–6
Eurobarometer 77, 199
Europe des patries 36
European Central Bank 39,
   94, 194
European Coal and Steel
   Community 13, 36
European Communities Act
   1972 50
European Company
   Statute 67
European Council of
   Foreign Relations
   198, 214
European Convention
   on Human Rights 4,
   33, 122
European Court of
   Auditors 159
European Court of Human
   Rights (ECHR) 4, 7, 33,
   118, 196, 210

European Court of Justice
   39, 155
European dream xviii
European Economic
   Community (EEC)
   8, 60
European External Action
   Service (EEAS) 125
European Free Trade
   Association (EFTA) 6
European Monetary System
   (EMS) 186–7
European Movement 40
European Parliament
   39, 69, 161, 205:
   1979 election 158:
   1989 election 55: 1994
   election 160: 2004
   election 98: 2009
   election 160: 2014
   election 7, 107, 160:
   legitimacy of 158
European People's Party
   (EPP) 114, 118, 124,
   162, 216
European Policy
   Institute 86
European Works
   Councils 197
Europe ministers 86
Eurozone: and George
   Osborne: lack of
   growth 16
'ever-closer union' 24
Exchange Rate Mechanism
   (ERM) 82, 189–90
exports 82

Fabian Society 54
Fabius, Laurent 37, 183
Falkland Islands 66, 70
Fallon, Michael 13
Farage, Nigel 7, 108, 120,
   143, 161, 164, 168, 181,
   213, 218, 224: admits
   pocketing £2 million
   in expenses 163: links
   to anti-Jewish Polish
   party 164
Federalist papers 157
Federation of Poles of Great
   Britain 169
Financial Times 162,
   168, 179
Fischer, Joschka 96, 105
Foot, Michael 40, 51
Ford, Glyn 25
Frachon, Alain 17

free movement of workers xxvi, 8, 19, 207
free trade 21, 74, 124
French Communist Party 12, 65
Fukuyama, Francis 201, 221

Gaitskell, Hugh 47: rants against EEC 48
Ganeesh, Janaan 20
Garton Ash, Timothy 87
Georgia 222
German Social Democrats 37
Germany: dominant in Europe in event of Brexit 9: East 93: 'Gestapo-controlled Nazi EU' 10
Giddens, Anthony 6
Giscard d'Estaing, Valéry 18, 37, 63, 157, 185
globalization 15, 54
Gnodde Richard 139
Godley, Wynne 137
Goldman Sachs 140
Gollan, John 153
Gonzalez, Felipe 54, 113, 202
Goodhart, David 18, 128
Google 92, 142
Gove, Michael 196
Grant, Charles 174
Greece 4, 197ff, 202
Greenspan, Alan 192
Grexit xi, 193
Grillo, Beppe 161, 164
growth 92
Guardia, Anton la 6
Guardian 95, 217: hostile to European economic integration 179

Habermas, Jürgen 21, 157, 217
Haffner, Sebastian 22
Hague, William 83, 88, 108, 115, 121, 124, 193: background, education 110: makes Euroscepticism Tory leitmotif after 1997 109: paid by Rupert Murdoch 111: unfunny jokes about Europeans 110
Hain, Peter 86

Hammond, Philip xx, 9, 11, 121, 214
Hands, Guy 127
Hannan, Daniel 127
Harrod, Roy 30
Hassan, King of Morocco 214
Hassan, Mehdi xxviii
Hattersley, Roy 50
Hayek, Friedrich 129
Healey, Denis 38–40, 187
Heath, Edward xxx, 49, 55, 60ff, 185: EEC negotiations 1961–2 60: takes UK into EEC 50
Heffer, Simon 174
Hegel, Georg 202
Heseltine, Michael 80, 91, 112
High Representative, EU 105
Hilton, Steve 213
Hitler, Adolf 10, 53, 60, 66
Hollande, François 208
House of Commons 158, 160, 213
Howard, Michael 81, 90, 112, 146
Howe, Geoffrey 74, 80, 188
Hurd, Douglas 79, 111, 135
Hurd, Nick 135

immigrant EU workers 15, 93, 101, 102
Independent 173
India 10
Institute for Economic Affairs 141
International Labour Organization xx
International Monetary Fund 51
Iraq war 71, 102, 105, 191
Ireland, problems with Brexit 20
Italy xviii, 10

Japan 10
Javid, Sajid 13
Jay, Michael 88
Jenkins, Roy 42, 48, 185: proposes referendum and resigns as Labour deputy Leader 51
Jennings, Ivor 153
Jobbik 149, 164
Joffrin, Laurent 203

John Paul II, Pope 161
Johnson, Boris xxiii, 16, 26, 29, 122, 210, 218: Brussels correspondent fabrications 172ff
Johnson, Lyndon 220
Johnson, Paul 146
Jospin, Lionel 89, 102
Juncker, Jean-Claude xxvi, 26, 27, 119, 121, 162: Cameron's attack on 120
juste retour, le xxiii

Kennedy, Charles 91
Keynes, John Maynard 223
Kielinger, Thomas 213
Kinnock, Neil 25
Kohl, Helmut 89, 127, 190
Konrad Adenauer Foundation 116
Kosovo 19, 82, 105

Labour Government 1945–51 37: hostile to European construction 44, 46
Labour MPs 90, 96
Labour Party 210: 2009 conference 104: adopts referendum tactically 51: anti-EEC 1970s 49: approach to Europe 37: failure to explain Europe 221: opposes joining EEC 1961 47: pro-EU in 1990s 42: supports withdrawal from Europe 54
Lafitte, Jacques viii
Lamont, Norman 82, 127, 168, 190
Lamy, Pascal 70
Landale, James 173
Laughland, John 136
Lawson, Nigel 74, 122, 123, 188
Le Figaro 168
Le Monde 17, 71, 168
Le Pen, Marine 12, 164
Lea, David 87
Leach, Rodney 146–7
Legrain, Philip 6
Leguiller, Pierre 117
Lemaire, Axelle 104
Leveson, Sir Brian, later Lord 170ff
Liberal Democrats 97, 118
Liberal Party 54

Libération 168
Libya 124–5
Liddle, Roger 6
Lidington, David 122
Lisbon Treaty 104, 106, 120, 223
Lloyd, John 167, 203
L'Obs (formerly *Nouvel Observateur* viz) 180
London Chamber of Commerce 144
Longworth, John 144

Maastricht Treaty xi, 81, 111, 190
Macmillan, Harold 30, 59, 111, 185: accuses France of duplicity 60
mad cow disease 73, 82
Madison, James 157
Magna Carta 153
Major, John 22–4, 55, 80ff, 123, 151
Mandelson, Peter 19, 45, 54, 106, 128, 219
Marconi, Cristina 167, 203
Margaret Thatcher Foundation 73
Marlborough, Duke of 223
Marsh, David 194
Marshall Plan 65
Marten, Neil 50
Marx, Karl 82
Maxwell Fyfe, David 33
McCarthy, Senator Joseph 163
McKnight, David 90, 175
McMillan-Scott, Edward 116
Mélanchon, Jean-Luc 219
Members of European Parliament (MEP) 158, 159, 163: Conservative, link with anti-Jewish Polish politicians 116: expenses 159, 167: Labour 10, 55, 104
Members of Parliament 161, 163: lack of knowledge of EU countries, languages 157
Merkel, Angela xxvi, 64, 105, 120, 163, 163, 198, 225
Messina conference 58
Middelaar, Luuk van 39, 201

Miliband, David 10, 94, 96, 105
Miliband, Ed xii, xiv, xxiv, 13, 106, 107, 191
Militant syndicalism 65
Milosevic, Slobodan 85
Miners Strike 1984–5 65
Mitterrand, François 15, 54, 113, 128, 157, 187, 188, 202
Monaco 19
monetary union 186
Monks, John 87
Monnet, Jean 32, 44
Mont Pélerin 130
Moore, Charles 2, 79
Morgan Stanley 8
Morrison, Herbert 45
Moscovici, Pierre 157
Murdoch, Rupert 91, 111, 122, 166, 169, 175, 191, 210

Nairn, Tom 218
national sovereignty 73
National Union of Journalists 66
NATO 43, 148, 154, 182
'Nazi European Union' 136
Nazism 10, 130
Neil, Andrew 180
Netherlands 10
New Europe 147
New Statesman 39
News of the World 166
Nice Treaty 85
Nicolaidis, Kalypso 141
Nissan 11
North Atlantic Free Trade Area (NAFTA) 74
Norton, Philip 50
Norway xvi, 3, 9, 221
Nouvel Observateur 14, 180
nuclear weapons 43, 60

oil shock 1973 61
Oliver, Jamie 196
Open Europe 147
opt-outs 82
Orban, Victor 120
Organisation for Economic Co-operation and Development (OECD) 39, 43, 214
Ortega y Gasset, José 203
Orwell, George 129
Ouest-France 168

Owen, David 18, 42
Oxbridge Conservatives 79

Paisley, Ian 161
Palmer, John 212
Papandreou, George 198
Parliament: supremacy 70, 151
parliaments, national 161ff
Partisan Review 129
Party of European Socialists (PES) 102
PASOK 198
Patten, Chris 81
Pearson, Lord 147
Peet, John 6
Persson, Goran 96
Piris Jean-Claude 197, 205
Pisani-Ferry, Jean 214, 225
PiS (Polish Law and Justice Party) 19
Pitt, William 123, 125
Pohl, Karl Otto 69
Poincaré, Raymond 184
Poland viii, xxv, 9, 20, 32
Policy Network 218
post-1968 leftism 65
pound sterling 96
Powell, Charles 146
Powell, Enoch 61, 168: helps win 1974 election for Labour 62: writes pro-European pamphlet 154
Preisbindung xxxii
Press Complaints Commission (PCC) 182
primary legislation xviii
prix du livre xxxii
Putin, Vladmir 222

Reagan, Ronald 72
Redwood, John 83, 112, 140, 168
referendum 165: 1975 2, 51, 150: 2010 broken promise by Conservatives, Liberal Democrats 3: 2011 Act 118, 216: EU Constitutional Treaty 85, 96, 97: Euro 86, 95: Scotland xxi: Swedish 96: voting reform 3
Reinfeldt, Fredrik 19, 116
Renzi, Matteo 120, 196
Retinger, Joseph 30

Reuters Institute for the
    Study of Journalism 167
review of competences 216
Reynolds, Emma 106
Ridley, Nicholas 35, 154
Rivers of Blood speech 61
Road to Serfdom 130
Robertson, George 55
Robinson, Nick 180
Rocard, Michel 14
Roma xxxi
Roubini, Nouriel 194
Rousseau, Jean-Jacques 201
Royal Bank of Scotland
    (RBS) 192
Rumpuy, Herman van 106
Russia 10

Saint Malo agreement 97
Sandys, Duncan 30
Sarkozy, Nicolas 105, 153
Schengen zone 25, 85
Schmidt, Helmut 52, 77,
    133, 157, 185
Schröder, Gerhard 89, 100,
    157, 198
Schuman, Robert
    33, 44, 45
Scottish National Party xxii
Sherwood, Michael 140
Siedentop, Larry 157
Sikorski, Radek 16, 126
Single European Act 1985
    64, 78, 85, 188, 202
single market 74
Sked, Alan 116
Smith, John 50
Soares, Mario 202
Social Chapter 85
Social Democratic Party 54
Social Europe 24, 55, 218
Soros, George 189
South Africa 10
South Korea 10
Soviet Union, compared to
    European Community 72
Spaak, Paul-Henri 29, 58
Spain 10
Spanish Succession,
    War of 222

'special relationship' 59
Spectator 79, 174, 175
Spencer, Michael 145
spread betting 145
Straw, Jack 42, 63, 97,
    104, 118
Südetenland 222
Suez 58
Sun 2, 76, 166, 171
Sun on Sunday 166
Sunday Times, The 166
Svenska Metall 20
Swiss People's Party 12
Switzerland xxx
Syriza 219

Tata 11, 150
Taylor, Paul 167
Tebbit, Norman 168
Thatcher, Margaret 2, 14,
    38, 55, 74, 84, 111,
    131, 188, 202: attacks
    Delors in Commons 74:
    Bruges speech (1988) 72:
    elected leader of
    Conservatives 62:
    and Exchange Rate
    Mechanism 188–189:
    opposed to trade
    unions 62ff: portrayed by
    Meryl Streep 77
third way 40, 89
Times, The 173, 179
Torreblanco, José
    Ignacio 199
Touhig, Don 87
Toyota 11
trade unions 24: help
    bring down Conservative
    government 1974 65
Trades Union Congress
    (TUC) 65, 87
Traynor, Ian 179, 212
Treasury 187
Treaty: new EU xvii: of
    Rome 1, 32, 36
Tribune 217
Trichet, Jean-Claude 94
Troika (International
    Monetary

Fund-European
    Central Bank-European
    Commission) 198
Turkey 10
Tusk, Donald 19

Ukraine 222
union, federal 132
United Kingdom
    Independence Party
    (Ukip) xi, 96, 104,
    109, 123, 160, 181,
    213, 224: links to
    anti-Jewish party,
    Poland 164
United States: of
    America xxx, 10: of
    Europe 29
Usborne, David 173
Utrecht, Treaty of 223

Valls, Manuel xvi
Vatican 19
Vaz, Keith 107
Verdun 128, 205
Verheugen, Günter 89
Verhofstadt, Guy 97,
    105, 214
Versailles, Treaty of 222
veto 210
Virgil 61

Walker, Martin viii
Wall, Stephen 100
Watson, Rory 173
Welt, Die 213
Werner, Pierre 185
Westerwelle, Guido 126,
    213
Westphalia, Treaty of 222
Wheeler, Stuart 145
White, Michael 123
Wilders, Geert 164
Williams, Shirley 42,
    219, 220
Wilson, Harold 38, 48
Wise, Tom 167
Working Time Directive 24
World Trade Organization
    70, 148, 154